THE FATHERS OF THE CHURCH

A NEW TRANSLATION

VOLUME 61

THE FATHERS OF THE CHURCH

A NEW TRANSLATION

ROY JOSEPH DEFERRARI
Editorial Director Emeritus

EDITORIAL BOARD

THE WORKS
OF SAINT CYRIL
OF JERUSALEM

Volume 1

Translated by
LEO P. McCAULEY, S.J.
Boston College
Chestnut Hill, Massachusetts

and

ANTHONY A. STEPHENSON
University of Exeter
England

THE CATHOLIC UNIVERSITY OF AMERICA PRESS
Washington, D. C. 20017

NIHIL OBSTAT:

JOHN C. SELNER, S.S., S.T.D.

Censor Librorum

IMPRIMATUR:

✠PATRICK CARDINAL A. O'BOYLE, D.D.

Archbishop of Washington

November 15, 1968

Library of Congress Catalog Card No.: 68-55980

Copyright © 1969 by

THE CATHOLIC UNIVERSITY OF AMERICA PRESS, INC.

First Paperback Reprint 2005
ISBN 0-8132-0061-X (cl)
ISBN 0-8132-1431-9 (pbk)
ISBN-13: 978-0-8132-1431-3 (pbk)

CONTENTS

v

GENERAL FOREWORD

Father Leo P. McCauley is responsible for the translation, with notes, of the Lenten (pre-baptismal) Lectures 1-12. Father A. A. Stephenson is responsible for the General Introduction and the *Procatechesis*. Except where otherwise noted, the text translated is that of the W. K. Reischl and J. Rupp edition of the works of Cyril (Munich 1848-1860).

Father Stephenson writes as follows on certain matters:

> My general introduction is heavily indebted to many scholars. While most of these debts are indicated, however inadequately and implicitly, in the Select Bibliography, I gladly mention here how much I owe to that great Cyrilline scholar, Dom A. A. Toutée, O.S.B., and to the *Patristic Greek Lexicon* edited by Dr. G. W. H. Lampe, who has conferred an inestimable boon on all students of the Greek Fathers. Instructive, however, as Toutée's dissertations, notes, and critical apparatus still are, there is as yet no modern critical edition of the works of Cyril, and it is good news that this need is very soon to be supplied by Père E. Bihain. Throughout the volume "Lecture" may stand for *Catechesis;* in the General Introduction, "Eusebius" is always Eusebius of Caesarea, "Basil" is always Basil of Ancyra, "the East" does not include Egypt, and "Eastern theology" refers to the tradition originated by Origen and continued by, among others, Eusebius.

A further volume in the series will contain, in addition to the *Sermon on the Paralytic* and the *Letter to Constantius,* the Lenten Lectures 13-18 and the lectures on the sacramental mysteries *(Mystagogicae)* delivered at Jerusalem during Easter week, although the balance of probability slightly favors the view that these Mystagogical Catecheses are, at least in their present form, the work of Cyril's successor, John of Jerusalem.

BERNARD M. PEEBLES
Editorial Director

SELECT BIBLIOGRAPHY*

Texts:

A. A. Toutée and P. Maran [Maurists] (Paris 1720; reprinted PG 33.331-1180).

W. K. Reischl and J. Rupp (Munich 1848/1860). Text with improvements based on Cod. Monac. gr. 394.

F. L. Cross, *St. Cyril of Jerusalem's Lectures on the Christian Sacraments* . . . (S.P.C.K. Texts for Students 51; London 1951). Text and English translation (by R. W. Church), with Introduction, of the *Procatechesis* and the Mystagogical Catecheses.

A. Piédagnel, *Cyrille de Jérusalem, Catéchèses mystagogiques* (Sources chrétiennes 126; Paris 1966).

English Translations:

R. W. Church, *The Catechetical Lectures of S. Cyril, Archbishop of Jerusalem* (Library of the Fathers of the Holy Catholic Church [LCF] 2; Oxford and London 1839). Contains Dean R. W. Church's classic translation of the Lenten Lectures (the prebaptismal *Catecheses*) and the Easter (Mystagogical) *Catecheses*, and a Preface by J. H. Newman, who apparently (cf. xxx) also revised the translation.

E. H. Gifford, *St. Cyril of Jerusalem and St. Gregory Nazianzen* (Library of Nicene and Post-Nicene Fathers [LNPF], Second series 7; London 1894; recently reprinted by Eerdmans, Grand Rapids, Mich.). E. H. Gifford's revision of Church's translation, with useful introduction and notes.

W. Telfer, *Cyril of Jerusalem and Nemesius of Emesa* (Library of Christian Classics [LCC] 4; London 1955). A new translation of extensive selections from the *Catecheses* with the *Letter of Constantius*. Contains very valuable introduction and notes.

French Translations:

J. Bouvet, [Cyrillus Hierosolymitanus] *Catéchèses baptismales et mystagogiques* (Les Écrits des saints; Namur 1962).

M. Véricel, *Cyrille de Jérusalem* (Collection Église d'hier et d'aujourd'hui; Paris 1957). Selections.

Historical:

G. Bardy *et al.*, *The Church in the Christian Roman Empire* I, English translation, by E. C. Messenger (London 1949), of the first two parts of A. Fliche and V. Martin (general editors), *Histoire de l'Église etc.* 3 (Paris 1947).

——————, "Cyrille de Jérusalem," *Dictionnaire de la spiritualité* (DSp) 2 (1953) 2683-2687.

——————, "Cyrille de Jérusalem," *Dictionnaire d'histoire et de géographie ecclésiastiques* (DHG) 13 (1956) 1181-1185.

---

* Where a work is cited only by the name of its author, the reference is to his work listed in this Bibliography.

E. Bihain, "La source d'un texte de Socrate *(Hist. Eccles.* 2.38.2) relatif à Cyrille de Jérusalem," *Byzantion* 32 (1962) 81-91.

⸻, "Le *Contre Eunome* de Théodore de Mopsueste, source d'un passage de Sozomène et d'un passage de Théodoret concernant Cyrille de Jérusalem," *Le Muséon* 75 (1962) 331-355.

⸻, "Une vie arménienne de S. Cyrille de Jérusalem," *Le Muséon* 76 (1963) 319-348.

H. Chadwick, *The Early Church* (The Pelican History of the Church 1; London 1967).

⸻, *The Circle and the Ellipse* (Inaugural Lecture; Oxford 1959).

Francis Dvornik, *The Idea of Apostolicity in Byzantium* (Cambridge, Mass. 1958).

F. J. A. Hort, *Two Dissertations* (London and Cambridge 1876).

X. Le Bachelet, "Cyrille (Saint), évêque de Jérusalem," *Dictionnaire de théologie catholique* (DTC) 3 (1908) 2527-2577.

Hans Lietzmann, *A History of the Early Church* II (containing vols. 3 and 4 of the German original) being the paperback edition (London 1961, 1963) of Bertram Lee Woolf's translation of Lietzmann's *Geschichte der Alten Kirche* (4 vols., 1961); references to the 4-volume edition of the Woolf translation are added in parenthesis.

A. P. Stanley, *Lectures on the History of the Eastern Church* (2nd ed., New York 1862).

J. Stevenson, *A New Eusebius: Documents Illustrative of the History of the Church* (London 1957).

Theological:

G. W. H. Lampe, *A Patristic Greek Lexicon* (Oxford 1961ff.).

J. Lebon, "La position de St. Cyrille de Jérusalem dans les luttes provoquées par l'arianisme," *Revue d'histoire ecclésiastique* 20 (1924) 181-210, 357-386.

G. L. Prestige, *God in Patristic Thought* (London 1952).

Archibald Robertson and John Henry Newman, *St. Athanasius: Select Works and Letters* (LNPF, Second series 4; London 1891).

G. C. Stead, "The Significance of the *Homoousios,*" *Studia Patristica* III (=Texte u. Untersuchungen 78; Berlin 1961) 397-412. (See also the discussion of the *homoousios* that has been carried on in recent years in the *Journal of Theological Studies.*)

A. A. Stephenson, "St. Cyril of Jerusalem and the Alexandrian Christian Gnosis," *Studia Patristica* I (=Texte u. Untersuchungen 63; Berlin 1957) 142-156.

H. A. Wolfson, "Philosophical Implications of the Theology of Cyril of Jerusalem," *Dumbarton Oaks Papers* 11 (1957) 1-19.

Creeds:

E. C. S. Gibson, *The Three Creeds* (Oxford Library of Practical Theology; London 1908).

F. J. A. Hort, *Two Dissertations (cit. supra)* 73-150.

J. N. D. Kelly, *Early Christian Creeds* (London 1950).

A. A. Stephenson, "The Text of the Jerusalem Creed," *Studia Patristica* III (=Texte u. Untersuchungen 78; Berlin 1961) 303-313.

I. Ortiz de Urbina, "La Struttura del simbolo Constantinopolitano," *Orientalia Christiana Periodica* 12 (1946) 275-285.

Other Works:

F. C. Conybeare and J. A. Maclean, *Rituale Armenorum* (Oxford 1905).

J. H. Greenlee, *The Gospel Text of Cyril of Jerusalem* (Copenhagen 1955).

A. Paulin, *S. Cyrille de Jérusalem, catéchète* (Paris 1959).

A. Renoux, "Les Cathéchèses mystagogiques dans l'organisation liturgique hiérosolymitaine du IVe et Ve siècle," *Le Muséon* 78 (1965) 355-359.

Hélène Pétré, *Ethérie, Journal de Voyage* (Sources chrétiennes 21; Paris 1948).

J. Quasten, *Patrology* III (Utrecht/Antwerp-Westminster, Md. 1960) 362-377, with excellent bibliography.

ABBREVIATIONS

Athanasius	The LNPF volume on Athanasius, by Newman and Robertson. See Select Bibliography.
C	The "Constantinopolitan" Creed.
Denzinger	H. Denzinger, *Enchiridion symbolorum* . . ., 32nd ed. by A. Schönmetzer, S.J. (Freiburg i. B. 1963).
DHG	*Documents Illustrative of the History of the Church*, ed. B. J. Ridel (2 vols., London 1938).
DTC	*Dictionnaire de théologie catholique*, ed. A. Vacant *et al.* (Paris 1903-1950).
GCS	*Die griechischen christlichen Schriftsteller* (Leipzig 1897ff.).
J	The Creed of Jerusalem.
LCC	*Library of Christian Classics*, ed. J. Baillie *et al.* (Philadelphia and London 1953ff.).

LNPF   *A Select Library of Nicene and Post-Nicene Fathers of the
            Christian Church,* ed. Ph. Schaff and H. Wace (Buffalo and
            New York 1886-1900; reprinted Grand Rapids 1952ff.).

LTK   *Lexikon für Theologie und Kirche* (2nd ed., Freiburg i. B.
            1957ff.).

Myst.   The (Easter) *Mystagogical Catecheses* of Cyril.

N   The Creed of Nicaea (325 A.D.).

P   Piédagnel's edition or text of *Myst.*

PG   Migne, *Patrologia Graeca.*

PGL   *Patristic Greek Lexicon,* ed. G. W. H. Lampe (Oxford 1961ff.).

PL   Migne, *Patrologia Latina.*

RR   The Reischl-Rupp edition of Cyril of Jerusalem. See Select
            Bibliography.

GENERAL INTRODUCTION

1. The Lenten Lectures

St. Cyril delivered his pre-baptismal catechetical lectures in the Lent of (probably) 349 A.D.[1] The audience consisted principally of the higher class of catechumens, i.e., those who, having decided to "take the plunge," had, before Lent, given in their names with a view to receiving Christian initiation through baptism by total immersion, chrism and Holy Communion in the night of Holy Saturday and the early morning of Easter Sunday. Since a common name for baptism was "enlightenment," the candidates were called *phōtizomenoi*, "those to be enlightened" or "those being enlightened." Adult baptism, except in emergency, was the rule in the fourth century. Among those present were also many baptized Christians, for whom the Lenten exposition of the creed served as a refresher course. Men and women were separated, occupying opposite sides of the church.[2]

Cyril never formally published his *Catecheses*. According to a scribal note,[3] we owe the preservation of their text to the fact that some of the *spoudaioi (dévots*, probably the local monks and nuns) reported Cyril in shorthand as he was speaking. According to this note, Cyril's lectures were taken down in one year only. This statement is a little difficult to square with the extensive variations in the manuscripts,[4] which suggests stratification there, i.e., that the manuscripts

---

1 For the year, see Telfer 36-38.
2 *Procat.* 14.
3 At the end of the *Catecheses* in the old Munich MS; RR 2.342-343 n. 20.
4 See especially Toutée's two recensions of *Catechesis* 2; there are two different versions of 2.16-20.

1

reflect the catechizing of more than one year. Similarly, the advanced theology of the Holy Spirit in *Catecheses* 16 and 17 also suggests a date considerably later than 350. Again, the one-year view is difficult to harmonize with the various indications of the season[5] and with Cyril's reference to "what has been said to previous classes,"[6] for Cyril very probably did not give the *Catecheses* before 349, the year represented by our text if it represents the lectures of only one year. Owing to the rule of the secret (attested by the scribal note following the Procatechesis), the *Catecheses* must have circulated privately at first, being available only to the baptized and *phōtizomenoi*. Towards the end of the century, St. Jerome mentioned their being in (public?) circulation: "Exstant eius Catecheses, quas in adolescentia composuit."[7] This perhaps implies Jerome's belief that the lectures had not been adequately revised.

Syllabus and Arrangement

The syllabus of the *Catecheses*, at least in the form in which they have reached us, is the exposition and "demonstration" of the Jerusalem Creed. The only exception is the second part (18-37) of Lecture 4, and Lecture 4 is somewhat exceptional. The fact that the Creed is delivered to the candidates only at 5.12 may seem to suggest that it was only part of the syllabus. But *Catecheses* 6-18 deal with the clauses of the Creed in order and, as Cyril points out in 18.22, *Catecheses* 1-3 have for their subject the clause in the Jerusalem Creed, "one baptism of repentance for the remission of sins." *Catechesis* 4.4-17 is a summary exposition of the Creed, and

---

5 At 18.7 ("The season is winter . . ."), Gifford says that this passage and 4.30 "show that the Lectures were delivered in the year when Easter fell early." But in 14.10, spring had already arrived, and not merely official spring, but also the spring flowers. 13.18 may be relevant to this problem.

6 6.21. Cyril apparently refers here to his own previous lectures; he usually refers to himself either by "we" or in the passive voice.

7 *De viris illustribus* 112.

Catechesis 5 deals with the "faith" by which we believe and "the faith (Creed)" which we believe. See also 4.3 and 18.32.[8] But while it is possible to establish by inspection the fact that the syllabus of the extant *Catecheses* is substantially the Jerusalem Creed, this proves that the entire syllabus of Cyril's Lenten preaching was the Creed, only if it can be assumed that the extant *Catecheses* are complete.

St. Jerome's *Contra Ioannem Hierosolymitanum* 11-13[9] probably implies that in 394 the syllabus was still, substantially, the Creed. The fifth-century Old Armenian Lectionary gives nineteen lessons for the Jerusalem Lenten preaching;[10] since these agree almost exactly with the eighteen lessons taken by Cyril as his texts, they imply an unchanged syllabus. The Armenian Lectionary represents the Jerusalem liturgy of *ca.* 440. A rather different picture of the syllabus is given by the western lady pilgrim, Aetheria or Egeria, who spent three years in the Holy Land probably within the period *ca.* 385-396.[11] While in Cyril's time the forty-day Lent probably meant six or seven weeks, in Egeria's time Lent lasted for eight weeks, since neither Saturdays nor Sundays, not being fast days, were counted. The syllabus as described by Egeria fell into two parts; the first five weeks were taken up by a Scripture course; the Creed was delivered at the end of the fifth week and its exposition occupied the next two weeks, there being no lectures during Holy Week. There appears to be some discrepancy between this account of the syllabus and that given by St. Jerome, which seems to agree with what we find in the extant *Catecheses.*

---

8 The description of the syllabus given in *Procat.* 11 is probably compatible with the syllabus being the creed.

9 PL 23.379-82, *al.* 363-66.

10 *Rituale Armenorum*, ed. F. C. Conybeare and J. A. Maclean (Oxford 1905), Appendix 2, esp. p. 518.

11 Though K. Meister and the philologists want to place the *Peregrinatio* considerably later, and E. Dekkers has advocated the date 415-417. The *Peregrinatio* (or *Itinerarium*) is now found (ed. E. Franceschini and R. Weber) in *Corpus Christianorum: Series Latina* 175 (cf. P. Geyer's ed., *Corpus scriptorum ecclesiasticorum latinorum* 39). For Egeria's account of the catechizing and its syllabus, see chapters 45-46.

How were the nineteen Lectures distributed over Lent? Lectures 6-8 belong to successive days (cf. 7.1; 8.1), as also do 10-12 (11.1; 12.4). Lecture 14 was given on a Monday (14.24) and there was one day's interval between Lectures 3 and 4 (4.32). In 18.32, after concluding his exposition of the last clause of the Creed, Cyril says that he has given as many lectures on the Creed as was possible during Lent. The Lectures vary considerably in length and the distribution of the subject matter is uneven, four lectures (6-9) being devoted to the words, "one God, the Father Almighty, Creator . . .," two lectures (16 and 17) to the Holy Spirit, while one lecture (15) covers the Resurrection, Ascension and Session, and one lecture (18) the Church, the resurrection of the flesh and life everlasting.

The most attractive suggestion so far made about the distribution of the Lectures is that of Telfer. Pointing out that Lecture 18 is really a double lecture, so that there were twenty lectures in all, he has suggested that Cyril gave twenty lectures in Greek to the Greek-speaking population and twenty in Syriac (Palestinian Aramaic) to the Syriac-speaking members of the community. Cyril would then have lectured on each of the forty days of Lent, as he perhaps claims in 18.32.[12]

The Jerusalem Creed and its Demonstration

In 5.12 the Creed is formally delivered to the candidates by the Church as represented by Cyril, the local bishop. Cyril's teaching was severely biblical. In 4.17, explaining that the substance of the Lenten course is the "demonstration" of the Creed from Scripture, Cyril says: "Concerning the divine and holy mysteries of the Faith, not even a casual statement must be made without the Holy Scriptures." For Aristotle, "opinion" was converted into genuine knowledge

---

12 Telfer 34-36. The hypothesis does not very well explain why Lectures 6-8 and 10-12 were delivered on consecutive days.

by a demonstration *(apodeixis,* Cyril's word) which, grounding particular propositions in indemonstrable, self-evident primary premises, made them luminous and evident. Cyril, apparently following the method of the Alexandrine school of Clement and Origen, keeps but transforms this pattern. Cyril's "demonstration" is highly paradoxical insofar as it shows that the Creed, itself culled from Scripture (5.12), is really contained in Scripture. This procedure grounds the Creed not in self-evidence but in authority and mystery. But the method of the Lectures is also apologetic. Cyril attached immense importance to the proof from miracles and prophecy. Especially from prophecy; in 13.9 he seems to say that the important thing about the miracles of Jesus was that they had been prophesied. Similarly in 14.17, engaging to produce "Scripture testimony" in proof of the Resurrection, Cyril says, "the Lord Jesus Christ himself supplies it in the Gospels"— and then quotes our Lord's appeal to the type of Jonah. It is not, of course (cf. 14.15), that Cyril regarded the New Testament as less authoritative than the Old; he stressed the argument from prophecy partly because it is a rational, apologetic argument (for prediction is miraculous) and partly because the Jews, against whom much of Cyril's argument was directed, acknowledged the inspired character of the Old Testament. Cyril's persistent polemic against the Jews is a blemish upon the *Catecheses,* but it must be remembered that in Palestine the Jews would have been the chief critics of Christianity and Cyril's age was not one that easily distinguished between religious error and bad faith. Cyril assumed that almost every detail of the birth, passion and resurrection of Jesus had been prophesied in the Old Testament; it was a principle of exegesis with him that "concerning Christ all things may be found written; nothing is doubtful, for nothing is without its text" (i.e., in the Old Testament).[13] Lectures 12-14 provide massive illustration of this method. It

---

13 *Cat.* 13.38; cf. 13.21.

must be admitted—indeed it is the weakness of the *Catecheses*
—that much of Cyril's exegesis of the Old Testament is im-
plausible and far-fetched; he produces some better arguments
for the truth of the Resurrection in 14.26. Controversial
reasoning against pagans is also to be found in Lectures 12-14
and (against the Samaritans also) in 18.1-21.[14] But the argument from prophecy is very prominent; it is probably con-
nected with an anti-Jewish polemic developed in the Church
of Jerusalem and may have originated in a collection of
"testimonies" and a tradition of exegesis similar to that
which K. Stendahl thinks lies behind St. Matthew's Gospel.[15]

2. Cyril and "Gnosis"

Gnosis in the early Christian tradition was a complex
concept especially associated with the Alexandrian school of
Clement and Origen. Gnosis ("knowledge") usually implies
a sublime sort of knowledge. The word was often used in a
quasi-technical sense. The object of gnosis was usually the
world, the self and, above all, God. Gnosis tended to combine mystical with philosophical or intellectualist elements,
the one or the other predominating. Since it was commonly
held to be obtainable only through a supernatural revelation,
it tended to be esoteric. The mystical variety of gnosis was
won through asceticism, detachment, and the prayerful study
of the Scriptures employing especially the allegorical method
of interpretation. It culminated in union with God through
love.

In 13.9 Cyril implies that there are two kinds of scriptural
exegesis:

---

14 Cf. *Procat.* 10.
15 Cf. K. Stendahl, *The School of St. Matthew* . . . (Uppsala Thesis;
Lund 1954). Stendahl thought Caesarea a possible place of origin for
such a manual of teaching. Cyril may have been trained in Caesarea.
Qumran and Alexandria also had their own special traditions of
exegesis. Cyril and the Alexandrians (Clement and Origen) had a
good deal in common with Irenaeus and the Apologists.

We are met together not now to make a contemplative (*theōrētikēn*) exposition of Scripture, but rather to be certified of the things which we already believe.

This implies that at least one style of the "ordinary preaching"[1] used the allegorical method of interpretation to bring out the hidden meaning of Scripture or, through a contemplative and mystical approach, sought to lead the Christian soul to the higher walks of the spiritual life. Of this quasi-mystical mode of contemplative exegesis of the Scriptures we appear to have a good example in Cyril's *Homily on the Paralytic*. Beginning abruptly with the words: "Wherever Jesus appears, there is salvation," the sermon constantly recalls Clement's picture of Christ who, as the heavenly Physician, cures the sick soul of its passions and then, as the Teacher, schools it, first by discipline, then by instruction, in the knowledge of Himself as the eternal Word.[2] In Chapter 2, Jesus is "the physician of souls"; in Chapter 4, salvation is of faith, faith depends on our willing, and Jesus freely gives the will; Chapter 5 has the theme of spiritual enlightenment; in Chapter 6 the Physician by a question leads the sick man on to the true saving knowledge (*gnōsis*) which the sequel soon shows to be the recognition of Jesus' divinity. It is not the three chapters (10-12) of allegorical exegesis that are so interesting and attractive in the *Homily*, but the contented contemplation of Jesus as the place of encounter with God, the place where Plato's *aisthēta* and *noēta* (earthly and heavenly realities) meet, the Jacob's Ladder of the Fourth Gospel. This is the *theōria* (contemplation) of Clement and Origen. So Origen taught that only through the Word can we contemplate God.[3] The whole *Homily* is impregnated with the spirit of Clement's saying that the highest *theōria* is to seek for God and strive to come to the knowledge of Him.[4] The sentence (Ch. 9), "Look into the strong depths of the

---

1 Cf. the "ordinary homilies" of *Procat.* 11.
2 *Paedagogus* 1.1-2 (GCS, Clem. 1.89-94).
3 Origen, *In Ioh.* 19.6 (GCS, Orig. 3.305; PG 14.536B).
4 Clement, *Stromateis* 2.10.

spring and glimpse God visible in the flesh," suggests that, as Jesus is reflected in the water, so He is Himself the reflection of God, especially of the creative power of the Father from whom, as the prime source of life and being,[5] His healing and saving power derives.

In Chapter 19 Cyril describes Jesus as "the Physician of gnosis," i.e., the physician who heals souls by imparting true knowledge, which is the knowledge of Himself and so of the Father. Similarly, "let us beg wisdom of Wisdom" recalls the conception, common to Clement and Origen, of Christian perfection as the true, supernatural wisdom.

Since the Lenten Lectures aim not at devotion so much as instruction, they are not concerned with gnosis in the sense of mystical or contemplative knowledge. It is not surprising, however, given Cyril's *attrait*, to find them once or twice modulating into *theōria*. Such a passage is that (13.30-31) where the eternal Light leads the Good Thief to the light. Another is 10.13, which introduces briefly many of the themes of the *Homily* and concludes with a reference to the paralytic of John 5.

More important is the question—and in determining it we must remember that gnosis is not *necessarily* a technical word for a special kind of knowledge—whether in the Lenten Lectures we find a relationship of *pistis–gnosis* (faith–knowledge) that corresponds, though transposed, to their relationship in the Alexandrine tradition.

Here it is a question of *gnōsis* in the sense of a systematic body of knowledge, a transcendent revealed synthesis. The Alexandrians did not separate faith and gnosis, but regarded gnosis as the perfection of faith. Clement thought that the whole gnosis was contained in the Old and New Testaments[6] and he defined faith as "a sort of concise gnosis of the essen-

---

5 Cf. Eusebius, *De ecclesiastica theologia* 2.7 (PG 24.913A).
6 *Strom.* 7.16.95 (GCS 3.67). Thus the earliest conception of "fides quaerens intellectum" and "credo ut intelligam" was of a movement not from the revelation to other knowledge, but "from faith to faith," i.e., to a deeper and fuller understanding of the revelation.

tials, while gnosis itself is a firm and solid demonstration of the truths of faith, being built upon faith by means of the Lord's teaching" (i.e., Scripture or the New Testament).[7] This is strikingly similar to the project of the Lenten Lectures, the demonstration of the faith from Scripture. Referring in the introductory lecture[8] to the Lenten enlightenment to which the candidates are looking forward, Cyril says: "We bring you the stones of gnosis." There is an analogy between the relation of Christian faith to knowledge *(gnōsis)* and the Platonic-Aristotelian conception of the relation of opinion or belief to knowledge *(epistēmē)*. In the latter system belief or opinion becomes real knowledge when, grounded in the indemonstrable and self-evident primary premises, it becomes incorporated into a systematic body of scientific knowledge. In the Christian system, faith becomes knowledge when "demonstrated" from the divine authority of Scripture. In the Clement-Origen-Cyril terminology this "demonstration" seems to be conceived variously in three ways: (a) The propositions of the creed are simply proved by the authority of Scripture; i.e., it is shown that Scripture contains and warrants them; (b) while it is possible to disbelieve the bare summary of Scripture contained in the Creed, the scriptural gnosis itself, when the whole synthesis is properly apprehended, is self-authenticating;[9] it stands revealed as a superior philosophy which uniquely satisfies the demands and aspirations of the mind, heart and spirit of man; truth shines in its own light; (c) the (rational) demonstration from miracles and (especially) scriptural prophecies. In all of these ways the propositions at first "taken on faith" are shown to be "warranted"; thus they become the content of "knowledge" (="excellent" or "enlightened" faith) and belief is converted into certitude.

So when formally "delivering" the Creed to the candidates in 5.12, Cyril says that "it embraces in a few words all the godly gnosis of the Old and New Testaments." Cyril's descrip-

---

7 *Ibid.* 7.10.57 (GCS 3.42).
8 *Procat.* 11.
9 In *Procat.* 11, Cyril stresses this systematic, synthetic aspect.

tion in 4.18 of the preceding[10] exposition (summary and un-demonstrated) of the Creed as a gnosis recalls Clement's re-mark[11] that faith may be allowed to be "a sort of concise gnosis of the essentials." The "demonstration" of the Faith in Lenten Lectures 6-18 corresponds to what Clement calls "the gnosis proper." But a genuine gnosis must be not only a theology but also a cosmology and an anthropology. Cyril gives the Christian answer to the great problems which con-cern men: the origin of the world, the origin, nature and destiny of man; the question of fate or necessity; the origin of sin; the reasons for the Incarnation; the question of death; the question of salvation.[12] Cyril several times says emphatical-ly that man is master of his destiny and that his salvation lies in his own power. Not even an overt act is necessary; he has only to will it, to make the decision to believe and be baptized. But it is God who saves us; at least in the *Homily* Cyril adds that the initiative lies with the gracious God who gives the will. But while we are justified by faith, works are also necessary; the Christian must keep the commandments; Cyril several times refers to the repentant Thief as an instance of the mercy of God.[13]

In the *Letter to Constantius* Cyril, announcing the miracu-lous appearance of the luminous cross over Jerusalem, bids the Emperor to build gnosis upon the faith which he already has.[14] Here the idea is that the apparition of the Cross, as the fulfillment of the prophecy of our Lord,[15] is proof of the truth of Christianity and should convert Constantius' faith into gnosis.[16]

To draw attention to this pistis–gnosis pattern in Cyril and

---

10 *Cat.* 4.4-17.
11 Quoted above, n. 7.
12 E.g., *Procat.* 3-5, 7, 8, 16; *Cat.* 1.1; 2.1-5; 3.10; 4.18-32; 8.4; 12.5; 13.2, 28, 35 *fin.*; 14.1 *fin.*; 15.3, 25-26; 18.1-8, 18-20, 29.
13 *Procat.* 8; *Cat.* 1.2; 2.5; 5.10; 13.3-31; 14.10; *Homily* 4-6.
14 *Ep. ad Const.* 5; cf. 2.
15 Matt. 24.30.
16 While the chief message conveyed in the *Letter* is the assurance that the occurrence of the portent in Constantius' reign is a guarantee of heaven's blessing upon that reign, Cyril may well be hinting also

its nominal correspondence with the pattern of faith and gnosis/enlightened faith in Clement and Origen is by no means to suggest that Cyril makes a third with these two powerful and original thinkers. Obviously they stand poles apart. Cyril was an apophatic theologian who repeatedly repudiated speculation. The denatured and formalized gnosis of the Lenten Lectures lacked the profound theoretical structure and presuppositions of the systems of Clement and Origen (for a masterly study of Clement's see T. F. Torrance, "The Implications of Oikonomia for Knowledge and Speech of God in Early Christian Theology," in F. Christ [ed.], *Oikonomia: Heilsgeschichte als Thema der Theologie* (Festschrift O. Cullmann) [Hamburg-Bergstedt 1967] 223-238). It is with the warm and affective Alexandrian mystical tradition, especially the Clement of the *Paedagogus,* that Cyril has some affinity. But now the authenticity of the "Homily on the Paralytic," which leads into the detection of this mode in Cyril is in jeopardy. Bihain has reported that the only works of Cyril known to the Armenian tradition are the Lenten Lectures and the *Letter to Constantius.* We shall see. In any case the data tabulated above remain intact.

J. H. Greenlee[17] has found that the Gospel text of the Lenten Lectures is predominantly the pre-Byzantine Caesarean text of Origen and Eusebius. Quotations of Mark are strongly Caesarean; the material, though small, indicates complete agreement with Origen and Eusebius. In quotations from Matthew the Caesarean character is unquestionable, though weaker in Mt. 1-11. In Luke, again, the Caesarean character of the quotations is clear; quotations show close agreement with Origen, but the relation to Eusebius is unclear. Quotations from John are substantially Caesarean, but here the agreement is with Eusebius rather than Origen. Where not

that it is high time that Constantius be baptized. In Ch. 2, in spite of the construction, *gnosis* is used in the systematic sense (see the next sentence).

17 J. H. Greenlee, *The Gospel Text of Cyril of Jerusalem* (Copenhagen 1955), especially the tables in Part III of this very valuable study.

Caesarean, the text is Neutral rather than Western. Agreement with the Palestinian Syriac is erratic; it is very high in quotations from John. Cyril's quotations are often allusive and he shows the ordinary patristic tendency, already apparent in the manuscripts of the Gospels themselves, to conflate and harmonize variations between the Gospels. Examples will be found at 15.23 (Luke 17.34=Mt. 24.40) and *Homily* 5, where Cyril conflates Matthew's two stories (9.27-28 and 20.30-32) of the healing of two blind men.

3. The Historical Situation

Little is known for certain[1] about Cyril except that he was bishop of the Holy City from *ca.* early 349 to 18 March 387,[2] was several times deposed and banished, for many a long year resisted the Nicene definition of the "consubstantial," attended the First Council of Constantinople in 381, and is the author of the first of the two series of Catechetical Lectures traditionally associated with his name. The ancient historians mention Cyril as seldom as do modern Church historians, and their references to him are often as obscure and misleading as they are rare. Moreover, by the fourth decade of the fifth century Church history had already been byzantinized; Socrates, Sozomen and Theodoret had little understanding even of the *Problematik* of the great Arian controversy, and they are particularly uninstructive just in those areas and at those moments which touch Cyril. St. Jerome, who had excellent sources of information, was blinded by his Western partiality and was particularly embittered against Cyril. The narrowly orthodox St. Epiphanius must likewise have been well informed, but his references to Cyril are also few, brief

---

1 Cf. Telfer, General Introduction, first sentence. But Telfer has himself solved some of the problems.
2 For the year of his death, cf. P. Nautin, "La date du *De viris illustribus*," *Revue d'histoire ecclésiastique* 56 (1961) 33-35.

and somewhat obscure. Again, though belonging to a camp embattled against the strict Nicaeans, Cyril never mentions Athanasius, nor Athanasius him.

It is, of course, possible that the explanation of the early historians' near-silence about Cyril is that he played no considerable part in the great theological struggle. But there are some signs—the animosity of the strict Nicaeans against him is one—that from Cyril a powerful influence radiated. It must be remembered that the key-words and formulas about which our Fathers quarrelled in the fourth century were obscure and ambiguous, and most of those who resisted the "consubstantial" resisted it for the most edifying reasons. Referring to the struggle between Homoousians and Homoeousians (the "moderate" or "semi-Arian" party) Socrates, in a moment of insight, or perhaps quoting a perceptive acquaintance, remarked: "It was like a battle in the dark, with both sides shooting at shadows."[3] Similarly Athanasius spoke of the moderate party as "those who hold the same doctrines as we do, and differ from us only about a word."[4] Wolfson has described the position well by saying that when heresy was introduced by Arius, the variety and inconsistency of Trinitarian terminology led to a "war of suspicion" among the orthodox.[5]

Jerusalem and Caesarea

The story both of Cyril's life and of the Arian controversy in Palestine is in a considerable degree the story of a conflict between Jerusalem and Caesarea. It is, therefore, impossible to interpret Cyril's life correctly without some picture of the relationship existing between Jerusalem and Caesarea, the capital (*mētropolis*) of the Roman province of Palestine and,

---

3 Socrates, *Hist. eccles.* 1.23.
4 *De synodis* 41.
5 H. A. Wolfson, *The Philosophy of the Church Fathers* I (Cambridge, Mass. 1956) Ch. 15, sect. iii (p. 337).

from the time when ecclesiastical administration based on the unit of the Roman province developed, the metropolitan church of at least most of Palestine. The ordinary, or at least majority, view is that Jerusalem had "always" (i.e., really from *ca.* 135) been subject to Caesarea[6] and that the seventh canon of Nicaea merely reasserted this position, while also confirming to Jerusalem certain unspecified honorary ancient privileges, so that Jerusalem had no reason to be discontented with the canon. The canon reads:

> Let the bishop of Aelia [Jerusalem] keep his honorary precedency, warranted as it is by custom and ancient tradition, without prejudice to the proper dignity of the metropolitan see.

This conception of the situation needs, I believe, a slight but important adjustment. I believe that although Caesarea may have gained a widely acknowledged metropolitan jurisdiction over Jerusalem in the twilight period comprising the fifty years before Nicaea, Jerusalem would not have gladly acquiesced in this situation nor have gladly accepted the Nicene canon confirming it. It is unlikely that the canon resulted from an amicable arrangement between the two bishops concerned; for Eusebius of Caesarea and Macarius were champions of opposing theological views before and at the Council. While Eusebius came to Nicaea under a provisional sentence of excommunication for his Arian sym-

---

6 Cf. F. Dvornik, *The Idea of Apostolicity in Byzantium* (Cambridge, Mass. 1958) 21-23. So also S. Vailhé, "Formation du Patriarcat de Jérusalem," *Echos d'Orient* 13 (1910) 325-336, held that Jerusalem had always been suffragan to Caesarea, that *ca.* 196 her apostolicity won her second place in the province and that so the position remained until Nicaea when it was confirmed by the seventh canon. Vailhé allowed a good deal of prestige to Jerusalem, but based this on a distinction between "honor" and "jurisdiction" and between the bishop and the see. I suspect that the seventh canon may have created some such distinctions but that they would have been anachronistic before the late third century. W. Telfer and F. L. Cross (*op. cit.,* n. on pp. xv-xvi) are in substantial agreement with Dvornik.

pathies, Macarius was one of the three "theological ignoramuses" whom Arius listed as his chief enemies.[7]

I suggest that the position of Jerusalem was not that of the first satellite of Caesarea, but of a second sun in Palestine; that Jerusalem was virtually a second, smaller metropolitan church in the south of Palestine. Not only did Constantinople I in 381 call Jerusalem "the mother of all the churches," as also did the *Apostolic Constitutions*, but Origen called Jerusalem a *mētropolis*.[8] Probably while Jerusalem may have been theoretically suffragan to Caesarea, she enjoyed not merely prestige but genuinely substantial privileges giving her a great deal of independent authority; she probably, though the evidence is not decisive, governed a ring of suburban and outlying churches around Jerusalem. Probably F. J. A. Hort appraised the situation accurately (if we give full force to the word "balanced") when he wrote: "All Palestine was subject to the supremacy of Antioch; and the metropolitan jurisdiction of Caesarea over the rest of Palestine was balanced by privileges peculiar to Jerusalem."[9] In particular Jerusalem appears to have enjoyed the very important privilege of special rights in determining the episcopal succession on the death of her own bishop and probably also in neighboring sees. Normally election was by the comprovincial bishops, although in early times the local people and clergy had a powerful voice. There was a gradual trend towards the transference of the power of election to the comprovincials and especially to the metropolitan, a trend consolidated by the fourth, and perhaps also by the sixth, canon of Nicaea. But it looks as if Jerusalem, like Rome and Alexandria,[10] had retained the

---

7 Letter of Arius to Eusebius of Nicomedia preserved in Epiphanius, *Panarion* 69.6; also in Theodoret, *Hist. eccles.* 1.5.1-4. A. P. Stanley, *Lectures on the History of the Eastern Church* (2nd ed., New York 1862) 260, suggested that the seventh canon reflected a "passage of arms" between Eusebius and Macarius, and he was probably right.
8 Origen, *Fr. 58 in Ierem.* (GCS, Orig. 3.277.11; PG 13.584A).
9 Hort, *Two Dissertations* 59.
10 At Alexandria St. Athanasius appointed his own successor before his death in 373.

rights of the local church in this matter, just as these were the three great churches in which government was originally collegiate.

While in general the rank of sees was determined by the place of the cathedral city in the imperial administrative divisions rather than by apostolicity (in the East apostolic sees were two-a-penny), the church of Jerusalem—the church of all the apostles, the church created by the Holy Spirit and situated in the city where the decisive events of salvation history had taken place—was unique; and Telfer has argued impressively that the disasters of 68-70 and 134-5 had not destroyed the continuity of the Jerusalem tradition. In any case the New Testament was an abiding witness to the glories of the church of Jerusalem.

While it is well known that both of Cyril's immediate predecessors had attempted, one successfully and one unsuccessfully, to appoint their successors without reference to Caesarea, the evidence of the *Church History* of Eusebius suggests that these events were not simply the result of the theological quarrel between the two churches at this time but reflected a long-standing claim on the part of Jerusalem. Eusebius' pages show Jerusalem behaving, especially in the matter of episcopal elections, in a high-handed way, flouting the customs by which other churches were bound and breaking more or less widely acknowledged rules. Eusebius also gives the impression that Caesarea and Jerusalem were a pair of approximately equally distinguished churches in Palestine.

The story of bishop Narcissus,[11] though he is no doubt largely a legendary figure, is suggestive. Said to have been 116 years of age in 216, he may have become bishop before the middle of the second century. His holiness made him enemies and he disappeared into the desert. "The neighboring (*homoroi*)[12] churches" ordained Dius in his place. Dius was

---

11 Eusebius, *Hist. eccles.* 5.12; 6.9-11.
12 If *homoros* ("marching with," "having common boundaries") is used strictly, it would refer not to Caesarea but to suburban parish churches and the dioceses in the immediate vicinity of Jerusalem. Similarly

succeeded by Germanio, who was succeeded by Gordius, during whose episcopate Narcissus reappeared and was immediately besought by "the brethren" to accept the episcopate. Unless Gordius died, he presumably either retired into the ranks of the presbyters, like Cyril's rival Heraclius later, or acted as auxiliary. For a see to have two bishops was a grave violation of Church law, and for a bishop to have an auxiliary was probably felt to savor also of ambition and aggrandizement. Narcissus may even have had two auxiliaries for a time, for Eusebius' account represents Alexander's arrival and election by acclamation *(ca.* 212) as occurring immediately afterwards. Alexander certainly, according to Eusebius' account, acted as Narcissus' coadjutor,[13] and his election also broke the rule against translations. Eusebius says that in ordaining Alexander, Jerusalem acted "with the unanimous consent of the neighbouring *(perix)* churches." Which are "the neighbouring churches"?[14] Perhaps Narcissus did consult Caesarea, the comprovincial bishops, and Antioch, beforehand; but could *they* have dispensed with canon law?

---

when (7.28), listing the illustrious bishops *ca.* 266, Eusebius uses the word again, speaking of "Hymenaeus of the church of Jerusalem and Theotecnus of the neighboring church of Caesarea," he is using the word accurately only if the reference is to two metropolitans whose provinces march together. Of course, in the former instance the word could precisely refer to Caesarea *if* the reference were to provinces.

13 Eusebius, *Hist. eccles.* 6.11.

14 For *perix* cf. Acts 5.16. Eusebius seems not to use the word *eparchia* (province) much. Perhaps it is an anachronism to read back the Nicene organization into pre-Nicene times, when law and custom were hardly distinguished. The organization by provinces originated as a *de facto* inevitable arrangement, gradually crystallized and became formally recognized. Then Jerusalem, the one church whose position was not based on its cathedral city being a capital, was left high and dry, as the Nicene canon mentioned but did not specify its traditional rights—indeed referred only to "honor" *(timē).* I believe that the seventh canon was a blow to Jerusalem. Macarius may have asked for a special canon—he would have been forced to after canon 4—but the effective part of the canon is clearly the final saving clause. For it is likely that the traditional privileges of Jerusalem *had* meant that Caesarea had not enjoyed (at least full) metropolitan rights in her regard, and consequently Jerusalem's traditional privileges were annulled by the clause which "saved" Caesarea's metropolitan authority in her regard.

Eusebius' account of the Origen episode would lead one
to suppose that Jerusalem and Caesarea enjoyed equal em-
inence and authority. In concert their two bishops acted with
marked independence of ecclesiastical rules. When in 216
Origen came to Palestine and stayed in Caesarea, "the bishops
of the country" invited him to preach, although Origen's
own bishop, Demetrius of Alexandria, thought this highly
irregular as Origen was not a presbyter. When Demetrius
protested, "Alexander of Jerusalem and Theoctistus of
Caesarea" (the second time we have seen Eusebius name the
sees in that order) wrote defending their action. When in 229
or 230 Origen again arrived in Palestine, "the bishops of
Caesarea and Jerusalem, the most eminent in Palestine"
ordained him in Caesarea, where he continued to reside for the
rest of his life. "Alexander of Jerusalem and Theoctistus
of Caesarea used to hang on his lips" and Firmilianus came
from Cappadocia and "visited him in Judaea [*sic*]."[15] In one
of his periodical lists of illustrious bishops Eusebius[16] mentions Theophilus of Caesarea immediately before Narcissus;
the churches listed are Rome, Alexandria, Antioch, Caesarea,
Jerusalem, Corinth and Ephesus, all apostolic sees and all
except Jerusalem capital cities.

Bright, who assumed that Jerusalem enjoyed "precedency
among the suffragan churches," wrote that "Caesarea was the
undoubted metropolis of Palestine: and its bishop Theophilus
had, in the latter part of the second century, presided over
a synod of Palestinian bishops" (Euseb. 5.23).[17] But, in fact,
what Eusebius says at 5.23 is that Theophilus of Caesarea and
Narcissus of Jerusalem presided. In the Paul of Samosata
episode (264-268/9) at Antioch, Jerusalem scores heavily:
Eusebius names Hymenaeus before Theotecnus; and in the
encyclical letter issued by the final synod, Hymenaeus' name

---

15 Eusebius, *Hist. eccles.* 6.8.1-5; 6.19.16-19; 6.23.4; 6.27; Jerome, *De vir.
illus.* 54.
16 Eusebius, *Hist. eccles.* 5.22.
17 W. Bright, *Notes on the Canons of the First Four General Councils*
(Oxford 1882) 22. The date of the synod was *ca.* 196.

stands second, immediately after Helenus of Tarsus, who was apparently president after the death of Firmilianus.[18] Vailhé,[19] however, wrote: "dans ce synode régional les préséances paraissent établies, non d'après la prééminence du siège, mais d'après la date d'ordination." Possibly the position had changed, to Jerusalem's disadvantage, by 300. Caesarea, but not Jerusalem, is listed among the sees represented at the councils of Ancyra (ca. 314) and Caesarea in Cappadocia (ca. 318); neither council, however, was restricted to metropolitans.[20] In any case, there seems to be no reason to believe that at least up to 270 Jerusalem was, at least in practice, subject to Caesarea.

Arius was hospitably received by Eusebius. Since his denunciation of Macarius, apparently written from Caesarea, belongs to the year 324, it is likely that Macarius took a leading part in the council of Antioch (early 325) which condemned Eusebius. Moreover, Hort may be right in his view that Macarius took a prominent part in the defeat of Eusebius at Nicaea.[21] Certainly from 324 until the death of Maximus in 348/9 relations between Jerusalem and Caesarea must have been extremely tense—indeed not far from a state of ecclesiastical war. The situation was aggravated by the fact that for eighty-five years from ca. 330 the patriarchal church of Antioch was paralyzed by schism and could do little or nothing to make peace.

Describing the succession of Cyril's predecessor, Maximus, to Macarius early in 335, Sozomen writes:[22]

> The story is that Maximus had earlier been ordained by Macarius to the see of Diospolis [=Lydda], but that the

18 Eusebius, *Hist. eccles.* 7.28; 7.30.2,5.
19 *Loc. cit.* Vailhé produces no evidence for this assertion.
20 There seems to be some doubt whether the lists for these two councils are complete. The see of Jerusalem may have been vacant at the time of Ancyra.
21 Hort 59 n. 2; cf. Theodoret. *Hist. eccles.* 1.18; cf. 2.4; Sozomen, *Hist. eccles.* 1.13.2; 2.20.
22 Sozomen 2.20; "the people" may have included the local clergy (presbyterate).

people of Jerusalem insisted on keeping him. For . . . he was already the people's tacit choice as Macarius' successor.

Claiming special knowledge of the facts, Sozomen (a Palestinian writing in Constantinople about 446) states that Macarius privately agreed with his people, judging Maximus a suitable successor on account of his sound Trinitarian doctrine, especially as he feared that otherwise Eusebius and Patrophilus of Scythopolis would on his death place an Arian in the see: "for even during Macarius' lifetime they had attempted a coup." So Maximus was retained by Macarius as his coadjutor and succeeded him. But what is so remarkable is that Macarius should, without consulting Caesarea, have ordained a bishop for a see twenty-five miles to the northwest of Jerusalem;[23] and this after Nicaea! The increasing prestige of Jerusalem after the rediscovery of the holy places in 326 may have affected Macarius' bold policy, yet the episode is in striking accord with the picture of Jerusalem's position as we have tentatively reconstructed it for the years 185-270. For Sozomen writes as if Jerusalem had the right to appoint to certain neighbouring sees and as if election to its own see were simply by "the Chapter."

There is no reason to believe that before 323 or 324 relations between Caesarea and Jerusalem had been anything but friendly. The quarrel was caused by the different attitudes of Eusebius and Macarius to the Nicene definition, and was probably exacerbated by the seventh canon of Nicaea. Soon after, when Eusebius was succeeded by his admirer, Acacius, in 340, the situation deteriorated still further. For when a great East-West council met at Serdica (Sofia) in 342, the Eastern bishops found St. Athanasius, whom they had deposed for canonical reasons, sitting with the Western bishops. They demanded that he withdraw and, when he refused, left the

---

23 Perhaps what really happened was that Eusebius defeated Macarius' attempt to place his nominee in the see of Diospolis, but failed to prevent Maximus's succession in Jerusalem.

assembly, and, holding a council separately, deposed Pope Julius and other Nicaean leaders. A very few of the Eastern bishops—Maximus among them—stayed at Serdica with the Western bishops, and this council deposed a number of the Eastern leaders, including Acacius.[24] Thus Maximus deposed his own metropolitan. It must be assumed that Acacius promptly retaliated.

4. Life of Cyril

Only within this context can the life of Cyril be understood. Cyril firmly believed in the true divinity of Christ, but he disliked the Athanasian theology. In 346 Cyril's predecessor, Maximus, reaffirmed his support of Athanasius by convening a small council of fifteen Palestinian bishops[1] who received Athanasius into communion and sped him on his way to Alexandria. Some time before his death in 348/9 Maximus, like his predecessor Macarius, appointed and consecrated his successor, one Heraclius, to prevent Acacius of Caesarea securing the appointment of an anti-Athanasian. The well informed St. Jerome, describing Cyril's election,[2] says that on the death of Maximus "the church of Jerusalem was invaded by Arians, first by Cyril . . . ." According to Jerome, Acacius and his allies in the province made it a condition, in giving the see to Cyril, that he renounce his priestly ordination by Maximus and submit to reordination. This is probably true, as by Eastern canon law Acacius' deposition of Maximus would have been valid and Maximus' subsequent ordinations invalid. Socrates and Sozomen say that Acacius and Patrophilus expelled Maximus and replaced him by Cyril.[3] This

---

24 Sozomen 3.11-13; Athanasius, *Apol. c. Arian* 50 *fin.*

1 Probably a few of them were from Syria outside Palestine; Socrates 2.24.1-2.

2 *Chronicle*, at the 11th year of the Sons of Constantine (PL 27.501-2). In the terminology of Jerome, Epiphanius and (usually) Athanasius, all non-Homoousians are Arians.

3 Socrates 2.38.2; Sozomen 4.20.1.

is unlikely. Up to 350 Constantius was held in check by the powerful Western emperor, Constans; it was only after Constans' assassination early in 350, indeed only after the defeat of Magnentius in late 351, that a strong anti-Athanasian policy became possible. E. Bihain has shown that Socrates 2.38.2 belongs between 2.27.7 and 2.28.1; we may probably infer that its strictly orthodox and bitterly "anti-Macedonian" source represented Cyril's installation in Jerusalem as part of the general anti-Nicene *revanche* of 351, which included the replacement of Paul by Macedonius in the see of Constantinople.[4] Consequently, Heraclius may have ruled the see of Jerusalem for a short time after the death of Maximus. Jerome's text suggests that on Cyril's accession Heraclius was persuaded reluctantly to retire into the ranks of the presbyters. This episode implies no unorthodoxy in Cyril; but (unlike his two immediate predecessors), a product of the Eastern theological tradition, Cyril was in decided sympathy with the determination of the Eastern Church to affirm the divinity of Christ in the terminology of its traditional formulas.

Not later than 355 Cyril quarrelled with his metropolitan Acacius:[5]

> After being entrusted with the bishopric of Jerusalem, Cyril quarrelled with Acacius of Caesarea concerning metropolitan rights, on the ground that he ruled an apostolic see. From that they proceeded to personal feuding, imputing to each other unsound doctrine. For even previously both had been suspect, surmise attributing Arian views to Acacius and to Cyril sympathy with the "homoousion." In this mood Acacius, acting with the bishops of the province who shared his views, got his blow in first and deposed him.

Socrates[6] does not know the charges against Cyril.

---

4 This, probably coincidental, association of Cyril with Macedonius at the beginning of his public life may explain why so often in the Socrates–Sozomen tradition he is later classified as a "Macedonian."

5 Sozomen 4.25.2. The emendation *homoiousion* for *homoousion* has been suggested.

6 Socrates 2.40.

Doctrinal differences, if relevant at all, were secondary. The issue was certainly the jurisdiction or privileges of Jerusalem. Sozomen apparently meant that Cyril claimed the metropolitanate of Palestine for Jerusalem. This, like the reference to the apostolicity of the see of Jerusalem, is clearly an anachronism. But a legal dispute was inevitable owing to the self-contradictory 7th canon of Nicaea, which at once guaranteed full metropolitan rights to Caesarea, and to Jerusalem ancient rights which (I suppose) had in ante-Nicene times qualified Caesarea's metropolitan rights in regard to Jerusalem. Since Theodoret[7] also describes the quarrel as a struggle "for the primacy" and Socrates reports that for two years Cyril refused to appear to stand his trial, it is fairly certain that, while a claim by Jerusalem to be the metropolitan of Palestine was at this time out of the question, the issue was some alleged infringement by Caesarea of Jerusalem's traditional rights or a revival by Cyril of an ancient claim by Jerusalem to be virtually a second metropolitan see in the south of Palestine. Since a metropolitan court could do nothing worse to Cyril than depose him, his refusal to attend it is most naturally interpreted as based on a denial of the competency of the court, apparently a Palestinian court convened at Caesarea. Cyril's appeal to a higher jurisdiction fits into the same picture; and the Emperor's sanctioning of the appeal is interesting.

While his appeal was pending, Cyril requested the Emperor to have his case tried by a higher court, i.e., by a more broadly representative council. Constantius assented. Meanwhile (357) Cyril found a friendly welcome with Silvanus of Tarsus. There were canons forbidding the reception into communion of a deposed bishop and Acacius took advantage of them to protest, but Silvanus neatly riposted with the remark that Cyril's preaching had made him such a favorite with the people that expulsion or suspension was impossible.

---

7 Theodoret, *Hist. eccles.* 2.26.

Towards Seleucia

In the fifties the Emperor used Sirmium, a fortress town and imperial residence in the Balkans, as a meeting-place for his theological advisers from East and West. The arianizing Eudoxius was now bishop of Antioch and the irreverent dialectician Aëtius had risen to notoriety. The year 357 saw the promulgation of the disquieting ambiguous Second Formula of Sirmium.[8] Banning discussions of "substance" and the formulas "homoousion" and "homoiousion," this creed confessed "one God, the Father Almighty . . . not two Gods"; the Son is "God of God, Light of Light," subordinate to the Father from whom He was begotten before the ages. "Likeness" was not formally asserted. The document, whose tone was agnostic rather than apophatic, raised the question whether it regarded the Son as God in a merely titular sense. The East took fright. Basil of Ancyra summoned a council (358) and, aided by George of Laodicea, campaigned successfully for the formula "homoiousion, of like substance," really probably "of the same generic substance or nature."[9] Basil converted the Emperor Constantius and Macedonius of Constantinople to this formula. Flushed with success, Basil banished over seventy "Arian" bishops, including Eudoxius. Constantius and the Homoeousians then decided to hold a general council to achieve unity in orthodoxy. East and West were to meet at Seleucia and Rimini respectively, and a theological commission from each council was then to repair to Constantinople, where it would be determined how far the decisions reached agreed with Scripture. But a reaction against Basil and his formula set in. The formula finally drawn up at Sirmium (the Fourth[10] [Third] of Sirmium, the "Dated Creed," 22 May 359) as a norm or basis for the conciliar dis-

---

8 Text in Hilary, De synodis 11; Athanasius, De synodis 28. Cf. Denzinger, nn. 138-39.

9 Text of Basil's encyclical conciliar letter in Epiphanius, Haer. 73.2-11; dogmatic epistle of Basil and George, ibid. 12-22.

10 Fourth, if one counts the unoriginal formula (Sirmium 358) as the Third.

cussions asserted not "like in substance" but "like in all things." At the critical moment Basil had been to some extent displaced in the Emperor's confidence by a group (including Acacius?) which stood somewhat to his left and disliked any formulas embodying *ousia*.

The Letter of Basil and George (allies of Cyril's friend, Silvanus) preserved by Epiphanius seems to show the Homoeousian leaders planning a line of argument in this situation. The relationship of Father and Son, it says, is better expressed by the terms Father and Son, which imply essential likeness (identity of specific or generic nature), than by "Unbegotten" (or "Unoriginate") and "Begotten," which imply some sort of unlikeness and contrast. Moreover "Unbegotten" is, like *ousia*, unscriptural. No doubt some or many (though their numbers are perhaps usually exaggerated) of the moderate party thought that Basil had made a fatal mistake in accepting the compromise "in all points." This Letter points out that "like in all points," i.e., "complete likeness," includes likeness in substance. The formula has now, Basil says, been accepted by all parties and approved by the Emperor; so it is the other side that has been outwitted.

The council of Seleucia (27-30 September 359) is unfortunately as obscure as it is interesting and important.[11] Cyril came to Seleucia under the wing of Silvanus and mingled with the Homoeousian leaders. Many of the leading bishops were deposed or had charges lying against them, and the council was intended to settle these questions also. The council could not agree and soon split into two parties. According to Philostorgius the Basilians, meeting separately, ratified the "homoiousion." This is improbable. According to Socrates and Sozomen, although there was a sharp debate about the "homoiousion," the Basilians adopted the Dedication Creed of Antioch (341). This account appears to be cer-

---

11 Socrates 2.39-40, Sozomen 4.22-23; Philostorgius, *Hist. eccles.* 4.11, Epiphanius, *Haer.* 73.23, 27; Athanasius, *De syn.* 29, Hilary (who claims to have attended the council), *Liber ad Constantium Augustum*, Theodoret 2.26.2-27.2.

tified by the preamble of the extant *ekthesis* of the Acacians. The Antioch formula was a good orthodox creed which had been accepted by Pope Liberius along with the First Sirmium.[12] The Acacian creed *(Syn.* 29) declared full agreement with the Antioch creed and anathematized the *anomoion* ("unlike"), but, rejecting *homoousios* and *homoiousios* as unscriptural terminology and affirming "God of God" with a weak "like" formula, it resembled the Niké formula, i.e., the weakened 4th (3rd) Sirmium finally accepted by Rimini. The omission of *kata panta* (Cyril's formula) was very regrettable.

The discussion included a debate of "likeness in substance," maintained by the Basilians, as against "like in will and action." The Basilians claimed that Acacius had previously committed himself in writing to "likeness in all respects" and (Sozomen) "likeness in essence." Sozomen's statement perhaps means that the Basilians argued that universal likeness included likeness of nature or substance. But the occasion referred to may be a written *votum* submitted by Acacius to Macedonius or Constantius in the course of the deliberations of the theological experts at Sirmium (358-359) in the period when the Basilians were in the ascendant.

Sozomen reports Eleusius, a moderate, as saying: "Any deal that Basil or Mark may have made on their own, or the mutual accusations made by them and the Acacians, are no affair of the Council. Neither need the Council concern itself with the question whether their credal formula is, or is not, a good one"; then he urged the reaffirmation of the Antioch creed.[13] The interpretation of this remark depends to some extent on the sequence of events, which is uncertain. Perhaps Acacius had accused the moderates of betraying him

---

12 Liberius' four letters in Hilary's *Fragmenta;* Denzinger, nn. 138, 141-143 (all new to the 32nd ed.); Athanasius, *Hist. Arian.* 41; Sozomen 4.15. Pressure had been brought to bear on Liberius, but he insists that he acted freely and in the interests of peace and unity. He seems genuinely to have come to see the Eastern point of view and to have recognized the legitimacy of their *Problematik* and terminology.

13 Sozomen 4.22.22; cf. 4.27.1 and Socrates 2.45 *init.* But see also Athanasius, *De syn.* 37-38.

by not accepting the Sirmium formula and Basil and Mark had countered that he had betrayed them by weakening that formula. But some of the moderates may have thought that to proclaim the "homoiousion" just when the West seemed ready to abandon logical and metaphysical mysteries in favor of the acknowledgment of the mystery of the divine Being itself, was to surrender everything they had fought for when they were in sight of victory. Alternatively it is possible that the majority were deterred from affirming the "homoiousion" by Sirmium's ban on *ousia;* in general, however, the Seleucian majority showed little respect for the imperial will. Moreover, bishops unable to be present themselves, and perhaps including some of the left-wing bishops banished by Basil, were allowed to vote by proxy at the council.

Theodoret represents the council as breaking down over the question of Cyril. When Acacius, he says, found Cyril among the assembled bishops, he demanded that, as being deposed, he withdraw, but, though his demand won some support, Cyril refused, and then Acacius left the assembly and joined the Eudoxians. This, however, is incredible. Such intransigence would have been suicide on Cyril's part, and the greater folly as he appears to have had the sympathy of the majority. Theodoret has been carried away by his liking for the dramatic and the personal. His reference, a little earlier, to Cyril as "a zealous champion of the apostolic decrees" (i.e., apparently of Nicaea) shows that he is thinking of the later Cyril of the Establishment and comparing his presence at Seleucia to the presence of Athanasius at Sardica, where the tactical situation was different. The presence of a number of deposed and accused prelates was clearly a cause of complaint at Seleucia, but there is no reason to doubt the statements of Socrates and Sozomen[14] that the complaint chiefly concerned the late arrivals, Macedonius and Basil, and that all the bishops challenged by Acacius withdrew.[15] Moreover Acacius

---

14 Socrates 2.40 *ad init.,* Sozomen 4.22.10-11.
15 See also Sozomen 4.22.25.

seems to have been in partial sympathy with the Eudoxians since 357.

Probably the difference between the Antioch creed and the Acacian formula, though superficially not very great, was critical. It was apparently Acacius' mission to win the council's assent to the same weakened Sirmium formula which was to be forced upon the West. For this purpose the Antioch formula would not quite serve. But the major episcopal trials pending were also an important issue (not unconnected with the doctrinal issue), and Acacius seems to have found himself facing a strong *bloc,* a *bloc,* moreover, that was planning to replace Eudoxius by Anianus at Antioch. Within this political pattern of personal and "cathedral" rivalries the question of Cyril was not unimportant—especially to the metropolitan of Palestine. Epiphanius, who in 359 was still living in his monastery near Eleutheropolis, states that Eutychius of Eleutheropolis, though a Nicaean, cast in his lot with the Acacians out of enmity for Cyril.[16] As Eleutheropolis lies to the southwest of Jerusalem, Cyril may have been interfering in Eutychius' diocese on the ground that it formed part of his "province" or sphere of influence.

Continuing to meet on their own after Leonas and the Acacians had signified their intention of boycotting the council, the majority deposed, among others, George, Eudoxius and Acacius—the bishops of Alexandria, Antioch and Caesarea! —and presumably acquitted and reinstated Cyril, and ordained Anianus bishop of Antioch. The Acacians and ten deputies representing the Seleucia majority repaired to Constantinople, where they met the ten deputies from Rimini and a number of other bishops who happened to be in the capital on business. The ten Seleucian deputies finally accepted the revised Rimini creed. Sozomen[17] reports that they abandoned the term "substance" only when the Acacians assured them on oath that the dropping of the term by no

16 Epiphanius, *Haer.* 73.23, deleting the negative with Petau.
17 Sozomen 4.23.5.

means implied the view that the Son was unlike the Father in substance, a doctrine which they were ready formally to condemn. We may perhaps accept the sincerity of the Acacians in this matter and the truth of Philostorgius' statement[18] that when (early 360) Acacius deposed both the (arianizing) Aëtians and the Basilian leaders, he deposed the former for their heterodoxy and the later because of his vendetta with them.

Among those deposed by this Acacian council and banished by the Emperor in 360 were Macedonius, Eustathius, Basil, Silvanus, Sophronius, Eleusius, Anianus, Neonas of Seleucia and Cyril.[19]

A.D. 360-387

Thereafter Cyril seems to have shared the fate of the Eastern "conservative" bishops. Recalled (January 363) under Julian, repossessed of his see under the orthodox Jovian (d. Feb. 364), he was banished by the Homoean Valens in late 366 or 367 and returned finally to his see when Gratian (autumn 378) recalled the bishops exiled by Valens.[20]

Cyril's activities and views during this long period are obscure. He was powerful enough to secure the appointment of his nephew Gelasius to the see of Caesarea on the death of

---

18 Philostorgius 4.1, 12; 5.1; 6.4. But if Socrates 2.45 and Sozomen 4.29 are accurate, I am probably wrong. Whereas Athanasius (De syn. 31) judged Acacius a secret Arian, Philosotorgius (who characterizes him as a liar and a master of Machiavellian arts) thought him a hypocritical Arian who double-crossed the Eudoxians by appointing "Homoousian" bishops in 360. Philosotorgius does not formally contradict Athanasius' statement that Acacius appointed Arian bishops, since in Athanasius' vocabulary "Arian" means anyone who does not accept the "homoousion," while in Philostorgius' vocabulary "Homoousian" means anyone who believes that Christ is God and not a creature. The only reliable evidence for anyone's belief in this period is the creeds he signed. The allegations of Acacius' Aëtianism in Antioch in 361 may arise from a popular misunderstanding of the favorite Homoean theme that there are not "two Unbegottens." It is rather surprising that both Constantius (who was in Antioch) and Acacius should so suddenly change from persecutors to adherents of Aëtianism.
19 Sozomen 4.25.1-5; Theodoret 2.27.2.
20 Socrates 4.35; Sozomen, 4.30.3.

Acacius in 366. Though soon ousted, Gelasius later regained the see and still held it at the time of the first council of Constantinople (381).

When did Cyril accept the "homoousion"? Hort's view that he accepted it in the years 362-364 rests largely on his assumption that Cyril was an ally of St. Meletius of Antioch, whose name headed the signatures to the Nicene confession sent to Jovian by the bishops assembled at Antioch in 363.[21] Tillemont had linked this event with Theodoret's story[22] of how between June 362 and March 363[23] Cyril received from Meletius at Antioch and smuggled over to Palestine the convert son of a pagan priest attached to the court of the apostate Julian. It seems certain, however, that Cyril did not sign the memorial to Jovian, since Socrates, drawing on Sabinus, apparently gives the complete list of signatories, and Cyril is not among them.[24] Moreover, there is far more evidence for a friendship between Meletius and Acacius than between Meletius and Cyril. Meletius voted with the Acacians at Seleucia,[25] and Epiphanius seems to say that his action was motivated by enmity towards Cyril. In 361 Acacius secured Meletius' nomination to the see of Antioch. Acacius was a cosignatory with Meletius to the memorial to Jovian in 363.

If Cyril during this period was an active member of any group, there is a stronger case for the conjecture that he was one of the homoeousian "Macedonians" who, anticipating the Meletians and led by Basil and Silvanus, petitioned Jovian in 363 and were rebuffed.[26] It seems to have been approximately the same group which, led by Silvanus and Eustathius, in the autumn of 365 or spring of 366 sent a deputation to the Western Emperor Valentinian, Pope Liberius and the Western bishops, accepted the Nicene creed and were re-

---

21 Hort, *Two Dissertations* 97-107, esp. 95-97; 106 n. 5.
22 Theodoret, *Hist. eccles.* 3.10.
23 Dates established by Clinton.
24 Socrates 3.25 (cf. 27, 28). This council at Antioch seems to have been in the late summer or autumn of 363.
25 Epiphanius, *Haer.* 73.23; Socrates 2.44.
26 Socrates 3.25 *init.;* Sozomen 6.4 *init.*

ceived into communion by Liberius.[27] The second name on the list of the addressees of Liberius' letter is "Cyril." But it is a common name, and Socrates and Sozomen, though they describe the "Macedonians" as led by those bishops of the Seleucia majority deposed by Acacius in 360, never actually mention Cyril among them. Sometimes, without characterizing his position, they seem to distinguish him from them. Again, if Socrates and Sozomen are at all correct in ascribing to the "Macedonians" heretical views about the Holy Spirit, Cyril (unless the *Catecheses* are more heavily stratified or interpolated than the evidence presently available suggests) cannot have belonged to their group.[28] In the years following 360 he may have played a lone hand. It is noticeable that Socrates, in describing the position on the accession of Valens, mentions Cyril without characterizing his doctrinal position.[29] If the "Niceno-Constantinoplitan" creed is a revision and expansion of the Jerusalem creed, and if the former's appearance in the *Ancoratus* of Epiphanius[30] is authentic, then Cyril must have accepted the "consubstantial" by 374.[31] Yet in this case it is surprising that neither Socrates nor Sozomen mentions Cyril's conversion to formal, as distinct from substantive, Nicene orthodoxy, for the overt gesture of the acceptance or the rejection of the "homoousion" is just the sort of thing

27 Socrates 4.12; Sozomen 6.10-11. In their letter to Liberius this group glossed the "homoousion" as meaning "Very God" and "like to the Father in all things," both characteristic Cyrillic phrases. For the later theological history of this group, see Socrates 4.12 *fin.*, 5.4; Sozomen 7.2.2-4.
28 That is, after they fell into heresy, in 361. Sozomen 4.25.1 (cf. 24.9, 16) suggests that Cyril's original trouble with Acacius stemmed from his association with the Homoeousian Seleucians including the eccentric ascetic Eustathius, whom in 358 a council at Melitene deposed in favor of Miletius. Was the group already the champions of the "homoiousion" before its banning by Second Sirmium in 357? The charge against Cyril in 360 was that he had held communion with Eustathius and Elpidius after their deposition (unless there were two councils of Melitene) and with Basil and George after his own deposition.
29 Socrates 4.1. *ad fin.*
30 *Ancoratus* 118.
31 And, if so, probably by 366.

they understand and are competent to record. In fact, however, both Socrates and Sozomen represent Cyril at Constantinople in 381 as a recent convert to the "homoousion,"[32] which suggests that Cyril accepted it only when Theodosius I became the Eastern Augustus (January 379) and made its subscription mandatory. The group which (above) accepted the "homoousion" in 365-6 soon recanted.

Cyril's substantive orthodoxy, of course, is attested from the first by the *Catecheses*. If we measure orthodoxy by the confession of the true divinity of Christ and not by acceptance of a philosophical term, Cyril never wavered in orthodoxy. The story of his life shows him steadfastly refusing all complicity with heresy and bears out the encomium of the Second Ecumenical Council, which in its synodal letter[33] of 382 to Pope Damasus and the West declared that Cyril had "on various occasions valiantly combated Arianism." In that first council of Constantinople (381 A.D.) Cyril probably played a leading part. Socrates names him second and Sozomen third among the leading prelates. It is probably an index not only of Cyril's personal prestige but also of the authority of his see that both Socrates and Sozomen[34] name him among the four leading prelates of the orthodox majority, the others being Timothy of Alexandria, Meletius of Antioch and Gregory of Nazianzus, whom Theodosius had transferred to the see of Constantinople, 27 November 380.

Cyril's influence was probably great at the later sessions of the council when Meletius had died, Gregory had left, Timothy had been discredited by his support of the claims of the adventurer Maximus to the see of Constantinople, Constantinople itself was represented by Nectarius who had been only a catechumen when the council opened, and Cyril's nephew Gelasius presided over the church of Caesarea. While Cyril was no doubt suspect in Western eyes (St. Jerome was

---

32 Socrates 5.8 *ad init.;* Sozomen 7.7.3.
33 Text in Theodoret 5.9.
34 Socrates 5.8; Sozomen 7.7.3.

still calling him an Arian in his *Chronicle, ca.* 380), it is very improbable, especially after his acceptance of the "homoousion," that (as Hort suggested) he needed to vindicate his orthodoxy at the Eastern council of Constantinople by producing the traditional creed of Jerusalem.[35] But, while the minutes of the council have for the most part perished, it is not unlikely that the Eastern bishops perceived the tactical usefulness of the unimpeachable creed of "the Mother of all the Churches" as a symbol of the orthodoxy of their non-homoousian past. The council may well, therefore, have commissioned Cyril to expand his creed into a form which should, taking into account present needs, represent the faith of the East. E. Schwarz suggested that the *tomos* mentioned in the council's reply to the West (382) referred to the "Constantinopolitan" creed (C); and it is significant that that reply implies that Cyril's theological respectability had been impugned by the West. While, then, it is not even certain that the "Niceno-Constantinopolitan" creed (i.e., the present liturgical creed of East and West, commonly miscalled the "Nicene" creed) was either composed or adopted by the council of Constantinople, the internal evidence for this great creed's being based on the Jerusalem creed (J) and possibly being the work of a committee chaired by St. Cyril at Constantinople, is briefly as follows. The first thirty-six (Greek) words of the two creeds are identical,[36] except that the phrase "true God" is held over in C; only ten words of J are not included in C, and of these three are accounted for by merely prepositional changes; while the amount of detail, or degree of expansion, in the key third clause of J is uncertain, all the phrases of C's very full third clause coincide with the phrases emphasized and "demonstrated" in *Catechesis* 12. In his main contention, therefore, Hort may well have been right.

---

35 And still more improbable if he had accepted the "homoousion" in 362-364; these two parts of Hort's hypothesis are mutually contradictory.

36 I.e., down to "before all ages" inclusive. The next thirty (Greek) words come from N.

Of the twelve clauses of the creed, all but the third and fourth are quoted verbatim in the *Catecheses* and can be reconstructed with considerable confidence from the following passages: 7.4, 9.4, 11.21, 14.24, 15.2, 17.3, 18.22.

Cyril died in 387.[37] Commemorated among the blessed in the Eastern Church since the fifth century,[38] Cyril was proclaimed a Doctor of the universal Church by Pope Leo XIII. His feast is kept on March 18th.

5. Cyril's Theology

Cyril's theology was highly apophatic. Pseudo-Denis the Areopagite spoke of an apophatic ("negative") theology as a way to the knowledge of God through negations. But by characterizing Cyril's theology as apophatic, I refer to his insistence that we can know of God only what has been revealed.[1] This position, implicit in the conception of a divine transcendent revelation, Cyril held in common with all the Fathers and classical theologians, and it was strongly reaffirmed by the First Vatican Council. It was probably this principle that caused Cyril to refuse for so long to accept the "consubstantial" as defined by the Council of Nicaea; it is likely that he held out until it was recognized that the "consubstantial" *(homoousion)* need not be interpreted as affirming anything more than is taught in Scripture. Not that in principle Cyril barred theological speculation, but he thought that its conclusions could not have the same certainty or authority as belonged to scriptural truth. In particular he emphasized (what, of course, all theologians assert) that the

---

37 P. Nautin, "La date du *De viris illustribus,*" *Revue d'histoire ecclésiastique* 56 (1961) 33-35; Jerome, *De vir. illus.* 112.

38 See the calendar in *Rituale Armenorum,* edited by Conybeare and Maclean.

---

1 Cyril thought of the revelation in a "propositional" way, i.e., as the imparting of mysterious truths. Nevertheless he also understood it as God's self-disclosure in history; he had some grasp of revelation as "salvation history" *(Heilsgeschichte).*

divine nature and "the mysteries of Father, Son and Holy Spirit" (i.e., the Creed) are profoundly mysterious and beyond man's comprehension. It is quite characteristic of Cyril to say (6.2): "For concerning God it is high knowledge to confess our want of knowledge." Significantly he continues: "Therefore glorify the Lord with me . . . ." Cyril thought that the purpose of the revelation was to guide aright our worship, devotion and conduct and that immoderate curiosity was doomed to remain unsatisfied and tended to produce strife in the Church. Such an apophatic theology tends to pile up negatives;[2] we can deny of God anything that implies imperfection, but of the nature of God's inmost being we cannot have exact positive knowledge. The reader will find illustrations of this apophatic approach at 4.17; 5.12; 6.2, 6.4-8; 7.5; 9.1-3; 11.9-12; 16.5.

In trinitarian theology Cyril belonged to the right wing of the Eusebian or Eastern school. This school, though its origins are obscure, seems to have been the product of the meeting of a diluted Origenist tradition with a (not very scientific) biblical theology, stressing the literal meaning and historical side of the scriptural record, as practiced at Antioch. While this school aimed at scientific exegesis, Cyril had rather more sympathy with the spiritual and allegorical senses of Scripture. To risk a generalization: while Latin theology translated into philosophical terms the biblical record of revelation as interpreted by tradition, this Eastern school constructed its theology more directly from the Scriptures. This procedure had its dangers on account of the great development within the New Testament's christology; if the biblical theologian failed to notice this development and the transformation in the New Testament, whether through their deepening, or hellenizing, of certain Old Testament Semitic categories (e.g., "Son of God" or "image"), he might find himself an Arian. But the method also had its advantages. It saved the theologian from what I. A. Richards has called, in

2 Cf. *Cat.* 7.5.

relation to poetry, the "stock response," i.e., the interpreting of a poem simply on the basis of one's previous experience instead of being open to what is unique, original and excitingly new in the poem and allowing that to re-create one's ways of thinking and feeling. Eastern theology was more aware of the highly personalist Hebrew categories in the Bible and of the functional and historical, rather than metaphysical, character of the revelation. It read the Bible as a "salvation history," a *story* in which the leading role in the creation and new creation of mankind is played by three very exciting and distinctive Persons. It reacted sharply against any suggestion that the Three were really "substantially one." Nor would it wish to see the story dissolved into philosophy.

Not only Cyril's silence about the "homoousion" shows that he belonged to the Eastern school. Though he was perhaps unaware of the logic underlying his position, he seems to have held the "Eastern" trinitarian theology approximately as described above. Cyril does not interpret John 10.30 as teaching a *numerical* unity of the (concrete) divine essence:

> He says, not "I am the Father," but "the Father is in me" . . . He did not say, "I and the Father am one," but "I and the Father are one" . . . "One" they are because of the dignity proper to the Godhead, since God begat God. "One" on account of the unity of their reign, for the Son's subjects are not different from the Father's, as if He were an Absalom in revolt. . . . "One" because of the absence of discord and disagreement, for their wills and purposes are the same. "One" because the handiwork of Christ is not different from that of the Father; rather there is a single production of the universe, the Father having made all things through the Son. "He spake. . .," for He who speaks speaks to one who heeds, and He who issues commands issues them to One who is present with Him.[3]

Although Cyril recognized a hierarchy in the Blessed Trinity, he recognized also that the three Persons all belong

---

3 *Cat.* 11.16.

absolutely to the side of the divine and the transcendent; they were partners in creation and redemption, together rule the world and history, and are uniquely the source of being, life and salvation. Their unity was a moral unity, a unity, Cyril explains (11.16), of rule or reign; again, they acted, as it were, as a team under the captaincy of the Father, and the Son's and Spirit's relations of origin to the Father gave the necessary ontic unity. The pattern of rule and action corresponds to the relations of origin. As the Father begets the Son, so He commands and sends Him, while the Son performs the commands of the Father. The being and dignity or status of the Three are known from their names and functions. Christ is God, but God the Son:

> The Son, then, is Very God, having the Father in Himself, but not changed into the Father; for the Father was not made man, but the Son. For let the truth be freely spoken: the Father did not suffer for us Himself, but sent Him who suffered. Let us beware *either* of saying that there was a time when the Son did not exist, *or* identifying the Son with the Father. Rather let us walk in the King's highway, turning aside neither to the right nor the left.[4]

We may, perhaps, find an analogy to this "unity of rule" in the system whereby the reigning Emperor admitted his sons to partnership in sovereignty, making them *consortes imperii*. In defining the divine unity, Eastern theology also sometimes toyed with the idea of a sort of "concrete universal,"[5] rather as Scripture regards mankind as a collective, in a profound sense a single Man, fallen in Adam and restored in Christ, the New Man. Again, the East emphasized that there is but one Unoriginated *(agenētos* or *anarchos)*, the Father. This hierarchy and differentiation in the Godhead is found also, of course, in Western theology, but there it is less prominent, being overshadowed by the substantial identity

---

4 *Cat.* 11.17.
5 Cf. Gregory of Nyssa, *Quod non sunt tres dii.* Gregory's final answer, however, is not this.

of the three Persons.[6] But in Eastern theology the full (generic) divinity of Son and Spirit is safeguarded and expressed by their coördination in the creed, the baptismal formula and the doxology.

Cyril's regular formula is not the "coessential," but "like the Father in all things."[7] Cyril teaches that the Son is *anarchos* (unoriginated) in the sense of "having no beginning in time." But the Father alone is *anarchos* in the sense of having absolutely no origin. In Cyril, "God" seems to be the proper name of the Father, though of course the Son is God.[8] The Father is. the Unbegotten, the Son the Only-begotten. "The Father is the beginning [origin, principle] of the Son, himself without beginning," i.e., the *archē anarchos*.[9] A glance at Toutée's *apparatus criticus* shows that *anarchos* has been interpolated in a number of places (e.g., 11.4, 5, 7, 13), presumably to make Cyril teach that the Son is in every sense Unoriginate. Cyril emphasizes that the Son's begetting was ineffable and "before all ages." He seems to have interpreted eternity in the Greek manner as a "timeless now," not as an infinitely long time (time in the sense of "a before and after"); certainly he makes it clear that "before all ages" means timelessly, outside time *(achronōs, aidiōs)*.

Origen sometimes said that the Son was begotten of the Father's will.[10] Athanasius seems to have held or implied that the begetting was by an essential necessity; without the Logos, he says, the Father would have been *alogos*. Did the Father beget "by nature" or by deliberation and free choice? The Arians argued that the Father cannot have begotten unknowingly or involuntarily, yet free choice presupposes de-

---

6 Similarly in Western, as in Eastern, theology the Father is principal agent in redemption as well as in creation, performing both through the Son. It is only "by appropriation" that the Son is "the Redeemer." The Father conceived and planned the operation and "sent" (commissioned) the Son, who is the executive, the "commander in the field."

7 *Cat.* 4.7; 11.4, 18.

8 *Cat.* 4.4, 7, 16 *fin.;* 11.4, 7, 20.

9 *Cat.* 11.20.

10 Origen, *De principiis* 4.4.1.

liberation. Cyril answered that the Father begot neither unknowingly nor after consideration involving an interval; God begot knowingly and (apparently) voluntarily, but eternally;[11] and the Son was a natural Son. Correspondingly the Father was a perfectly free agent *(autoproairetōs)* in bestowing the Lordship upon the Son, but the Son was the natural heir to it. Moreover, while the Lordship was "delivered unto Me of my Father," there never was a time when He was not Lord; He ever shares His Father's throne.[12] The whole thing is beautifully balanced. For Cyril's doctrine of the "Monarchy" (the singleness and single rule of God) see *Catecheses* 6.1-11, 7.1 and 16.4. Here are two typical excerpts:[13]

> Let the thought of "Father" accompany the thought of "God," that the praise of the Father and the Son be indivisible. For Father and Son have not two different glories, but one and the same. For the Father has an Only-begotten Son who, when the Father is glorified, shares his glory. For the glory of the Son flows from the Father's dignity.

> Our hope is in Father, Son and Holy Spirit. Not that we proclaim three Gods . . .; no, we preach one God, with the Holy Spirit and through one Son. The faith is indivisible, the worship inseparable. . .

O. Perler (LTK 6.710) is correct in saying that Cyril is somewhat subordinationist, as the following passages show: 7.5; 10.5, 7, 9f.; 11.10, 12-23; 12.16; 14.27; 15.25, 30. But although Cyril's theology is subordinationist in a pejorative sense by the norms, and within the pattern, of Western theology, need we pass the same judgment when we view it within the different pattern and presuppositions of Eastern theology?

In spite of the (original) Nicene Creed, Cyril never speaks of the Son being generated "from the substance of the Father," but simply "from the Father." He emphasizes strongly

11 *Cat.* 11.4, 7, 8, 20. The formula which has prevailed is "neither by necessity nor by free will, but by nature."
12 *Cat.* 10.9; Matt. 11.27.
13 *Cat.* 6.1; 16.4.

that neither men nor angels can know anything of the
Father's essence, and that the generation of the Son is particularly mysterious, altogether ineffable: the Son is born
as God "himself only knoweth."[14]

What is the relation of the Trinitarian theology of the
Lectures to that of St. Athanasius and the West? It is notorious
that the word "of-one substance" (homoousios) does not occur
in St. Cyril's writings. But that may not be very significant,
since St. Athanasius himself made little use of the word, even
in his anti-Arian writings, before the revival of Arianism in
357-8. And in those same earlier writings Athanasius quite
often used formulas equivalent to Cyril's "like the Father in
all respects." In an article that is very illuminating on the
historical side, Msgr. J. Lebon[15] has maintained that, while
"politically" Cyril was for many years arrayed with the central
Eastern bloc that was critical of the Nicene formula, theo-
logically his position was indistinguishable from that of the
Athanasian-Western party; while for adventitious reasons (e.g.,
because of reluctance to introduce a non-scriptural word into
the Creed) Cyril eschewed the "homoousion," actually his
theology was implicitly that of St. Thomas Aquinas and later
Scholasticism, insofar as he distinguished sharply, though not
explicitly, between nature and person and even implied the
doctrine of the "numerical" identity of the divine nature of
the three divine Persons. But little evidence, and no convincing evidence, has been produced for this widely accepted
view.

In what direction does the external evidence point? Apart
from his silence about the "homoousion," Cyril flatters Constantius II, in his letter to him, more than courtly politeness
demanded, saying (Ch. 3) that he surpasses the piety or
orthodoxy (eusebeia) of Constantine. Again, although the date
of Cyril's acceptance of formal Nicene orthodoxy is debatable,
both Socrates and Sozomen seem to say pretty clearly that he

---

14 Cat. 11.8, 11.
15 Op. cit. (supra, Bibliogr.), in Rev. d'hist. eccl. 20 (1924) 181-210, 357-
386.

accepted it only on the eve of the second ecumenical council (only when the Emperor made it mandatory?). The Lectures themselves give some indirect clues to Cyril's position when he says repeatedly (4.8; 11.13, 16, 18; 16.4; 17.34) that orthodoxy stands midway between two heretical extremes. The two extremes are obviously those of the Arian and Sabellian type, but since, as Toutée noted,[16] in 15.9 Cyril describes them as *widespread and disguised,* they cannot have been overt and explicit Arianism and Sabellianism. Presumably, therefore, one extreme was represented by the "Eastern" party or some group in it (Eusebius of Nicomedia? Acacius?), and the other was the Athanasian-Western party or some group in it, presumably Marcellus' since Cyril attacks him strongly in 15.27-30. It is possible, however, that Cyril attacked Marcellus openly only because he could be attacked with safety, but was in fact also somewhat suspicious of the Western school.

Passages like 11.12 can only be directed against the Nicaeans. Cyril's own orthodoxy can hardly be doubted, since he followed Scripture almost verbally and is a Doctor of the Church. The basic requirement for Trinitarian orthodoxy seems to be the recognition that the Son is truly, in the proper and strict sense, God. This requirement refers especially to the Son's divine nature; as a Person, precisely as the Son, it is allowable to say that He is, while truly divine, in some sense subordinate to the Father. The equality of nature means (at least) that the Son has all the same attributes or predicates (omnipotence, eternity, etc.) as the Father, and shares the Father's divine titles and functions as creator and ruler of the universe and source of all saving grace. If, however, a distinction should not be drawn between nature and person, the requirements of orthodoxy may perhaps be safeguarded in a different way.

There are three *prima facie* possible ways in which the three divine Persons may be related to the divine nature. On any orthodox theory They must have "the same" nature; i.e., they

16 PG 33.43-44.

must be *homoousioi;* they must, in Aristotelian language, have the divine nature in common. But the unity of the divine nature might be specific, numerical, or generic. If the Three had "the same" specific nature, They would have it in common in the same way as three men have "the same" human nature. But this is impossible because (a) since individual instances of a species are distinguished from one another by their matter, no spiritual (immaterial) species can have more than one instance; hence St. Thomas Aquinas taught that every angel constitutes a species of its own;[17] (b) originatedness (begottenness or procession) would on this analysis have to be classified as a merely "accidental" differentia, whereas it seems to be more than that; (c) the theory would be, or involve, tritheism.

To say that the divine Persons have *numerically* the same nature is to say that They have in common literally the same identical concrete nature. This is St. Thomas's theory and the theory which Lebon thinks Cyril held implicitly. On this theory a sharp distinction is drawn between person and nature, and the Three, while different ("distinct") as Persons, are yet each identical with the same thing, the one divine essence. The Persons are held to be subsistent relations. St. Thomas's synthesis is brilliant and profound, but it seems to leave us ultimately (as the Orthodox East complain) with one thing instead of three. Moreover it is not easy to see how it does not involve a contradiction in terms. If in defence of the theory it is urged that the Three possess the identical nature in different ways, the First Person as begetting (it?), the Second as begotten, and the Third as proceeding, this seems to make some concession to the specific or generic view.

It is the third, the *"generic* unity or identity," view which

---

17 *Sum. theol.* I, 76, 2, ad 1: "multi autem angeli unius speciei omnino esse non possunt." Not that St. Cyril supposed that *angels* are immaterial; in common with the Bible (at least usually) and a learned tradition that continued up to the seventeenth century (e.g., Milton), he held that angels are composed of a fine, subtle, spiritual substance; for the relevant passages, see Index, s. v. "angels."

provides the logical framework that, though never made explicit, seems to be required by all, or almost all, Cyril's Trinitarian expositions. On this view the divine Persons are three, not individual instances of a species (like three men), but three individual subsistent species which are members of the same genus (deity); They have the same *generic* nature. The Trinitarian logic, on this view, will be broadly similar to that governing three Thomistic angels. The relationship of the Persons to the divine nature will follow the same general logic as the relationship of a Cherub, a Seraph and a Domination to the (generic) angelic nature, or (if it may be said with reverence) as the relationship of the three species of triangle, isosceles, scalene and equilateral, to the genus triangle. In the three logics the relationship of the individuals' distinguishing characteristics *(idiotētes, gnōrismata)* to the common nature is different. When, as in three men, the common nature is a species, it differs concretely in the three only accidentally. If three beings have numerically the same common nature, clearly it does not differ in the three at all. But the distinguishing characteristics of individual species of one genus may modify the common nature internally; in any case they are likely to be of more than "accidental" importance. A Cherub, a Seraph and a Domination are three different ways of being an angel, and perhaps the same applies to the three types of triangle. On this logic Father, Son and Holy Ghost will be three different ways of being God. While each will be God in the proper and true sense, They will be God in the same generic sense, but not in the same specific sense. This logic does not allow the strong distinction between nature and person which enables one to draw sharp distinctions between the Persons in regard of origin while at the same time stressing the identity of nature. For on this logic the personal distinguishing characteristics (which are related to the question of origin) determine the nature and modify it internally. But the interrelationship of the members of a genus is not uniform; it depends upon the particular case. That is perhaps why St. Cyril did not make explicit the genus–species model of his thinking. For it is open to abuse, as St. Athanasius pointed out when he remarked that the divine nature could not be paralleled with that of "animal," with its species of man, lion and wolf, or illustrated by three kinds of metal, for instance, the royal metal, gold, silver and base metal, copper. The advantage, for theology, of the genus–species logic is that it is flexible. It does not, as the choice of the logic of specific or numerical identity of nature does, predetermine the whole pattern; the precise pattern is filled in accordance with the biblical data. Cyril, of course, by refraining from specifying any logic, retained a sovereign freedom to expound the doctrine of the Holy Trinity in entire fidelity to Scripture. But his exposition is compatible with, even seems to require, the genus–species logic; certainly within that framework it can be best understood. This also seems to be the logic of the Cappadocian Trinitarian theology, though even the Cappadocians never spelt it out fully.

A theology implicitly based on something like this genus–species logic will be pluralist in the Eastern way of Origen. It will take seriously the Son's character as the Son and the mystery of the divine begetting, and it will be, by the standards of modern Scholastic notions, somewhat subordinationist. Cyril's Trinitarian theology clearly has three characteristics. It is pluralist insofar as Cyril stresses that Son and Spirit are independent substantial beings (4.7, 8; 11.10; 17.5). Msgr. Lebon[18] has singled out 11.16, Cyril's exposition of John 10.30 ("I and the Father are one") as a clear illustration that Cyril held implicitly the doctrine of numerical identity. But 11.16 offers four expositions of this text, and none of them approaches the idea of numerical identity. The point does not need discussion. Indeed 11.16 is one of the passages noted by Perler in the LTK as subordinationist. Its subordinationist and pluralistic character come out in the last sentence of the section.

18 *Op. cit.* (n. 15 *supra*) 376-381.

Passages (e.g., 11.10-12, esp. 11.11) emphasizing the ineffability of the Son's generation and of the Father's substance *(ousia)* probably provide the explanation of the puzzle why Cyril could not accept the *homoousion.* It is a puzzle because *homoousios can* designate community of generic as well as specific nature. But apparently by 350 it was naturally taken to refer to unity of specific nature *or* to sameness of *concrete* substance. Both interpretations would present difficulties for Cyril. The latter might be judged to be implied by N's "begotten from the Father, that is, from the substance of the Father." For Cyril, "God" was the proper name of the Father (even though Christ was properly and strictly God), and the divine substance was identical with the Father. For Cyril, it was this divine substance which was entirely transcendent, incomprehensible and ineffable, known only by the Son and the Spirit, and before which human speculation must be silent (6.5). Moreover, if the divine substance is defined as identical with God the Father, then the Father will beget according to (divine) genus, not according to species; else the Son too would be Unbegotten—a proposition which Cyril denies a score of times.

This ineffable mystery of the divine generation is central in Cyril's theology. The Arians held that the Son was begotten in the same, improper or metaphorical, sense as the creatures. Orthodoxy says that the divine begetting is literal and proper though analogical. Cyril insists that this must be taken seriously; a son owes his existence to his father and (consequently) is bound to obey him. Moreover there is one important difference between human and divine begetting. A human son has exactly and specifically the same nature as his father. For his father too is a son; he is not unbegotten. Cyril discreetly makes this point in the many passages where he insists that the Son is not unbegotten; there is only one Unbegotten, God the Father; see 4.4; 7.10; 11.2, 4.

The nature and pattern of Cyril's theology roughly corresponds to the logic of three angelic species/individuals; the

divine Three have proper names which are also descriptions
of the Individuals who own them (7.1; 8.1; 10.1, 2, 5). Thus
the name of the first Person is God. He is further described
as the Unbegotten or Ingenerate, the Father of the Son, and
the Creator. *Cat.* 4.4 provides a good example: "There is but
one God; He is unbegotten, unoriginate . . . not begotten
of another. . . There is one only God . . . the Father of the
Only-begotten Son." Compare 11.13: "neither two Unbegottens nor two Only-begottens . . .; to be unbegotten is to have
no father." The last clause is significant; here, as often elsewhere, Cyril is trying to open our eyes, blinded by custom, to
the significance of the New Testament's language. There is
only one Unbegotten, Cyril insists; to be Unbegotten is not
to have a father. The Only-begotten also is unique, not in
having no Father, but in having no brother. Thus Cyril emphasizes the doctrine of the Monarchy, but not in a modalist
(Sabellian) but in an anti-modalist sense.

The Second Person is the Only-begotten: the Son, or God
the Son, or the Son of God, or the Lord, or "the begotten
God"; only the eternal Son became man and suffered; Cyril
protests against Patripassionism; 4.4, 7, 8 and *passim*. According to Socrates (1.23) and Sozomen (2.18; cf. 3.18) very soon
after 325 many Eastern bishops reached the view that Nicaea's
"consubstantial" and "begotten from the substance of the
Father" were a blasphemy against the Son and destroyed His
hyparxis—presumably either by implying His numerical identity with the Father, or by asserting the specific identity of
two immaterial Beings, or, more likely, by denying His distinctive characteristic as the Son.[19] The name of the Third
is the Holy Spirit. Cyril insists on the uniqueness of each:
"There is only one Holy Spirit, the Paraclete. . . There is

---

19 Of course, the Nicene "consubstantial" ("homoousion") *need* not
   have these implications. It depends on the meaning assigned to that
   highly ambiguous word. Cyril equivalently teaches the "coessential" in
   two senses: (1) "having the same essential predicates (or description)"
   and (2) "of the same divine nature," nature or essence being understood, as it must be in the case of spirits, as a genus.

one God, the Father . . . and one Lord, Jesus Christ . . . and one Holy Ghost" (16.2).

It is a magnificent theology, a brilliant statement. Free from the self-conscious theorizing of the splendid Cappadocian theology which it essentially anticipates, it is concrete, attractive, devotional, biblical, Johannine in the tradition of Origen, but having a higher doctrine of the Son than Origen, whose theology, excessively dominated by the Logos concept and occasionally influenced by Middle Platonism, was somewhat minimizing. Cyril's concept of the "begotten God" somewhat resembles Origen's distinction between the supreme and absolute God *(autotheos)* and the second *(deuteros)* God. Similarly, Cyril is influenced by Origen when he says (4.8; contrast 11.16 etc.) that the Son is creator of all who partake of reason; Origen taught that, while the Father was universal creator, the Logos made all rational creatures. Cyril's Trinitarian theology is also approximately that of Milton's *Paradise Lost*. It is a masterly achievement; Cyril's superb theological style masks the extraordinary precision and finesse with which he expounds the central orthodoxy, the Royal Road (11.17). His theology is a tritheism qualified and redeemed by subordinationism, and a subordinationism qualified and redeemed by tritheism. The two criticisms cancel out. The Eastern party was accused of teaching polytheism (Socrates 1.23) *and* subordinationism.

Cyril taught that the Son is perfect Son of the perfect Father, that He is Very God and perfect *(teleios:* 4.7; 7.5; 11.18) God. He is creator and Lord of all without exception. While (16.4) "we preach not three Gods . . . but one God, with the Son and the Holy Ghost," yet "their worship is inseparable." This is all very right. The Son is the natural Son of God, and like begets like; the Father "begat God" (11.18). As the "express image of the Father's substance," the Son has exactly the same attributes or predicates (eternity, etc.) as the Father. Therefore the "description" of the Son is the same as that of the Father. For "description," or sum of predicates, may logically refer to essence and prescind from existence, the question of origin and existential status. As St. John said, the Father is in the Son, and to see the Son is to see the Father. Moreover the Father has conferred upon the Son all His prerogatives, such as lordship, and has associated the Son with Himself in the creation and rule of the universe. But if unoriginatedness be included among the list of predicates, then, Cyril repeatedly emphasizes that the Son is neither unbegotten nor absolutely unoriginated *(anarchos)*. The Son is, however, both eternal and uncreate; and for Plato eternity was the hallmark of deity. Yet while, unlike the creatures, the Son has no *archē* (beginning, principle, origin) in time, He has an eternal *archē* in the Father. The Father alone is absolutely *anarchos*, the unbegun beginning or unoriginated origin *(archē anarchos:* 11.14, 18, 20). The unhappiness of the copyists at this doctrine is reflected by their interpolating (the manuscripts so far edited suggest) the word *anarchos* at 11.4, 5, 7, 13, 14, to make Cyril conform to the orthodoxy of a later, scholasticizing age. But Cyril's doctrine is the paradox of the derived, the begotten, though not created, God. "Son," alike in Scholastic and Hebraic thinking, implies on the one hand the inheritance of nature and rank, but also dependency and subordination. God begets God, but He cannot beget an Unbegotten. Certainly "there is nothing lacking (in deity)" to the Son (4.7; 11.13), but this refers to content, not the existential status or origin. Similarly in creation, the Son created all things "at His Father's bidding"; He rules the universe because the Father has committed to Him all authority. His rule is eternal and divine and by birthright *(ek physeōs)*, but it is delegated; He sits as Crown Prince at the Father's right hand, who alone has absolute sovereignty *(authentikē exousia)*. Everywhere in his exposition of the Son's role as creator, lord and judge Cyril emphasizes that He is invested with these offices by His Father, holds them in dependence on the Father, and exercises them in submission to the Father (7.5; 10.5, 9; 11.10, 22, 23). The

Son's status and activity correspond exactly to His nature and being as the Only-begotten. It was not that Cyril was unaware of possible distinctions between the Son's person and nature, or between His divine and human nature; no, *en pleine conscience* he expounds his doctrine. For Cyril the Son's title, the Son or the Only-begotten, tells us both who and what He is. He emphasizes that the Son Himself glories in His position: "He was not ashamed to call His Father 'His God' " (11.18).

When (11.16) Cyril quotes John 14.11, "the Father is in me," he explains it (11.18), with his profound feeling for Johannine theology, as meaning that, as the living image of His Father, the Son reflects and reveals Him; he correctly relates it to John 14.9. Similarly in 11.18, which is a magnificent summary of his position, Cyril explains the meaning of "separate" in his common formula, "we must neither confound nor separate Father and Son." In Cyril, as in most patristic Trinitarian contexts, "separate" means of a foreign or contrasting nature; the Only-begotten is not a creature, but "own Son" *(idios)* of the Father. It is decidedly not a question of God and god, though perhaps of GOD and God. A score of passages show that St. Cyril regarded any interpretation of the Son as a mode, manifestation or "presentation" of the Father as Sabellian. "Separate" has also a kind of local, or even social, sense in Cyril; he thinks of the Three Inseparables, for the Holy Spirit is always around too *(aei symparon,* cf. *Procat.* 15; *Cat.* 15.24; 17.5).

The puzzle is that so many of Cyril's formulas can be paralleled almost verbally in Athanasius, even some of his "subordinationist" passages, e.g., his quoting the Fourth Gospel to the effect that "the Son can do nothing by himself, he can only do what he sees the Father doing" (John 5.19; cf. 5.21, with C. K. Barrett's commentary). But the emphasis in Athanasius is usually a little different, and in his later writings the trend is towards "numerical" identity, though he usually, perhaps always, avoids committing himself to it unambiguously. He may have come to think that the line as drawn by Cyril could not be held, it was too subtle. But probably he never quite grasped the Cyrilline position; he could not quite match Cyril's intellectual distinction. The metaphysical approach was explicitly developed in the so-called Athanasian Creed, but this was never a recognized standard of orthodoxy in the East and scholarly opinion is hardening in the view that it was the theology of St. Cyril and the Cappadocians that was canonized by Constantinople I (A.D. 381), when, ratifying the Nicene "homoousion," it interpreted it in the sense of "three hypostases and one *ousia*," a formula which, like St. Cyril himself, was anathema to St. Jerome, the admirer of Athanasius.

Is monotheism safeguarded in Cyril's system? The Greek Fathers' approach to the problem of the divine unity was not primarily arithmetical. In Cyril's system the "Monarchy" is safeguarded in many ways: (1) There is a single source of deity. (2) The divine Trinity is a single source of created being. (3) The Three possess a generic unity. (4) "God" is the proper name only of the Father. (5) There is a single harmonious and hierarchical divine action in creation, world-rule and salvation: the Father does all things by the Son in the Holy Spirit. (6) While standing absolutely on the divine side of the gulf dividing God and creatures and possessing all the essential predicates of deity, the Only-begotten and the Holy Spirit derive their sovereignty from the Father. (7) There is a kind of (analogical) unity of "race" *(genos)*. (8) The Three are Inseparables, and Their worship is indivisible. Howbeit, if haply I err in this matter, I declare my submission and adhesion to the holy Catholic and Apostolic faith.

The Cappadocian theology, which took up the torch, was probably more Eastern than Western, though its distinction between nature and *idiotētes* (the distinctive characteristics and relationships of the Persons) might presuppose the concept of either specific or generic nature. The definition by Constantinople I in 381 of "three hypostases in one *ousia*" was probably a compromise between Eastern and Western

trinitarian theology. Nicaea had used *ousia* and *hypostasis* as
synonyms in its anathematism, and as late as 376 St. Jerome,
a strong Westerner, was imploring Pope Damasus to resist a
definition in these terms. Many, but probably not all, Roman
Catholic theologians hold that the Fourth Lateran Council
(1215 A.D.), with its formula *una summa res* ("one supreme
reality"), finally settled the question in favor of (numerical)
substantial identity. Yet the Church made Cyril a Doctor of
the Church quite recently.

It is regrettable that Cyril was not content with distinguishing sharply between revelation and speculation, but seems to
have eschewed systematic theological reflection. For his trinitarian theology could be related in interesting ways to other
dogmas, notably the incarnation and work of Christ and
the restoration of man. Highlighting the functionally differ-
entiated and hierarchical pattern within the Trinity and
taking with full seriousness the eternal obedience of the
Son, this theology suggests an intelligible inner continuity
between the preëxistent and the incarnate Christ "obedient
unto death." Especially is this true when the redemption is
conceived as the restoration in man of the divine image; for
it is precisely as the obedient Son that the Word is the
eternal Image, and it was precisely by disobedience that man
lost the divine image-by-grace and divine sonship, and by
his obedience as the second Adam and new Israel that Christ
restored it. Again, if we think of man's task in Eastern terms
as his divinization by grace, the Eastern theology, with its
emphasis on the three Persons rather than the one divine
nature, reminds us that God is not only the infinite Good
but also the obedient and loving response to divine generosity
and goodness.

Cyril reminds us that by his ascension Jesus is not removed
from us, but rather is made universally available:[20]

He both sits on high and is here present together with
us . . . His absence now in the flesh does not mean that

---

20 *Cat.* 14.30.

He is absent in the Spirit. He is here present in the midst
of us . . .

Thus Cyril concludes *Catechesis* 14 with Bonhoeffer's "transcendent in the midst." But it is in the "contemplative" or
"mystical" exegesis,[21] employing imagination in Coleridge's
profound sense of the word, rather than in the catechizing,
that such "existential" themes are best explored. Cyril's
Homily on the Paralytic is a study in encounter with the
Transcendent historically revealed in Christ. The dramatic
suspense of this homily depends on the enigmatic personality
of the Healer and the success or failure of the various char-
acters to penetrate the disguise of Him who is "the true
Bread," "the Light which lightens every man," "the resurrection," "the physician of souls" and "the Lawgiver." The
opening sentence abruptly proclaims Jesus as "the Man for
others": "Wherever Jesus appears, there is salvation." This
Jesus "makes himself all things to all: to the hungry, bread,
to the sick, a physician, to sinners, absolution," and He comes
bringing not empty words but deeds, especially to those in
desperate straits.[22]

Sozomen has an interesting passage: the emperor Constantius, he says, at first followed the Nicene beliefs of his father
Constantine, but was later converted to Homoeousianism. For
the Eusebians and other Eastern bishops of the same generation whose life and intelligence commanded admiration drew
a distinction between *homoousios* and *homoiousios,* teaching
that the former properly applies only to material things like
men, animals, and trees, which (severally) have the same
specific nature and reproduce after their specific kind. But
in the case of immaterial beings, such as God and angels, the
proper term to express corresponding relationships is *homoiousios,* for here no species can include more than one
member, but each existent individual is unique.[23]

---

21 *theōretikē, Cat.* 13.9.
22 *Homily on the Paralytic* 1, 5, 7, 9.
23 Sozomen 3.18.1-3. It may be suspected that, quite soon after Nicaea,

The Eastern theologians were aware of the biblical usage by which a proper name is the clue to function, and function the clue to nature. They knew, too, that "father" in the Bible connotes authority, and that the essential characteristic of a son is to obey;[24] and they thought of divinity to a large extent in terms of authority rather than ontologically. Again, the idea of "father" and "unbegotten" is close to the idea of creator, the "self-existent" "uncaused" or "unoriginate," which common sense and philosophy both asserted to be an essential predicate of God. Thus they reached the idea that Christ, as the Son and heir of his Father's nature, has the divine nature and is truly and properly God, yet the Father (the Old Testament Creator God, Jehovah, the Lord of Hosts) is God *par excellence*. Here one can see how the divine begetting created a problem, and why Cyril insisted that it must be left shrouded in mystery. For while we have empirical knowledge about procreation in the human and animal world, where reproduction is according to species and "like begets like," the Father's *specific* nature includes Fatherhood; his genus is deity, but his specific differentia is to be a Father and the Unbegotten. But presumably as an individual member of a species begets according to his species, so an individual species begets according to genus. Therefore, the Father will beget God, but God the Son, not the Unbegotten but the Only-begotten. Yet "God" is the Father's proper name, and moreover one had begun on the assumption that to be self-existent, unoriginate and unbegotten was at least a primary predicate of deity. Still, reflection guided by revelation suggests that absolute and unqualified unoriginateness need be a predicate only of God *par excellence;* the unique Son of the Unbegotten and Unoriginate is truly God; for the Father has communicated to Him all his divine

---

Constantine changed over to the "Homoiousian" doctrine, though not then so called.

24 Israel's claim to sonship depended on its obedience, and by his obedience our Lord showed Himself, and created, the new Israel.

nature except unbegottenness; the Son remains within the charmed circle of deity. To be begotten by the Self-existent in such wise as to have exactly the same generic nature as He, is certainly to be God. This exact sameness of (generic) nature is sometimes illustrated by the Fathers by the image of two torches or lights, one of which has been kindled from the other. They are exactly alike, indistinguishable, "Light from Light." St. Athanasius, however, was not satisfied with this metaphor. One can see St. Cyril's Seleucian ally, Basil of Ancyra, reflecting on the question and the linguistic problem in his synodical epistle (358) and invoking the biblical distinction between *theos* and *ho theos* as exemplified in Philippians 2.6-11.[25]

Just as Christ, he says, "born in the likeness of men," was truly man, though not man in all respects (for He was not born, like men, from human seed and through marital intercourse), so He who before the ages was the Son is God, as being the Son of God, just as, incarnate, He was man, as being the Son of Man:

> So being "the Son of God (*tou theou*)" and "being in the form of God (*theou*)" and being "equal to God (*theōi*)," He had the essential predicates of Divinity, being like the Father in incorporeality, deity and the divine operations . . . [Paul does not say that] He is "the form of *ho theos*," but "of *theos*," nor that He is "equal to *ho theos*" but "to *theos*" . . . Those who deny the *essential* likeness of the Son to the Father make Him not a Son but a creature . . . The concept of "likeness," however, does not imply total likeness to the Father as an individual,[26] but likeness in nature, just as "the likeness of sinful flesh"[27] does not imply total similarity to historical man (who is a sinner) but *specific* sameness.

---

25 Epiphanius, *Haer.* 73.9. My translation abbreviates and paraphrases a little.

26 *tautotēta*. So Origen (*Contra Celsum* 8.12) speaks of *tautotēti boulēs*, i.e., not a single will (as faculty), but of several wills having the "same" decision or resolution.

27 Rom. 8.3.

Only the Father, Basil also says in this passage, is God *authentikōs*, that is, "principally," *par excellence* or "as an original" (of which the Son is a replica). This passage incidentally illustrates what seems to be the normal meaning of *tauto* and *tautotēs* in the Fathers in this context, i.e., *specific* identity or exact likeness without exception or qualification—and not, as is often assumed nowadays, the literal identity of two things. Similarly *homoios* seems *normally* to mean not some degree of resemblance, but exact likeness in *all respects under consideration,* though the likeness may be *understood* to be limited in range, intensity or substantiality.[28] The passage probably also shows the nature of the orthodox Eastern objection to the "homoousion." Apparently by the fourth century the natural and usual meaning of *homoousios* was "of the same specific nature." Now, while the Father's generic nature was deity, his specific nature, they thought, included paternity. Moreover, as Basil goes on to say,[29] *Ousia* ("Being") is practically the Father's name and indicates his personal and incommunicable identity.[30] Hence, within this terminological pattern, *homoousios* implies a Sabellian *huiopatoria* (Son-Fatherhood). Origen, however, had used *homoousios* in the sense of generic unity (a natural meaning of the word, since Aristotle had used [second] *ousia* for both species and genus) to express the common unity of the three Persons, whom he regarded as three real individual species.[31] The learned Eusebius conveniently recalled this fact when called upon to sign the "homoousion" formula at Nicaea,[32] as probably Acacius and Meletius also did when they accepted the "homoousion" in 363. In this pattern of thinking Father, Son and Holy Spirit are three different individual species, but have generically the same (divine)

---

28 The likeness or image may be only a picture or a reflection in water. It may, further, be only analogical.
29 *Ibid.* 12.
30 Exod. 3.14 as (almost certainly) misinterpreted in LXX: "I AM he who Is." So also Athanasius.
31 Wolfson I 321.
32 Socrates 1.8.7 *fin.*

nature. The council reached the "homoousios" formula under the guidance of Constantine who, lately come from the West and knowing that Christian doctrine teaches the divinity of Christ, had been told by the Spanish theologian Hosius that the proper way to state this truth, within the context of Trinitarian doctrine, was to say that the Son was "consubstantial" with the Father. The East objected to the term because it was unscriptural and was commonly believed to have been misused by Paul of Samosata and, in consequence, to have been condemned by a great Eastern council at Antioch in 268. Moreover, both *ousia* and *homoousios* were philosophical words with a wide range of possible meanings, and several *possible* meanings of *homoousios* in this context were highly unorthodox.

Even one like Cyril, who presumably only signed the "homoousion" in the sense of generic unity, had always, even before he signed it, emphasized the *adiairetotēs* (inseparability) of the Three in power, worship, sovereignty, and also in some further sense. The further sense he would have interpreted less ontically than Athanasius; "the Inseparables" would have had for him a more personal suggestion. But he thought of the Three also as seated together on the same throne. Probably Athanasius would have allowed this view. Personally I prefer the image of a mystic dance whose weaving pattern provides a sufficient ontic unity; and the Cappadocians, with their *ex halyseōs*,[33] would have accepted this. Such metaphorical or mythological language is as far as we can get in the mystery of the divine Unity and Trinity—which is not to deny that for the more metaphysical mind the conception of a physical or mathematical unity may have its value. Or one may suggest the analogy of the way three chords combine into one musical phrase, or the question whether a Greek Trilogy may not with equal fitness be called either one or three, or the way in which in an orchestra the percussion,

---

[33] Indeed this image ("linked") rather suggests a spiritual dance in which Power, Wisdom and Love commingle.

strings and wind form an essential and functional unity and co-create a single world of harmony. It is enough that we adore the Triune God.[34]

Eastern patristic theology had its roots in biblical and Platonic rather than Aristotelian thought-forms. Where Western theology, in its search for final statements, moves on to ontology, the Eastern Fathers, while not questioning the primacy of ontological categories, found it more fruitful to explore the biblical revelation in the symbolic, personalist, and functional categories in which it was given. Thinking of divinity in terms of spiritually creative and redemptive power, Eastern theology found no difficulty in finding room in the divine nature, at least among "the weak things of God," for filial devotion and obedience. On this view the Trinitarian dialogue already foreshadows the biblical "address (demand) and response," and a continuity is established between the eternal and the incarnate Word. We shall misunderstand both the Bible and the Greek Fathers if we invariably interpret their thought ontologically; it is, commonly, broader, open-ended, polyvalent. In this way of thinking God is revealed in what He does, and especially in what He did in Christ: "My Father worketh until now, and I work," "I am in the midst of you as one that serveth," "He who sees me sees the Father." Jesus is God, but also God is Jesus.

Athanasius comes very near to saying, perhaps unclearly or ambiguously says, that the Son has numerically the same being as the Father. His profound discussion of the Son's eternal generation regards this generation as the Father's total communication of his own being to the Son, and Athanasius perhaps regarded this communication on the model of the replication of a Platonic "form." The question would then

---

34 Greek patristic theology would be prevented from interpreting John 10.30 in terms of a mathematical unity by such texts as Gen. 2.28, Eph. 2.13-18, 1 Cor. 6.18. Similarly in the Greek Fathers *achoristos* may mean "not separate socially" or "in rank"; cf. Gal. 2.11f., where Peter for a time "practised apartheid" *(aphorizen heauton)*.

arise whether the "replica" was numerically the same as the
original or not. But why, then, did the orthodox Eastern
bishops resist the Nicene and Athanasian theology? Apparently
because the Nicene and Athanasian "homoousios" could be, in
the fourth century, understood as asserting that Father and
Son shared a common *specific* nature. This, excluding the
Eastern distinction between the specific and the generic,
seemed to make the Son exactly the same sort of being as the
Father, whereas, if we are right in our reconstruction of the
Eastern trinitarian logic, the East regarded the three Persons
as Aquinas regarded angels—as being each a different and
unique species and having only a generically common nature.
For the East, the fatherhood of the Father was part of his
specific nature. Consequently the assertion of a common
specific nature would destroy the Second and Third Persons.
Sozomen, abridging Socrates,[35] wrote:

> The bishops had another tumultuous dispute concerning
> the precise meaning of the term "consubstantial." One
> party thought that it could not be admitted without
> blasphemy, that it implied the non-existence of the Son
> of God, and that it involved the error of Montanus and
> Sabellius. The champions of the term, on the other hand,
> regarded their opponents as Greeks [pagans], and con-
> sidered that their views led to polytheism.

Further evidence of the hypothesis that the dispute between the Homoousians and the Homoeousians centered
in the genus–species question may be found in those passages where Athanasius *(Decr.* 23, *De Syn.* 41, *Tom. Ant.* 5),
instancing a dog and a wolf or gold, silver and copper,
says that such generic identity of nature is insufficient: a
dog does not father a wolf; yet wolf, dog (and man) belong
to the same genus (animal), just as base metals and the
royal metal, gold, belong to the same genus (metal). Both
examples, however, are unfair. The Eastern conception could

---

35 Sozomen, 2.18; Socrates, 1.23. The passage shows incidentally that
Eusebius of Caesarea and Eustathius of Antioch were the respective
champions of the two theological schools just after Nicaea.

not be generalized; it was unique and determined by revelation: one divine Father, one divine Son and one divine Holy Spirit; the great dividing line runs between God and creatures. Where Arianism viewed Christ as a uniquely noble creature, this Eastern theology coördinates Him in worship with the Father, though always second after the Father. Like the Father, the Son is an uncreated source of creation and redemption. As regards his being, He is "begotten, not made." He does not derive his being from an "'external" act of creation, but is by nature the Son of the Father, who communicates to Him his (generic) divine nature with all his divine attributes except Unoriginatedness. His action in creation and redemption corresponds to his being; though dependent on the Father, it is intrinsically creative and redemptive. He is the Son.

In one sense this theology is polytheistic. The existence of several Divine Persons ("Gods") would be absurd if they were in conflict. Athanasius[36] shows the impossibility of dualism; two Gods "that are contrary to one another" cannot exist either together or apart. Can there be two Infinities? The Greek philosophers usually regarded infinity as a mark of imperfection; perfection they equated with form, which has bounds. Quantitative infinity is inapplicable to God; the analogy of works of art is more relevant. Athanasius does not, at least usually, include infinity when he lists the divine attributes.[37] Two Unoriginates and universal sources of being would be impossible, but the Eastern theology did not teach this.

Undoubtedly the Eastern theology has its problems; but the Blessed Trinity is mysterious. The Latin theology has its problems too. Cardinal Newman (?) wrote on the "numerical identity" solution: "Such a statement indeed is not only a contradiction in the terms used, but in our ideas, yet not

---

36 *Against the Heathen* 7. But the Christian Trinity can exist together, and this may be the meaning of *achōristos* (i.e., "not divided or existing apart").
37 E.g., *Or. c. Ar.* 1.21; *Afr.* 8.

therefore a contradiction in fact.[38] Moreover, the English formula, "three Persons and one nature," is somewhat misleading, since intellect and will follow nature, so that there is but one divine will and intellect.[39] Constantinople I seems not to have defined the numerical unity; the Council of Chalcedon defined that Christ is "in His divinity consubstantial with the Father, and in His humanity consubstantial with us."[40] Finally, for the interpretation of the Gospel according to St. John it is important to observe that, according to Eastern theology, it is not that the Son comes "instead of" the Father, but precisely to present or re-present Him, rather as, when the Bonnie Prince unfurled the Royal Standard on his native shores, loyal Scots were not only aware that they stood in the presence of the blood royal, but from his bearing, face and glance knew that in him the King, his father, lived again.

6. The Creed of Jerusalem ("J")

A sentence in a footnote in a recent article by E. Bihain, who has been collating the unedited manuscripts (which are the majority) of the pre-baptismal *Catecheses,* seems to express doubts about the reliability of quotations from J in the present editions of Cyril. Dr. J. N. D. Kelly, therefore, may prove to have been presciently right in describing J, in his monumental *Early Christian Creeds,* as "a largely artificial construction." Nevertheless, pending further clarification by Bihain of the position of the manuscripts, we may provisionally summarize the present position regarding the relation of J to C (the "Constantinopolitan" Creed, i.e., the Creed

---

38 *Athanasius* 366 n. 1.
39 Was Prestige aware that this is the teaching of Latin theology when he wrote that, while both theologies teach the numerical identity of the divine substance, the Eastern theology teaches only one divine "subject" but Western theology three?
40 Denzinger, n. 301 (148). But see PGL s.v. homoousios, II, c, 4.

recited at Mass on Sundays in East and West, and often miscalled the Nicene Creed). Our discussion of Cyril's life and
theology makes this question of great interest. We shall speak
of three articles (corresponding to the Trinitarian division)
and twelve clauses in the Creed.

Regarding the possibility of collecting the text of J from
the Lectures: while quotations of J in the titles of the individual lectures are, though probably usually right, un-
reliable, on the evidence of the manuscripts *so far edited*
quotations of J in the text of the Lectures are reliable; they do
not seem to have been conformed by the copyists to the Creed
(C) familiar to them. Ten clauses of J can be easily collected
from the Lectures. Some slight uncertainty, however, attaches
to the third clause, and the fourth clause, on which everything turns in establishing the relation of C to J, is definitely
problematic.

In a very learned article Fr. I. Ortiz de Urbina has sought
to derive J from the Old Roman Creed. But the Eastern
creeds seem to be a different, parallel growth, and C seems to
be Eastern. Until two generations ago C was commonly assumed to be a revision of the Creed of Nicaea (N). Then in
a brilliant and persuasive article, F. J. A. Hort championed
the derivation of C from J. Hort's connection of his thesis
with an interpretation of St. Cyril's history is unconvincing.
The two theses that Cyril accepted the "homoousion" *ca.*
362 and that he presented his creed, J, at Constantinople
(A.D. 381) as evidence of his orthodoxy seem mutually destruc-
tive. Nor, I think, did Hort present in the most logical or
convincing pattern the evidence for J's being the base of C.
But he showed brilliant insight in discerning the evidence,
and he may well have been right in his main thesis.

J is physically incorporated in C to the extent that only
nine or ten (Greek) words of J fail to appear in C. While the
third *article* in C is largely a new construction, not com-
parable with any early baptismal creed, the reader of Lectures
16 and 17 will see how much of it is emphatically and verbally

taught by Cyril. The main alleged difficulty to J's being the base of C is the brevity of the third *clause* in J as it is found in most reconstructions of J. These reconstructions assume that this clause is quoted, and fully quoted, in 12.13, " (Let us believe in Jesus Christ as) having come in the flesh and been made man." But even assuming that Cyril is here quoting the Creed, it is extremely doubtful whether he is quoting it completely; the words seem only to summarize the position so far reached in Cyril's exposition of the third clause. While it is impossible to detail the argument here, Lecture 12.3 and especially 4 (end) show that Cyril is going to proceed systematically, breaking up the third clause and taking it point by point. In fact the rest of the Lecture expounds and "demonstrates" the whole of the long third clause as it is found in C. This tips the balance decisively.

It is doubtful whether C had any connection with Constantinople I. Apart from other problems, a creed ("Ep. I") almost identical with C appears in Epiphanius' *Ancoratus* 18, written in 374. If C (= Ep. I) is an expansion of J, the case for Cyril's having accepted the "consubstantial" by 374 or earlier is strengthened. This is not in itself unlikely. Athanasius' allowance, in the sixties, of the "three hypostases" formula and his conciliatory emphasis that the "homoousion" was not intended to assert more than the Scriptural data must have been important concessions for Cyril. Only the evidence of Socrates and Sozomen makes it unlikely. Is Ep. I authentic? There is no sign of corruption or interpolation in the only manuscript of the *Ancoratus*. But Epiphanius' description of Ep. I as the Creed of the whole Church and as authorized by "all the holy bishops, above 310 in number," and the terms in which he compares it with Ep. II (Ch. 19), make it very probable that N, not C, originally stood in the text—as E. Schwarz, Papadopoulos, and Kelly (p. 319) have argued. If so, then C could have been drafted at Constantinople in 381 by a small committee chaired by the great Bishop of Jerusalem and using J as its basic model.

THE TEXTS

The Nicene Creed ("N")[1]

We believe in one God the Father almighty, maker of all things visible and invisible;

And in one Lord Jesus Christ, the Son of God, begotten of the Father, Only-begotten—that is, of the substance of the Father—God of God, Light of Light, true God of true God, begotten not made, consubstantial with the Father; through whom all things were made, things in heaven and things on earth; who for us men and for our salvation came down and was incarnate, and became man, suffered, and rose on the third day, ascended into Heaven, is to come to judge living and dead;

And in the Holy Spirit.

And those who say . . . (Concludes with the Nicene anathematism.)

The Jerusalem Creed ("J")[1]

I We believe in One God the Father almighty
   maker of Heaven and earth
   of all things visible and invisible

II And in one Lord Jesus Christ the Only-begotten Son
    of God
    begotten true God of the Father before all ages
    through whom all things were made

---

1 Translated from Hort's text. Cf. Denzinger, n. 125.

1 Reconstructed from the *Catecheses*, esp. 7.4; 9.4; 11.21; 14.24; 15.2; 17.3; 18.22, ignoring the titles. The text of ten clauses (i.e., of all but III and IV) seems to be certain, though there is perhaps a little doubt about "all" in I. (Cf. Denzinger, n. 41.)

III[2]   who came in the flesh (?) (and) was made man . . . (?)

IV   and was crucified (?)[3] and was buried (?)[4]

V   who rose on the third day

VI   and ascended into Heaven
       and sat down on the right of the Father

VII   and is to come in glory to judge living and dead
       of whose reign there will be no end

VIII   And in one Holy Spirit and Paraclete
       who spoke in the prophets

IX   and in one baptism of repentance unto the remission
       of sins

X   and one holy Catholic Church

XI   the resurrection of the flesh

XII   and life everlasting.

The "Constantinopolitan" Creed ("C")[1]

(the so-called "Nicene")

We believe in one God the Father almighty, maker of
heaven and earth, of all things visible and invisible;

And in one Lord Jesus Christ, the only-begotten Son of God,
begotten of the Father before all ages,[J] Light of Light, true
God of true God, begotten not made, consubstantial with the

---

2 Cf. *Cat.* 12.13.
3 Cf. *ibid.* 13.38.
4 Cf. *ibid.* 4.11; 13.39; 14.3, 11, 17, 18.

---

1 Translated from E. Schwartz's text of C. (Cf. Denzinger, n. 150.) J
  marks the end of the Jerusalem beginning, N the end of the Nicene
  insertion. Only nine or ten words of J fail to appear in C.

Father, through whom all things were made; who for us men and for our salvation came down[N] from Heaven, and was made flesh of the Holy Spirit and the Virgin Mary, and became man, and was crucified for us under Pontius Pilate, and suffered and was buried, and rose on the third day according to the Scriptures, and ascended into Heaven, and sits on the right hand of the Father, and will come again with glory to judge living and dead, of whose reign there will be no end;

And in the Holy Spirit, the Lord and Life-giver, who proceeds from the Father, who with the Father and the Son is together worshipped and together glorified, who spoke through the prophets;

In one holy Catholic and Apostolic Church:

We confess one Baptism unto the remission of sins. We look forward to the resurrection of the dead and the life of the world to come. Amen.

ANTHONY A. STEPHENSON

THE INTRODUCTORY LECTURE

(*Procatechēsis*)

Translated by

ANTHONY A. STEPHENSON

University of Exeter
England

THE PROCATECHESIS

or

PROLOGUE TO THE CATECHETICAL LECTURES

LREADY, MY DEAR CANDIDATES for Enlightenment,[1]
scents of paradise are wafted towards you; already
you are culling mystic blossoms for the weaving of
heavenly garlands;[2] already the fragrance of the Holy Spirit

---

1 I.e., Baptism; also intellectual "enlightenment," for pre-baptismal
instructions impart the revealed system of (supernatural and esoteric)
knowledge; cf. 6.29. Light is a prominent theme in the Bible from the
second verse of Genesis to the last chapter of the Apocalypse. Particularly important in the Johannine writings, the symbol was used
also by the Qumran community (cf. the war between "the Sons of
Light and the Sons of Darkness") as well as in Zoroastrianism and the
Greek mystery religions. Cf. T. Halton, "Baptism as Illumination,"
Irish Theol. Quart. 32 (1965) 28-41.

For literary and rhetorical reasons (note the anaphora, the thrice
repeated *ēdē*, "now," "already"), the "paradisal scents" and "mystic
blossoms" seem to refer to the candidates' recent enrollment and subsequent ceremonies rather than to the graces of the lower grade of
the catechumenate. Cyril means that the candidates' registration has
brought them so close to the Paradise of which the sacramental
initiation will seize them that already its exciting scents are sometimes
borne to them along the breezes. Compare the "yet brighter and
more fragrant meadow of this Paradise" of *Myst.* 1.1. The imagery,
inspired by the Song of Songs, favorite reading of Cyril, would be
more appropriate and natural if spring had already appeared in the
land—implying a later Easter. But in 14.10, four or five weeks later,
Cyril says the date is about March 25th and this implies an early
Easter. In 18.7, he says the season is "wintry" and adds: "The trees
now stand as if they were dead: where are the leaves of the fig-tree?
. . ."

There is no contradiction if the language in *Procat.* 1 is purely
metaphorical. For other evidence about the season, cf. 4.30; 13.18.
2 The garlands are probably those worn at banquets, especially marriage feasts. Cyril refers to the nuptials between the soul and Christ
(the Bridegroom) at Baptism, a spiritual wedding consummated in
the Eucharist, itself the pledge and foretaste of the marriage-feast of

has blown about you. Already you have arrived at the outer
court of the palace:[3] may the King lead you in! Now the
blossom has appeared on the trees; God grant the fruit be
duly harvested! Now you have enlisted; you have been called
to the Colors.[4] You have walked in procession with the
tapers[5] of brides in your hands and the desire of heavenly
citizenship in your hearts; with a holy resolve also, and the
confident hope which that brings in its train. For He is no
liar who said: "For those who love Him, God makes all things
conspire to good." Yes, God is generous and kind; nevertheless He requires in every man a resolve that is true. That is
why the Apostle adds: "For those who are called in accordance with a resolve." It is the sincerity of your resolution that
makes you "called."[6] It is of no use your body being here if
your thoughts and heart are elsewhere.

---

the Lamb; cf. *Procat.* 3 and 4, *Cat.* 3.1.

"Mystic": *noēta*, intelligible. Thus early Cyril introduces the Platonic
category of the sensible–intelligible, adapted to Christian spirituality
and sacramental theory.

3 I.e., at the threshold of Baptism, which is the portal of the Paradise
of the Church conceived eschatologically. Cf. *Procat.* 15-17, *Cat.* 18.34.

4 In *Myst* 1.2-9, the candidates, immediately before Baptism, renounce
Satan and take Christ for their Lord and Master. Roman army recruits
took an oath *(sacramentum)* pledging their personal fidelity to the
emperor. For the adaptation of this idea to the Christian mysteries
(called *sacramenta*, "sacraments," in the West) cf. Tert., *Ad Mart.* 3.
The Latin New Testament translated *mystērion* by *sacramentum.* Cf.
Col. 1.13, Eph. 2.1-2, 1 Pet. 2.9; and St. Augustine's doctrine *(City of
God)* of the two kingdoms or realms, each with its own king, laws,
goods, destiny, principle, and life.

5 Apparently, therefore (for this passage seems to be the chief or only
evidence), at some ceremony following their registration, perhaps, in
a formal entrance procession into the church for the opening lecture,
the candidates carried lighted tapers or torches, "a significant symbol
both of the marriage of the soul with Christ, and of its enlightenment by faith" (Gifford, xvii)—and also of the heavenly teaching
which, as *illuminandi*, they were about to receive.

6 Cyril stresses the importance of human effort to the point of mis-
interpreting Rom. 8.28. His successor, John, refused to condemn
Pelagius at a diocesan synod at Jerusalem, July 28, 415, as a
Palestinian synod at Diospolis (Lydda) also did in December 415;
cf. John Ferguson, *Pelagius* (Cambridge 1956) 82-89. This is not to say
that John was a Pelagian, still less Cyril, who is not asking whether
sincerity too is not God's gift, but only rhetorically insisting upon
the necessity of cooperation with grace. Cf. also Ch. 8. and *Sermon*,
Ch. 4 and 5 *fin.*

(2) Why, there was a Simon the Sorcerer[7] once who approached the baptismal waters: he was dipped in the font, but he was not enlightened. While he plunged his body in the water, his heart was not enlightened by the Spirit;[8] physically he went down and came up, but his soul was not buried with Christ, nor did it share in His Resurrection. If I mention these examples of falls, it is to prevent *your* downfall. "Now all these things happened to them as a type, and they were written for the correction"[9] of those who approach the font to this day. Let none of you be found tempting grace, "lest some bitter root spring up to poison"[10] your heart. Let no one enter saying: "I say, let us see what the believers[11] are doing; I'm going in to have a look and find out what's going on." Do you expect to see without being seen? Do you imagine that while you are investigating "what's going on," God is not investigating your heart?

(3) We read in the Gospels of a busybody who one day decided to "investigate" a wedding-feast.[12] Without dressing

---

7 Although, according to Acts 8.13, Simon Magus "believed," Cyril invariably assumes that he had been insincere from the first, at least in the sense that he had not "believed from the heart" (which implies more than an intellectual response); cf. 1 John 2.19.

8 Cf. Origen, *Hom. in Num.* 3.1: ". . . neque omnes qui loti sunt aqua, continuo etiam Spiritu Sancto loti sunt." Origen illustrates from the hypocrisy of Simon.

9 1 Cor. 10.11.

10 Cf. Heb. 12.15.

11 I.e., apparently the upper class of catechumens, i.e., the candidates *(phōtizomenoi—illuminandi)* who, contrary to the custom of other churches, at Jerusalem were assimilated to the faithful and no longer called catechumens.

12 Cf. Matt. 22.1-14, esp. verses 11-13. Perhaps what was originally a separate parable begins at verse 11. If the two parables are read as one, it is not clear—since the guests have been hastily collected from the highways and by-ways—how one could be blamed for not being in his "party clothes." Cyril, without mentioning the difficulty, offers an answer: "Should not your eyes have informed you?" Or perhaps (Telfer) Cyril realized that the two parables were independent and felt free to invent the circumstances of the unmannerly guest's entry. K. Stendahl thinks that there is no problem in oriental parable, where the details can be forgotten once they have served their purpose or be supposed to change appropriately as required by the unfolding story (Peake's *Commentary on the Bible* [London-New York 1962] *ad loc.*). The defective dispositions which mark Cyril's "intruder" seem

correctly for the occasion, he entered the dining room and,
unchallenged by the bridegroom, took his place at table.
Etiquette, of course, demanded that, seeing everybody's white
garments, he should conform; but in fact, though fully the
match of his fellow-guests as a trencherman, he did not match
them in his dress (I mean, his resolve). The bridegroom, for
all his large-heartedness, was not undiscerning and, while going
the rounds of the company and observing his guests indi-
vidually (it was not what they ate, but the correctness of
their behavior and dress that interested him),[13] he saw a
stranger without a wedding garment, and said to him: "Pray,
sir, how did you get in? What a color! What effrontery![14]
The doorkeeper did not stop you in view of the liberality of
the host? Quite so. You didn't know the correct dress for a
festive occasion? Quite. Nevertheless, you came in; you saw the
glittering clothes of those at table. Should not your eyes have
been your teachers? Should not a timely exit then have been
the prelude to a timely return? As it is, your untimely entrance can lead only to your untimely ejection." Turning to
his attendants, he ordered: "Bind those feet" which pre-
sumptuously intruded; "bind the hands" which had not the
wit to put a bright garment on him; and "cast him into the
outer darkness"; for he is not worthy of the bridal torches.

---

to be not so much imperfect faith as moral: the lack of the determination to make a decisive break with the old life in favor of
the new life with the ethical quality demanded by the Gospel. See
Ch. 3. In the era introduced by Constantine's conversion, when Christianity became first a tolerated and then a privileged religion in the
Empire, the merely curious or the dilettante might be found among
the candidates. In first-century Palestine, "the wedding garment was
not, apparently, a special garment, but ordinary clean clothes"
(J. C. Fenton, *Saint Matthew* [Pelican Gospel Commentaries, 1963]
ad loc.). While on the night of their Baptism the candidates would
be literally all in white (the Easter color, as Lancelot Andrewes
observed), in the Greek Koine "white garments" meant simply
"dressed in one's best" (Telfer). In Ch. 4, Cyril explains and applies
the metaphor; cf. 3.2.

13 Reischl encloses this parenthesis in square brackets, presumably as an
   interpolation, but his justifying note is obscure.

14 Or, keeping the apparently universal meaning of *syneidesis*, "What
   a conscience!" Then the phrase is probably either Cyril's interpretation
   of, or a scribal gloss upon, "What a color!"

Ponder, I bid you, the fate of that intruder, and look to your own safety.

(4) For our part, as Christ's ministers we have given a welcome to every man and, in the role of porter, have left the door ajar. You, maybe, have come in with your soul befouled with the mire of sin and with your purpose[15] sullied. You came in; you were accepted;[16] your name was entered in the register. Do you see the majesty of the Church? Do you behold, I ask, its order and discipline, the reading of the Scriptures, the presence of the ecclesiastical orders, the regular sequence of instruction? You are on holy ground; be taught by what you see. Withdraw in a good hour now, and come back in a right good hour tomorrow. If the fashion of your soul was avarice, put on another fashion, and then come in. Put off, I say, lewdness and impurity; put on the bright robe of chastity. I give you timely warning before Jesus, the Bridegroom of souls, comes in and sees the fashions. You cannot plead short notice; forty days are yours for repentance; you have opportunity in plenty for undressing, for laundry-work, for dressing again and returning. If you persist in an evil

---

15 *Proairesis* (resolve, intention, motive, project) is important in the *Catecheses* as also in first-century Jewish proselyte baptism, where conversion had to be intended or chosen for its own sake and not as a means, or as incidental, to something else; cf. D. Daube, *The New Testament and Rabbinic Judaism* (Oxford 1956).

16 *(Katexiōthēs)* Apparently, therefore, in Cyril's time acceptance for registration was not automatic. In Aetheria's time (ca. 390?; *Peregrinatio* 45) intending candidates, having previously given in their names to a priest who jotted them down, on the eve of Lent attended a formal scrutiny by the bishop who inquired of their neighbors whether they could give them a good character. If so, he formally entered their names in the register; else "he told them to go out and reform themselves . . . and then approach the Laver." Cyril probably means that, like his imaginary door-keeper in the parable, he had given the candidates the benefit of any doubt, reflecting no doubt that only God can read the heart. He regularly (cf. Telfer) puts the responsibility on the candidates; cf. 1.3. Nevertheless, the first sentence of Ch. 15 reminds us that in most churches there were periodical scrutinies during the final stages of preparation for Baptism. Candidates for admission to the Qumran community were examined to test their "spirit and learning"; while they practiced periodical ritual bathing, it is disputed whether admission to the order was by a bath after a period of instruction and probation.

purpose, the preacher is guiltless, but you must not expect
to receive the grace. Though the water will not refuse to
receive you, you will get no welcome from the Spirit.[17] If
anyone is conscious of a wound in himself, let him have it
dressed; if any has fallen, let him rise. Let there be no Simon
among you, no hypocrite—and no Paul Pry.

(5) Perhaps you have come with a different motive: perhaps you are courting, and a girl is your reason—or, con-
versely, a boy. Many a time, too, a slave has wished to please
his master, or a friend his friend. I allow the bait, and I
welcome you in the trust that, however unsatisfactory the
motive that has brought you, your good hope will soon save
you. Maybe you did not know where you were going, or
what sort of net it was in which you were to be caught. You
are a fish caught in the net of the Church. Let yourself be
taken alive: don't try to escape. It is Jesus who is playing you
on His line, not to kill you, but, by killing you, to make you

---

17 Here as in Ch. 2, Cyril seems to attribute the reception of the
Spirit to water (rather than to chrism). In 3.3 also, the "spiritual
grace" is given "with the water," and it is natural to read 3.3 as saying that it is in the baptismal bath that the Holy Spirit seals souls,
as is said explicitly in 3.4. In 3.5, "the gift" of "grace" *(charis)* is
"given through water," the fairest of the four elements, and Cyril
quotes Gen. 1.1. In 1.2 also, "the grace" is given, along with the
new birth, in the "Holy Bath," and 1.5 shows that "the grace" includes "the communication of" (or "participation in") the Holy Spirit
as well as the forgiveness of sins (3.2, 12, 15, 16). It is natural to read
1.2 and 3.3 as meaning that the Seal, like regeneration and adoption,
is given in "the Holy Bath," as is stated explicitly in 3.4. Thus, while
the *Catecheses* think of the Holy Spirit as working in the Baptismal
water, in the *Mystagogica,* by contrast, the descent of the Holy
Spirit upon Christ at Jordan is (3.1) distinguished from His actual
baptism, and (3.1-2) in the sacramental initiation the unction is
correspondingly distinguished from water-baptism and it is in the
post-baptismal unction that the Holy Spirit descends. In the *Mystagogica,* therefore, the Chrismation rivals Baptism in importance and
it is (3.5) only after Chrismation (Confirmation) that one becomes
really entitled to the name of "Christian." Many scholars, however,
have argued that the *Catecheses* and *Mystagogica* can be harmonized
by supposing that in the *Catecheses* "Baptism" often refers to the
whole initiatory rite and thus includes Chrismation. To settle this
question, one must notice what effects the *Catecheses* ascribe not
simply to "Baptism," but to the water. It is, I think, impossible to
harmonize the two works on this point.

alive. For you must die and rise again. Did you not hear the Apostle say: "dead to sin, but living to justice"?[18] Die, then, to sin, and live to righteousness; from today be alive.

(6) What honor Jesus bestows! You used to be called a catechumen, when the truth was being dinned into you from without:[19] hearing about the Christian hope without understanding it; hearing about the Mysteries without having a spiritual perception of them; hearing the Scriptures but not sounding their depths. No longer in your ears now but in your heart is that ringing; for the indwelling Spirit henceforth makes your soul the house of God. When you hear the texts from Scripture concerning the Mysteries,[20] then you will have a spiritual perception of things once beyond your ken.

Do not suppose that it is a small thing that you are being given. You, a pitiable creature, are receiving the family name of God. Listen to Paul saying: "God is faithful."[21] Listen to another Scripture saying God is "faithful and just."[22] It was because he foresaw this—because men were to bear a name which belongs to God—that the Psalmist, speaking in the person of God, said: "I have said: you are gods, and all of you the sons of the Most High."[23] But take care that you do not, while rejoicing in the name of "faithful," have the resolve of the faithless. You have entered for a race: run the course; you will not get the like chance again. If it were your wedding day that was fixed, would you not, ignoring everything else, be wholly engaged in preparations for the marriage

---

18 Cf. Rom. 6.11; 1 Pet. 2.24.

19 The word-play of the Greek depends on the derivation of "catechumen," etc., from *ēchē*, "a ringing sound" (cf. "echo"), *katēchō* then means "sound a thing in a person's ears," hence "teach by word of mouth," and finally, "instruct in the elements (of Christianity)."

20 "Mystery" in the Greek Church corresponds to the word "sacrament" in the Latin Church, especially the initiatory rites. In Cyril, "mysteries" also covers (e.g., 6.29) the doctrine of the Holy Trinity, which Cyril equates with the Creed. In this broad sense, "the Mysteries" cover the subjects of both series of *Catecheses*.

21 1 Cor. 1.9.

22 1 John 1.9.

23 Ps. 80.6.

feast? Then, on the eve of consecrating your soul to your heavenly Spouse, will you not put by the things of the body to win those of the spirit?

(7) A man cannot be baptized a second and a third time. Otherwise, he could say: "I failed once; the second time I shall succeed." Fail once, and there is no putting it right. For, "one Lord, one faith, one Baptism." It is only heretics who are rebaptized, and then because the first was no Baptism.[24]

---

24 Here we abandon RR, who adopted M 1's "splendid text" ("praeclara lectio"), "*some* heretics," and follow the great majority of MSS and Toutée. Toutée judged that Reg.'s omission of this sentence was due to haplography and not to the scribe's being shocked by Cyril's contradicting the teaching of the (medieval Western) Church. There seems, however, little doubt that Reg.'s omission and M 1's variant ("too good to be true") *are* due to some such scruple. If M 1's text were the original, the variants would be inexplicable. But, whereas since Augustine and probably since the Council of Arles (314; can. 9 [8]) heretical Baptism, if administered in the Name of Father, Son, and Holy Spirit, has usually (but see Nic. Can. 19) been deemed valid in the Western Church, Eastern practice has been much less uniform. Even the decision of Nicaea (Can. 19, and cf. 8) that convert Paulianists, though not Novatians, must be rebaptized *(anabaptizesthai)*, explained by Athanasius *(Orat. c. Arian.* 2.42-43) in relation to their defective Trinitarian faith, is much closer to Cyril's principle, than to Arles' since most fourth-century heresies were Trinitarian.

Telfer takes Cyril to mean that certain heretical sects do "repeat baptism," i.e., practice frequent ritual ablutions. This, though ingenious, seems less probable. The PGL seems to show no parallel for this meaning of *baptizomai;* rather, the *ana* implies the repetition (cf. *anablepō, anapneō)* of an act or state conceived of as normally unrepeatable or unrecoverable. Cyril seems to interpret "One Lord, one Faith, one Baptism" as excluding both the repeatability of a Baptism associated with the one Faith and the possibility of a true Baptism apart from it. Lest, however, we rashly judge Cyril a bigoted rigorist, we must remember that for him *(Cat.* 4.3-18; 5.12) "the Faith" was almost synonymous with the Creed. The "heretics" to whom he refers were no doubt the far-out Gnostic sectaries and particularly, perhaps, the Manichees, who were scarcely Christians at all (6.12). For in 6.14 he says: "The inventor of all heresy was Simon Magus" (the reputed founder of Gnosticism) and in 6.20 he speaks of hating "all heretics" but especially Mani, though the Manichees (6.21) were "not of Christian origin." To the groups whom he thought of as "heretics," Cyril's attitude was uncompromising: 4.37; 6.35; 15.9 (probably referring to both Arians and Sabellians, cf. 4.8; 11.13, 16, 17); 4.2. For an English translation of the principal documents in the third-century re-baptism controversy, cf. J. Stevenson, *A New Eusebius* (London 1957) 251-257, 323, 360-364.

(8) God requires of us only one thing, sincerity. Do not go on saying, "But how are my sins blotted out?" I answer: "By assenting, by believing." Could any answer be more succinct? If, however, not your heart but only your lips proclaim your assent, well, it is the "Reader of hearts"[25] who is your Judge. From today cease from every evil deed; let not your tongue speak unholy words, nor your eye commit evil or rove after vanities.

(9) Let your feet take you swiftly to the catechetical instructions. Submit to the exorcisms devoutly.[26] Whether you are breathed upon or exorcised, the act spells salvation. Imagine virgin gold alloyed with various foreign substances: copper, tin, iron, lead. What we are after is the gold alone; and gold cannot be purified of its dross without fire. Similarly, the soul cannot be purified without exorcisms, exorcisms which, since they are culled from the divine Scriptures, possess divine power. The veiling of your face is to foster recollection, lest a roving eye make your heart also stray. But the veiling of the eyes does not hinder the ears from receiving salvation.[27] Just as goldsmiths with their delicate instruments direct a blast upon the fire and, by agitating the surrounding flame, cause the gold hidden in the crucible to bubble up and so gain their object, in the same way when the exorcists inspire fear by means of the divine Spirit[28] and regenerate the soul by fire in the crucible of the body, our enemy the Devil flees, and we are left with salvation and the sure prospect of eternal life; and henceforth, the soul, purified of its offenses, has

25 Cf. Acts 1.24; 15.8.
26 In Aetheria's time (*Peregr.* 46), the candidates were exorcized daily by "the clerics" after the dawn service in the Church of the Resurrection. The exorcizing and teaching (in the Great Church, i.e., "Golgotha" or "The Martyry") occupied three hours, from six to nine.
27 Whereas for Greek philosophy, knowledge tends to be the analogue of visual perception of form and so objective, impersonal and universal, in the biblical tradition saving knowledge is a matter of a personal response of faith, and obedience to an audible word of invitation and command.
28 In Hebrew (cf. Gen. 1.1 and 2.7), Greek, and Latin, the same word means "spirit" and "breath."

salvation. Let us, then, my brethren, persevere in hope; let us commit ourselves in hope: so will the God of all, seeing our resolution, cleanse us from our sins, grant us a good hope of our estate, and bestow on us repentance unto salvation. It is God who has called, and it is you that He has called.

(10) Be faithful in your attendance of the catechizing. Even though we protract our discourse, do not let your mind yield to distraction. You are taking up arms against the enemy. You are taking up arms against heresies, against the Jews, against the Samaritans, against the Gentiles. Your enemies are many: take plenty of ammunition; you have targets in plenty. You must learn how to shoot down the Greek and do battle with heretic, Jew, and Samaritan.[29] Your weapons are sharp, and sharpest of all is "the sword of the Spirit."[30] But your own right hand must strike with a holy resolution, to fight the fight of the Lord, if you would conquer the opposing powers and make yourself proof against every stratagem of heresy.

(11) Let this also be included in your battle orders: study what you are told and guard it forever. Do not confuse the pre-baptismal instructions with the ordinary sermons. Ex-

---

29 This could suggest (cf. Toutée, *ad loc.*) that the program of the *Catecheses* is largely apologetics. For apologetics against the pagans by rational argument, cf. 12.27 and 18.5-10; against the Samaritans, Cyril could appeal to the authority of the Pentateuch (18.11-13); against the Jews, he appeals to the Old Testament and the fulfillment of its prophecies in the New; against heretics, he argues from all Scripture as handed down in the Church (4.35) from the Apostles. Ch. 11, however, suggests rather a program of systematic theology. Since even of the groups mentioned in Ch. 10 only the pagans (not important in the *Catecheses*) are routed by rational argument, and even they can only be taught the revealed truth through the exposition of the inspired Scriptures, the method of the *Catecheses* is predominantly systematic in a broad sense (they have the same sort of unity as the Creed) and dogmatic. Essentially, the *Catecheses* are the "demonstration" of the Creed, itself regarded as "collected" from Scripture (5.12; 4.17 and *passim*); this is the saving knowledge. But the argument, prominent in the *Catecheses*, from miracles and especially prophecy, is predominantly "apologetic," though Cyril handles it somewhat dogmatically, everywhere assuming the inerrancy of Holy Scripture.

30 Eph. 6.17.

cellent and reliable as those are, still, if we neglect their lessons today, we can learn them tomorrow. But the systematic instruction about the laver of regeneration—if that be neglected today, when shall the loss be made good? Imagine it is the season for planting trees: unless we dig, and dig deep, when can the tree be planted aright that has once been planted amiss? Or let me compare the catechizing to a building. Unless we methodically bind and joint the whole structure together, we shall have leaks and dry rot, and all our previous exertions will be wasted. No: stone must be laid upon stone in regular sequence, and corner follow corner, jutting edges must be planed away: and so the perfect structure rises. I bring you as it were the stones of knowledge; you must be instructed in the doctrine of the living God, of the Judgment, of Christ, of the Resurrection. Many things have to be said in order, which are now being touched upon at random but will then be brought together into harmonious system.[31] Unless you achieve this unity of design, holding the beginning and the sequel in your mind together, the builder may do his best, but your house will be a ruin.

(12) If after the class a catechumen asks you what the instructors have said, tell outsiders nothing. For it is a divine secret that we deliver to you, even the hope of the life to come. Keep the secret for the Rewarder. If someone says, "What harm is done if I know about it too?," don't listen to him. So the sick man asks for wine, but, given to him at the wrong time, it only produces brain-fever, and two evils ensue: the effect on the sick man is disastrous, and the doctor is maligned. So with the catechumen, if he is told the Mysteries by one of the faithful: not understanding what he has been told, the catechumen raves, attacking the doctrine and ridi-

---

31 The time-notes favor Toutée's (different) interpretation: the *Cate-cheses* systematize what the candidates have heard in the ordinary sermons. But how can they have heard the doctrines of the Creed in the ordinary sermons? Cf. Ch. 12. Is there, then, after all (cf. Ch. 14 and 16.27), something in Cabrol's theory that, as in Aetheria's time *(Peregr.* 46), the Lenten teaching fell into two parts? Improbably, on the evidence at present available.

culing the statement, while the believer stands condemned as a traitor.

You are now a man standing at a frontier: so, no careless talk, please. Not that these are not fit subjects for discussion, but that your interlocutor is not fit to hear them. You yourself were once a catechumen; I did not then describe to you the country which lay ahead. When you grasp by experience the sublimity of the doctrines, then you will understand that the catechumens are not worthy to hear them.

(13) All you who have been enrolled are the sons and daughters of one Mother. When you come in before the exorcisms are due to begin, let the conversation of each of you be such as to excite devotion. If anyone is absent, make search for him. If it were to a feast that you had been invited, would you not wait for your fellow guest? If you had a brother, would you not seek what is good for your brother?

Finally, do not indulge in idle curiosity—no asking "what the city has done," or the ward, or the Emperor, or the Bishop, or the priest. Lift up your eyes: now, as your hour strikes, you need Him who is above. "Be still, and know that I am God."[32] If you see the believers not recollected when they are ministering, well, they are safe; they know what they have received; they possess the grace. Your fate is still in the balance, to be accepted or not. Instead of copying the carefree, cultivate fear.

(14) During the actual exorcism, while waiting for the others, let men be with men, and women with women. For now I need Noe's ark, that I may have Noe and his sons together, separate from his wife and his sons' wives.[33] For, although the ark was one and the door was closed, yet decorum was observed. So now, though the church doors are barred and you are all inside, let distinctions be kept: men with men, women with women. Let not the principle of salvation be made a pretext for spiritual ruin. Keeping close

32 Ps. 45.11.
33 Cf. Gen. 7.7-9, 13.

together is a good rule, provided that passion is kept at a distance.

Furthermore, let the men have some profitable book in their hands while they sit waiting, and let one read from it and another listen. Or, if there is no book available, let one pray and another talk about something useful. Let the virgins likewise form a separate band, singing hymns or reading; silently, however, so that, while their lips speak, no other's ears may hear what they say. For, "I suffer not a woman to speak in church."[34] Let the married woman imitate them: let her pray, and her lips move, but her voice not be heard. So shall Samuel come among us: your barren soul, that is to say, shall bring forth the salvation of "God who has heard your prayers."[35] For that is the meaning of "Samuel."

(15) I shall be watching the earnestness of each man and the piety of each woman. Let your heart be fired to piety; let your soul be tempered like steel, as the stubborn metal of unfaith is hammered on the anvil till the dross scales off and the pure iron is left. Let the rust flake away, leaving the authentic metal.

May God one day show you that night whose darkness is daylight, the dark of which it is said: "Darkness shall not be dark to thee, and night shall be light as the day."[36] Then, may the gate of Paradise be opened to every man of you and every woman. Then, may you enjoy the fragrant, Christ-bearing waters. Then, may you receive Christ's name[37] and

---

34 1 Cor. 14.34; cf. 1 Tim. 2.11-12.
35 Cf. 1 Kings 1.12-14.
36 Ps. 138.12. The reference is to Holy Saturday night during which the candidates were baptized in the Church of the Resurrection, brilliantly illuminated to symbolize the return of the risen light and their own sacramental enlightenment.
37 This (cf. Ch. 13 *fin.* and *Myst.* 3.5) suggests that it was only proleptically and by courtesy that the candidates were styled "believers." Still, the evidence (*Procat.* 6, 12, 13, 17; *Cat.* 1.1, 4; 3.15; 5.1; 10.16; 11.9; 18.26), though it does not prove that at Jerusalem (unlike other Churches) the candidates were quite consistently classed as "believers," does show that the important distinction there was between the catechumens on the one hand and the candidates and believers on the other.

the power of things divine. Even now, I beseech you, in spirit lift up your eyes; behold the angelic choirs, and the Lord of all, God, on His throne, with the Son, the Only-begotten, sitting on His right hand, and the Spirit, too, and the Thrones and Dominations ministering, and every man of you and every woman receiving salvation. Even now let there ring in your ears that excellent sound which you shall hear when the Angels, celebrating your salvation, chant: "Blessed are they whose iniquities are forgiven,"[38] on the day when, like new stars of the Church, you will enter, your bodies bright, your souls shining.

(16) Great is the prize set before you in Baptism: ransom for captives, remission of sins, death of sin, a new, spiritual birth, a shining garment, a holy seal inviolable, a Heaven-bound chariot, delights of Paradise, a passport to the King-dom, the grace of the adoption of sons. But a dragon lies in ambush for the traveler; take care he does not bite you and inject his poison of unbelief. Seeing this numerous company winning salvation, he selects and stalks his prey.[39] In your

---

38 Ps. 31.1.
39 Cyril refers to the "roaring lion" of 1 Pet. 5.8. Ps. 90.13 couples the dragon and the lion. Is this dragon who "lies in wait" (*tērei*) for the foot of the initiate traveling to "the Father of souls" related to the serpent of Gen. 3.15? Cf. also "the croucher" (sin or the Tempter) of Gen. 4.7. There are perhaps traces in the *Catecheses* of Gnostic as well as apocalyptic and mystery-religion language and imagery. Jerusalem was not far from Samaria, the home of Simon Magus (Acts 8.9), whom Cyril (6.14), like other Fathers, over-simplifying, made the origin of Gnosticism. But many Christian Gnostic ideas were themselves borrowed from much older sources. Cyril's suggestion that the dragon may bite without hurting is interesting. The same dragon reappears just below (and cf. 3.11-12) as the sea-dragon Leviathan of Isa. 27.1 (cf. 51.9 and Job 41) who is related to the chaos-dragon of the Gilgamesh epic (who stole the hero's herb of immortality when he was bathing), who is related to Tiamât of the Babylonian creation epic, baptized as Tehom (chaotic abyss), the symbol of disorder and evil in Gen. 1.1 (cf. Ps. 73.13-14). The home of the dragon was the Jordan (Job 40.23, *lect. dub.*), though prob-ably his earlier dwelling was "old Nile." The dragon is important in the Apocalypse, but Cyril for some reason excluded the Apoca-lypse from the Canon (4.36). While Cyril's strong doctrine of the divine transcendence (not to mention 9.7 and the *Blitzkrieg* on Gnosticism in *Cat.* 6) excludes any suspicion of Gnostic dualism. *Myst.* 1 takes very seriously the (biblical) theme of the Christian's

journey to the Father of souls, your way lies past that dragon. How shall you pass him? You must have "your feet stoutly shod with the gospel of peace,"[40] so that, even if he does bite you, he may not hurt you.

With Hope invincible for your sandals and with Faith the guest of your heart, you may pass through the enemy's lines and enter into the house of the Lord. Prepare your heart for the reception of teaching and the fellowship in the holy Mysteries. Pray more frequently, that God may count you worthy of the heavenly and eternal Mysteries. Never be idle, day or night, but so soon as sleep falls from your eyes let your mind occupy itself with prayer. If you notice that an evil thought has entered your mind, hold tightly to the saving remembrance of Judgment. Apply your mind to learning, that it may forget low things. If you find someone saying to you: "So you are to go down into the water? What's wrong with the new public baths?," be sure that this is a ruse of "the Dragon that is in the sea." Attend not, then, to the lips of the speaker of guile, but to the Spirit of unbelief and deceit who works in him.[41] Guard your own soul if you would

---

war against the Powers of Darkness. For the (thoroughly Scriptural) "up and down" theme in the *Catecheses*, see, e.g., 4.1, 9, 11-15; 11.10; 15.1; 12.2, 5, 10; 14.3, 25; 17.13-15; 18.15; 3.12, and perhaps cf. Aetheria's report *(Peregr.* 42) that the Church of Jerusalem, probably *ca.* 390, went to Bethlehem to keep the vigil of the Ascension, and "the bishop and presbyters preached sermons appropriate to the day and the place." But for Dekkers' alternative explanation of this surprising Bethlehem "station" (which incidentally would date the Pilgrimage to 415-417), cf. Cross, p. xviii n. 1.

40 Eph. 6.15. The weapons and equipment mentioned here and in Ch. 10 echo the theme of the Christian warfare visualized in Eph. 6.10-20 as a conflict against evil angelic powers—"virtually the sole significant remnant of Jewish apocalyptic" in Ephesians (H. Chadwick, *ad. loc.* in Peake's *Commentary of the Bible* [London-New York 1962]). The "panoply" or "whole armor of God" reappears in the *Myst.,* where (3.4) it is completed by the "mystical Chrism," so that only after the Chrismation can the neophyte challenge and vanquish the Adversary; cf. *Cat.* 3.13. The Powers of Darkness are probably thought of as embodied in the heretics, Jews, Samaritans and Greeks (pagans) whom the candidates are being armed against; cf. 4.1 and 6.35 and the reading adopted at the end of this chapter; see next note.

41 Deserting RR and Toutée for the Paris MS (cod. Reg.): cf. Eph. 2.1; 2 Thess. 2.7-12. Most MSS have: "Attend not to the lips of the

avoid being trapped and would inherit, after standing fast in
hope, everlasting salvation.[42]

(17) These, then, are the instructions, these the battle
orders, that I (so far as a man may) give to you. To make
our house "hay, straw" and chaff is to risk its total loss by
fire; no, make the work of "gold, silver, precious stones."[43]
For it is mine to speak, yours to translate my words into
action,[44] and God's to perfect the work. Let us prepare our
hearts, straining every nerve and sinew of soul and mind.
The race is for our souls; we have set our hearts on an eternal
prize. God, who knows your hearts and discerns who is
genuine and who is only acting a part, is able both to keep
the sincere safe and to make a believer of the hypocrite. Yes,
even of the unbeliever God can make a believer if only he
gives his heart.[45] May He "cancel the decree against you";[46]
may He grant you an amnesty for your former sins; may He
set you as His sons in His Church and enlist you in His own
service, arraying you in the armor of righteousness. May He
fill you with the heavenly treasures of the New Covenant
and sign you with that seal of the Holy Spirit which no man
shall break forever, in Christ Jesus our Lord, to whom be
glory forever and ever. Amen.

TO THE READER[47]

These Catechetical Lectures, addressed to candidates for Enlightenment, may be given to those going forward for Bap-

---

speaker, but to God working in him," where "the speaker" is the
preacher. But Cyril seems to mean that the serpent speaks in the
tempter.
42 Cyril's emphasis on hope is notable. As Gabriel Marcel has shown,
this Christian theme needs stressing in our time.
43 1 Cor. 3.12, 15.
44 Diffidently following Toutée instead of RR with most MSS, "to
resolve."
45 Or perhaps "if only He give the heart."
46 Col. 2.14.
47 The work referred to in this note clearly did not include the *Mystagogical Catecheses*. The authorship and date of the note, for which

tism and to the already baptized faithful. They may, on no account, be given to catechumens or to other classes of non-Christians. Anyone making a copy is hereby adjured, as in the sight of the Lord, to preface it with this warning.

---

cf. Ch. 12, are uncertain. The "rule of the secret" excluded pagans and ordinary catechumens from the Lenten lecturing in the Jerusalem of 350; cf. *Procat.* 12, *Cat.* 5.12 (where, incidentally, the copyists omitted the text of the Creed); 6:29; 16.26 *fin.*

LENTEN LECTURES

(*Catechēses*)

I-XII

Translated by

LEO P. McCAULEY, S.J.

Boston College
Chestnut Hill, Massachusetts

FOREWORD TO THE CATECHESES

HE FIRST THREE DISCOURSES of Cyril develop the topic, "and in one baptism for the remission of sins," though the first *Catechesis*, like the *Procatechesis*, is largely introductory in character. There is great diversity in the manuscripts which have preserved the second *Catechesis*. Worthy of note is the opinion of Cyril *(Cat.* 3.7) that the baptism of John remitted sin.

The fourth *Catechesis* is a summary exposition of the fundamental Catholic doctrines. The details concerning the separate cells of the translators of the Septuagint, and the miraculous agreement of their versions (Ch. 24) were apparently an invention of Philo Judaeus, but accepted by some of the Fathers.

Cyril proceeds to discourse on Faith (5), the Unity of God (6), God the Father (7), Omnipotent (8), and Creator (9). There follow the lectures on One Lord Jesus Christ (10), the Only-begotten Son of God (11), who was made flesh (12), and was crucified and buried (13), and rose from the dead, ascended into heaven, and sits at the right hand of God the Father (14), and who is to come with glory to judge the living and the dead, of whose kingdom there is no end (15). Cyril devotes two lectures to the Holy Spirit (16-17), and concludes the *Catecheses* on the Creed with a discourse on the words: "And in one Holy Catholic Church, and in the resurrection of the flesh, and in life everlasting" (18). The bizarre story of the Phoenix (cf. Herodotus 2.73), advanced as an argument for the resurrection of the flesh *(Cat.* 18.8), seems to have been believed by some of the Fathers.

As he completes the exposition of the Articles of Faith,

Cyril promises further instruction on the reception of Baptism on Easter day itself, and on the days following Easter other discourses on the various mysteries of which the baptized are to become partakers.

To the modern reader Cyril's accommodation of Scripture texts will often seem strained or farfetched. Assuming that the record of the Old Testament is prophetic, he is constantly discovering what he believes to be prophetic anticipation of the events in the life of our Lord. This is particularly true in connection with His passion, death, resurrection and second coming. As for Cyril's position on the Trinity, I would here state that I do not accept some of the findings set out in pp. 34-60 above.

In the rendering of Cyril's biblical quotations into English, use has been made of the version published under the patronage of the Confraternity of Christian Doctrine. When the Confraternity rendering is based on texts that do not correspond with Cyril's Greek, the necessary adaptations have been made.

LEO P. McCAULEY, S.J.

CATECHESIS I

An Introductory Discourse to the Candidates for Baptism

"Wash yourselves clean! Put away the misdeeds of your souls from before my eyes . . ."[1]

(1) Disciples of the New Testament, sharers in the mysteries of Christ—as yet by calling only, but presently by grace as well—"make for yourselves a new heart and a new spirit,"[2] that you may become a subject of joy for the citizens of heaven. For if there is joy "over one sinner who repents,"[3] according to the gospel, how much more will the salvation of so many souls gladden the blessed saints? You have entered upon a good and glorious course: run the holy race in good earnest. Eager for your redemption, the Only-begotten Son of God is present among us; He says: "Come to me, all you who labor and are burdened, and I will give you rest."[4] Clothed as you are in the rough garments of your offenses and "held fast in the meshes of your own sins,"[5] listen to the prophet's voice saying: "Wash yourselves clean! Put away the misdeeds of your souls from before my eyes,"[6] that the angelic choir may chant over you: "Happy they whose faults are taken away, whose sins are covered."[7] Guard unquenched in your hands the torches of faith you have just lighted, that He who of old here on all-holy Golgotha opened

---

1 Cf. Isa. 1.16.
2 Ezech. 18.31.
3 Luke 15.7.
4 Matt. 11.28.
5 Cf. Prov. 5.22.
6 Cf. Isa. 1.16.
7 Ps. 31.1.

91

up Paradise to the robber because of his faith, may grant you
grace to sing the bridal song.

(2) If any man here is a slave of sin, let faith fit him for
the new birth of adoption that will set him free. Exchang-
ing the ignoble bondage of his sins for the blessed bondage of
the Lord, let him be counted worthy to inherit the kingdom
of heaven. By confession,[8] "put off the old man which is
being corrupted through his deceptive lusts,"[9] to put on the
new man which is being renewed unto perfect knowledge of
his Creator.[10] Attain by faith the pledge of the Holy Spirit
that you may win admittance into the everlasting taber-
nacles.[11] Come forward for the mystical seal, that you may be
recognizable by the Lord. Be numbered in the holy, spiritual
flock of Christ, that you may be set apart on His right hand
and inherit the life prepared for you. For the lot of those still
clothed in the rough garments of their sins is on His left
hand, because they did not attain the grace of God, which is
given through Christ, in the regeneration of Baptism. I do
not mean corporal regeneration, but the spiritual regeneration
of the soul. For bodies are born of visible parents, but souls
are reborn through faith. For, "the Spirit breathes where he
will."[12] Then you may hear, if you are worthy: "Well done,
good and faithful servant,"[13] when you have been found free
in conscience from hypocrisy.

(3) If there is any man here who thinks of tempting God's
grace, he deceives himself and knows not its power. Let
every man keep his soul free from deceit, because of Him
who searches hearts and reins.[14] For just as those who set
about levying an army examine the ages and constitutions

---

8 "confession": The confession referred to here and elsewhere in the
   Catecheses is obviously not secret auricular confession, but a public
   acknowledgment of sins and faults committed in the past.
9 Eph. 4.22.
10 Cf. Eph. 4.24; Col. 3.10.
11 Cf. Luke 16.9.
12 Cf. John 3.8 (Douay).
13 Matt. 25.21.
14 Cf. Ps. 7.10.

of those who enlist, so the Lord, when He raises His levy of souls, examines their motives; and where He finds a secret hypocrisy, He rejects the man as unfit for the true service. But if He finds a man worthy, He readily bestows His grace upon him. He does not give what is holy to the dogs, but where He discerns a worthy motive, there He confers the wonderful seal of salvation. Before this demons tremble whereas angels acknowledge it, so that the former are put to flight while the latter honor it as something kindred. The recipients of this spiritual and saving seal must have the proper disposition. For as the pen or the dart requires the hand of the user, so grace also demands believers.

(4) The armor you receive is not corruptible but spiritual. The paradise into which you are to be planted is not seen by the eye. You are being given a new name you did not possess. Instead of catechumen, you will now be called a Believer. From now on, you are grafted upon the stock of the spiritual olive, like a slip transplanted from the wild olive into the good olive tree, from sin to righteousness, from corruption to purity. You are to be made partaker of the holy vine.[15] If you abide in the vine, you will grow as a fruitful branch; if you will not abide, you will be consumed by fire. Let us then bear fruit worthily. May we be spared the fate of the barren fig tree; may Jesus not come even now and curse us for our barrenness. Grant that all may be able to say: "I, like a green olive tree in the house of God,"[16] an olive tree not visible to the eye, but spiritual and luminous. While it rests with Him to plant and water, it is your part to bring forth fruit. It rests with God to bestow grace, but with you to accept and cherish it. Do not despise the grace because it is freely given, but rather cherish it with reverence once you have received it.

(5) Now is the time for confession. Confess your transgressions, whether in word or deed, by night or day. Con-

15 Cf. John 15.1, 4, 5, 6.
16 Ps. 51.10.

fess at the accepted time, and on the day of salvation receive the treasure of heaven. Be earnest about the exorcisms. Be constant in attending the catecheses and be mindful of their teachings. For they are delivered not merely that you may listen to them, but that you may seal by faith what you have heard. Banish from your mind all human concerns, for the race you are running is for your soul. You are forsaking completely the things of the world: little are the things you leave behind, great are those bestowed by the Lord. Lay aside things of the present and put your trust in things to come. You have passed through so many cycles of years in the vain service of the world: will you not spare forty days for the sake of your soul? "Desist! and confess that I am God,"[17] says Scripture. Renounce idle gossip; do not slander nor listen readily to the slanderer, but be prompt to prayer. Show in ascetic practice the firmness of your heart. Make clean your vessel that you may receive more grace. For though the remission of sins is granted to all alike, the communication of the Holy Spirit[18] is granted in proportion to the faith of each. If you labor little, you will receive little; if you work hard, your reward will be great. You are running for yourself, so look to your own advantage.

(6) If you have aught against any man, forgive it him. You are coming forward to receive the remission of your own sins; you must, in turn, pardon him who has offended you. Else with what face will you say to the Lord: "forgive me my many sins," if you yourself have not forgiven the few sins of your fellow-servant? Be zealous in your attendance at Church, not only now when the clergy demand diligence,

---

17 Ps. 45.11.
18 Chapter 5: "Communication of the Holy Spirit": Cyril distinguishes two effects of baptism, first the remission of sins, which all who sincerely approach the sacrament receive; secondly, positive graces, or as he puts it, "the communication of the Holy Spirit." The second effect will vary, he feels, according to the fervor of faith and intensity of love of God on the part of the recipient. Note that the baptism of John (*Cat.* 3.7) grants remission of sin but not the communication of the Holy Spirit.

but after receiving the grace. For if before its reception it was a good practice, is it not good thereafter? If before your engrafting it is a safe course to be watered and tended, is it not far better after the planting? Sustain the struggle for your soul, especially in these days. Nurture your soul with holy readings; for the Lord has prepared for you a spiritual table. Repeat in the words of the Psalmist: "The Lord is my shepherd; I shall not want. In verdant pastures he gives me repose; beside restful waters he leads me; he refreshes my soul";[19] that the angels, too, may share your joy, and Christ Himself, the great High Priest, ratifying your purpose, may offer all of you to the Father, saying: "Behold, I and my children whom God has given me."[20] May He keep all of you well-pleasing to Himself, to whom be glory for the endless ages of eternity. Amen.

---

19 Ps. 22.1-3.
20 Heb. 2.13.

CATECHESIS II

On Repentance, the Remission of Sin, and the Adversary

"The virtuous man's virtue shall be his own, as the wicked man's wickedness shall be his. But if the wicked man turns away from all the sins he committed, [if he keeps all my statutes and does what is right and just, he shall surely live, he shall not die]."[1]

(1) Sin is a terrible thing, and the most grievous disease of the soul is iniquity, which corrodes the fibre of the soul and makes it liable to eternal fire. It is an evil freely chosen, the product of the will. For that we sin of our own free will, the Prophet clearly declares: "I had planted you, a choice vine of fully tested stock; how could you turn into bitterness, a spurious vine?"[2] The planting was good, but the fruit of set purpose evil; and, therefore, the planter is blameless, but the vine shall be burnt with fire, since it was planted for good, but its product was evil with malice prepense. "God made mankind straight," according to Ecclesiastes, "but men have had recourse to many subtleties."[3] For "His workmanship we are," says the Apostle, "created in Christ Jesus in good works."[4] Though the Creator, being good, created unto good works, the creature of its own free will turned aside to wickedness. Therefore, sin, as we have said, is a grievous evil, but it is not incurable, being grievous to him only who cherishes it, but easy of cure for him who puts it away by

---

1 Ezech. 18.20, 21.
2 Jer. 2.21.
3 Eccles. 7.29.
4 Eph. 2.10.

repentance. Imagine a man holding fire in his hand. So long as he grasps the burning coal, of course he is burned, but suppose he puts away the coal, then he has automatically cast away the flame with it. If any man thinks that he is not being burned when he is sinning, Scripture says to him: "Can a man take fire to his bosom, and his garments not be burned?"[5] For sin burns; it cuts the sinews of the soul, and crushes the spiritual bones of the mind, and darkens the light of the heart.

(2) Yes, and someone will say: "What, then, is sin? Is it an animal? An angel? A demon? What is this which infects us?" Rest assured it is not an enemy attacking from without, but an evil springing up within you. "Let your eyes look straight ahead,"[6] and there exists no evil desire. Steal not the property of others, and robbery is at an end. Be mindful of the judgment and neither fornication nor adultery nor murder nor any wickedness will prevail over you. It is when you forget God that you begin to entertain evil thoughts and commit wicked deeds.

(3) Yet you alone are not the source of the trouble, but there is also one who instigates you, the accursed devil. He makes his suggestions to all,[7] but he does not prevail by force over those who do not give way to him. Therefore Ecclesiastes says: "Should the anger of the ruler burst upon you, forsake not your place."[8] If you shut your door, you will be out of his reach and he will not harm you. But if you are so careless as to admit the lustful thought, reflection will cause it to strike roots within you; it will capture your mind and drag you down into an abyss of sins. But, you may say: "I am a Believer and no evil desire will overcome me, even though I dwell upon it often." Are you unaware that ofttimes a root by twining itself around a stone will crack it? Do not admit the

---

5 Prov. 6.27.
6 Prov. 4.25.
7 Translating the Maurist *pasin* (to all), rejected by Reischl-Rupp on stylistic grounds.
8 Eccles. 10.4.

seed, since it will shatter your faith. Before it has a chance to blossom pluck out the evil by the roots. Remissness at first leads in the end to the ax and to the fire.[9] When your eyes first trouble you, have them treated betimes, else you will be consulting the oculist after you have lost your sight.

(4) The chief author of sin, then, is the devil, the begetter of all evil. This not I, but the Lord has said: "The devil sins from the beginning."[10] Before him no one sinned. Nor did he sin because by nature he was of necessity prone to sin—else the responsibility for sin would reflect upon Him who created him thus—but after being created good, he became a devil by his own free choice, receiving that name from his action. Though he was an Archangel, he was afterwards called devil (slanderer) from his slandering,[11] and though he was once a good servant of God, he was afterwards rightly named Satan, for Satan is interpreted "the adversary." This is not my teaching, but that of the inspired Prophet Ezechiel. For, taking up a lament against him, he says: "You were a seal of resemblance, and crown of beauty; you were begotten in the Paradise of God," and a little further on: "Blameless you were in your conduct from the day you were created until evil was found in you."[12] The phrase, "was found in you," is most appropriate, for the evil was not brought in from without, but you yourself begot it. Thereafter, he mentions the reason: "You became haughty of heart because of your beauty: for the multitude of your iniquities you were wounded, and I cast you to the earth."[13] Similarly, the Lord says in the gospels: "I was watching Satan fall as lightning from heaven."[14] You see the harmony of the Old Testament with the New. When he fell, he drew many

---

9 Cf. Matt. 3.10.
10 1 John 3.8.
11 Cyril repeats in *Cat.* 8.4 that the devil was an archangel. His name of devil, i.e., slanderer, comes from the fact that he falsely charges men before God and God before men.
12 Cf. Ezech. 28.12-15.
13 Cf. *ibid.* 17.
14 Luke 10.18.

away with him. To those who hearken to him, he suggests evil desires, whence arise adultery, fornication, and every kind of evil. By his agency our forefather Adam was cast out and exchanged for a Paradise that untilled produced fruits, a soil bringing forth thorns.

(5) "Well, then," you will say to me, "are we betrayed and lost?" Is there no salvation henceforth? We have fallen. Is it impossible to rise again? We were blinded. Can we never recover our sight? We have become lame. Can we never walk aright? In a word, we are dead; is there no resurrection? Will not He who raised up Lazarus, already four days dead and fetid, far more easily raise you? He who poured out His precious blood for us will free us from sin. Let us not despair, brethren, nor give ourselves up as lost. For it is a grievous thing not to believe in the hope of repentance. He who despairs of rescue increases his evils beyond measure, but once a man has placed his hopes in a cure, he readily shows concern for himself. For the robber who looks not for mercy proceeds to despair, but when he has hope of pardon, he often comes to repentance. If the serpent can rid itself of its old skin, shall we not rid ourselves of sin? And if thorny ground, when well tilled, has been changed into fruitful soil, shall salvation be irretrievable for us? Nature, then, admits of salvation, but the proper disposition is a requisite condition.

(6) God is a lover of man, and a lover in no small measure. For do not say: "I have been a fornicator and an adulterer, I have committed grievous sin, and not once but very often; will He not forgive? Will He not grant pardon?" Listen to what the Psalmist says: "How great is the multitude of your sweetness, Lord."[15] The sum of your sins does not surpass the magnitude of God's mercies. Your wounds are not beyond the healing skill of the great Physician. Only surrender to Him with faith, tell the Physician of your malady. Repeat the words of David: "I said, I will confess against myself my iniquity to the Lord," and in like manner will be verified

15 Cf. Ps. 30.20.

the second part of the verse: "And you forgave the wickedness of my heart."[16]

(7) Do you, who have but lately come to the catechesis, wish to see the loving-kindness of God? Would you see the loving-kindness of God and the extent of His forbearance? Listen to the story of Adam. Adam, the first creature of God, was disobedient. Could He not have condemned him to death at once? But see what the Lord in His great loving-kindness does. Though he casts him out of Paradise—for he was not worthy, because of his sin, to live there—He settles him over against Paradise, that seeing whence and from what bliss he had fallen, he might be saved thereafter through repentance. Cain, the first-born man, became a fratricide, from whose wicked designings first stemmed murder and envy. Yet consider his sentence for slaying his brother. "Groaning and trembling shall you be upon the earth."[17] Though the sin was great, the sentence was light.

(8) This was truly an example of God's loving-kindness, but it is small compared to the sequel. Consider the story of Noe. The Giants sinned and great iniquity was then spread over the earth, and because of it, the deluge was foreordained. In the five-hundredth year, God utters His threat; in the six-hundredth, He brings the deluge upon the earth. Don't you see the breadth of God's loving-kindness, how he delays execution a hundred years? Could He not have done at once what He did a hundred years later? But He purposely delayed, granting a reprieve for repentance. Do you see the goodness of God? And if the men of that time had repented, they would not have failed to experience the loving-kindness of God.

(9) Pass now, pray, to the others who were saved by repentance. Perhaps even among the women someone will say: "I have committed fornication and adultery. I have defiled my body with every excess. Can there be salvation for me?" Fix your eyes, woman, upon Rahab, and look for salvation

16 Cf. Ps. 31.5.
17 Gen. 4.12 (Sept.).

for yourself too. For if she who openly and publicly practiced fornication was saved through repentance, will not she whose fornication preceded the gift of grace be saved by repentance and fasting? For observe how she was saved. She said only this: "Since the Lord, your God, is God in heaven above and on earth below."[18] "Your God," she said, for she did not dare call Him her God, because of her wantonness. If you want scriptural testimony of her salvation, you have it recorded in the Psalms: "I will think of Rahab and Babylon among those who know me."[19] O the great loving-kindness of God, which is mindful even of harlots in Scripture. He did not say merely: "I shall think of Rahab and Babylon," but added, "among those who know me." The salvation procured by repentance is open to men and women alike.

(10) Even a whole people's sin does not defeat the mercy of God. The people fashioned a calf but God did not abandon His loving-kindness; men denied God, but God did not deny Himself. "These are your gods, O Israel,"[20] they said, and yet the God of Israel, according to His wont, became their Savior. It was not the people alone that sinned, but also Aaron, the high priest. For Moses says: "And the wrath of the Lord was upon Aaron"; "and I prayed for him," he says, "and God forgave him."[21] Now if Moses, making supplication in behalf of the high priest who sinned, prevailed upon the Lord by his importunity, will Jesus, His Only-begotten Son, imploring God in our behalf, not prevail? If He did not prevent Aaron, because of his falling away, from acceding to the high priesthood, can it be that he will prevent you, coming from paganism, from attaining salvation? Repent in like manner, brethren, and grace will not be withheld from you. Manifest henceforth a blameless habit of life. For God is a lover of man, and all time cannot worthily recount His loving-kindness. Nay, if all the tongues

18 Jos. 2.11.
19 Cf. Ps. 86.4.
20 Exod. 32.4.
21 Cf. Deut. 9.20.

of men were gathered into one, not even thus could they tell in part of the loving-kindness of God. For we relate in some measure what has been written of the mercy of God towards man, but we do not know how much He forgave the angels as well.[22] For he pardoned them also, since there is only one without sin, Jesus, who cleanses us from our sins. But of the angels, enough.

(11) If you want further instances from among men, come to blessed David and take him as a model of repentance. He fell, David the great, fell, when, after sleeping in the afternoon and while walking on the roof, he was careless with his eyes and nature had her way with him.[23] The sin was consummated, but with it his honesty in avowing his sin did not pass away. Came the Prophet Nathan, swift censor, healer of the wound. "The Lord is wroth," he said, "and you have sinned,"[24] he, the subject, speaking to the king. But David the king was not indignant, for he regarded not the speaker, but Him who sent him. He was not dazzled by the throng of his attendant soldiery, for his mind traveled to the angelic host of the Lord, and as though he saw Him who is invisible, he trembled, and he replied to him who came, or rather, through him to Him who sent him: "I have sinned against the Lord."[25] You see the humility of the king, you see his confession. For had he been convicted by anyone? Did many share the guilty secret? The deed was done quickly and the Prophet was at hand at once to accuse him. The sinner acknowledged his sin and, because of his frank avowal, was quickly healed, for the Prophet Nathan who threatened him said at once: "The Lord also hath taken away thy sin."[26] You see the swift relenting of God in His loving-kindness.

---

22 Some see here an echo of Origen. Cyril's teaching on the angels is orthodox, but he seems to imply here venial faults in the good angels, possibly derived from the second and third chapters of the Apocalypse, where faults are found with the angels of the churches.
23 Cf. 2 Kings 11.2.
24 Cf. 2 Kings 12.1ff.
25 2 Kings 12.13.
26 Ibid.

Yet Nathan said: "Thou hast greatly provoked the enemies of the Lord."[27] Time was when you had many enemies because of your uprightness, but your self-control protected you. Now that you have given up your strongest armor, you have enemies standing ready to rise up against you.

(12) Thus, then, did the Prophet comfort him, but blessed David, though he heard most surely the words: "The Lord hath taken away thy sin," did not cease from repentance, despite his kingly office. He put on sackcloth[28] instead of purple, and quitting the throne inlaid with gold, sat upon ashes on the ground. Nor was he content to sit upon ashes; he fed upon the ashes as he himself says: "For I eat ashes like bread, and mingle my drink with tears."[29] He melted his lustful eye with tears, saying: "Every night I flood my bed with weeping; I drench my couch with my tears."[30] When the magistrates of his people urged him to eat bread he refused and prolonged his fast for seven days. If a king made his confession in this way, ought not you, a private individual, to confess? After the revolt of Absalom, when there were many roads of escape open to him, David chose to flee by the Mount of Olives, as though his prophetic spirit invoked the Redeemer, who would one day ascend into heaven thence. And when Semei cursed him bitterly he said: "Let him alone,"[31] for he knew that to him who forgives it shall be forgiven.

(13) You see what an excellent thing is confession. You see that there is salvation for the penitent. Solomon also fell; but what does he say? "Afterwards I repented."[32] Achab, too, the king of Samaria, was an iniquitous idolater of surpassing wickedness, a murderer of the Prophets, an enemy of piety, a coveter of the fields and vineyards of others. Yet when he

---

27 Cf. 2 Kings 12.14.
28 Cf. *ibid*. 16, 17.
29 Ps. 101.10.
30 Ps. 6.7.
31 2 Kings 16.11.
32 Prov. 24.32 (Sept.). Solomon's penance is not generally accepted.

slew Naboth by Jezebel's hand and the Prophet Elias came and merely threatened him, he rent his garments and put on sackcloth. And what does the merciful God say to Elias? "Hast thou not seen Achab humbled before me?"[33]—as though urging the fiery spirit of the Prophet to condescend towards the penitent. "I will not bring the evil in his days."[34] Though after his pardon Achab was not to desist from his wickedness, the forgiving God forgives him, not that He was unaware of the future, but granting forgiveness in keeping with the current moment of repentance. For it belongs to the just judge to pass sentence consonant with each several deed.

(14) Again, Jeroboam stood sacrificing to idols upon the altar. When he gave the order for the arrest of the Prophet who censured him, his hand withered on the instant; but having learned by experience the power of the man before him, he says: "Entreat the Lord for me";[35] and because of these words his hand was again restored. If the Prophet healed Jeroboam, will not Christ be able to heal and free us from our sins? Manasses, too, was a heinous sinner. He cut asunder Isaia,[36] was defiled with all manner of idolatry, and filled Jerusalem with innocent blood. Led captive to Babylon, by experience of suffering he learned his lesson, and repenting drew healing from his affliction. For Scripture says: "Manasses was humbled before the Lord, and he prayed and the Lord heard him and brought him again into his kingdom."[37] If he who had sawn asunder the Prophet was saved, will you who have committed no such enormity not be saved? Take care that you do not, without reason, underrate the efficacy of repentance.

(15) Would you know the power of repentance? Would you understand this strong weapon of salvation and the might of confession? By confession Ezechia routed a hundred and

---

33 3 Kings 21.29.
34 Ibid.
35 Cf. 3 Kings 13.6.
36 This is not stated in Scripture, but derived from Jewish tradition.
37 Cf. 2 Par. 33.12, 13.

eighty-five thousand of the enemy.[38] That was important, but it was little compared to what shall be told. The same king's repentance won the repeal of the sentence God had passed on him. For when he was sick, Isaia said to him: "Give charge concerning thy house, for thou shalt die, and not live."[39] What expectation was left? What hope of recovery was there, when the Prophet said: "For thou shalt die"? But Ezechia did not cease from penitence, for he remembered what was written: "In the hour that you turn and lament, you shall be saved."[40] He turned his face to the wall, and from his bed of pain his mind soared up to heaven—for no wall is so thick as to stifle reverent prayer—"Lord," he said, "remember me."[41] "For it is sufficient for my healing if You remember me. You are not subject to circumstances, but are Yourself the legislator of life. For not on birth and conjunction of stars, as some vainly say, does our life depend. No, You are the arbiter, according to Your will, of life and the duration of life." He whom the Prophet's sentence had forbidden to hope was granted fifteen further years of life, the sun turning back its course in witness thereof. Now while the sun retraced its course for Ezechia, for Christ it was eclipsed, the distinction marking the difference between the two, I mean Ezechia and Jesus. Now if even Ezechia could revoke God's decree, shall not Jesus grant the remission of sins? Turn and lament, shut your door, and beg for pardon, that God may remove from you the scorching flames. For confession has the power to quench even fire; it can tame even lions.

(16) If you doubt it, consider what happened to Anania and his companions. What streams did they pour out? How many measures of water were needed to quench a flame forty-nine cubits high? But wherever the fire threatened to overwhelm them, there their faith gushed rivers, as they repeated the words that worked like a charm: "You are just

38 Cf. 4 Kings 19.35.
39 4 Kings 20.1.
40 Cf. Isa. 30.15.
41 Cf. Isa. 38.2, 3; 4 Kings 20.2, 3.

in all you have done to us: for we have sinned and committed iniquity."[42] And their penitence subdued the flames.
If you do not believe that penance can quench the fire of
Gehenna, learn that from the story of Anania and his
companions. But some keen listener will say: "In their case,
God justly delivered them. Because they refused to commit
idolatry, God gave them this power." Since this objection
has in fact been raised, I shall go to a different example of
repentance.

(17) What think you of Nabuchodonosor? Have you not
heard from Scripture that he was bloodthirsty, fierce, with
the disposition of a lion? Have you not heard that he dis-
interred the kings?[43] Have you not heard that he brought the
people away into captivity? Have you not heard that he put
the king's sons to the sword before his eyes and then blinded
him?[44] Have you not heard that he shattered the Cherubim?[45]
I do not mean the invisible Cherubim—it were blasphemy
to think it—but the sculptured images, and the mercy-seat
in the Holy of Holies, from the midst of which God was wont
to speak with His voice. He trampled upon the veil of
sanctification, he took the censer and carried it away to a
temple of idols; he seized all the offerings; he burned the
temple to its foundations. What punishment did he not
deserve for slaying kings, for burning the holy objects, for
reducing the people to captivity, for putting the sacred vessels
in the temples of idols? Did he not deserve ten thousand
deaths?

(18) You have seen the enormity of his crimes. Turn now to
the loving-kindness of God. Nabuchodonosor was turned into
a wild beast; he dwelt in the wilderness; God scourged him
to save him. He had claws like a lion's, for he had preyed
upon the saints. He had a lion's mane, for he had been a

---

42 Cf. Dan. 3.27, 29.
43 Cf. Jer. 8.1; Bar. 2.24, 25.
44 Cf. 4 Kings 25.7.
45 Again an assumption on the part of Cyril.

ravening, roaring lion. He ate grass like an ox, for he had behaved like a brute beast, not knowing Him who had given him his kingdom. His body was drenched with dew, because, after seeing the fire quenched by the dew, he had not believed. And what happened? Afterwards he says: "I, Nabuchodonosor, raised my eyes to heaven, . . . and I blessed the Most High, and I praised and glorified him who lives forever."[46] When therefore he acknowledged the Most High, and uttered words of thanksgiving to God, and repented of his past wickedness, and recognized his own weakness, in that hour God restored to him his royal dignity.

(19) What then? If God granted pardon and a kingdom to Nabuchodonosor after such terrible crimes, when he had made confession, will He not grant you the remission of your sins if you repent, and the kingdom of heaven, if you live worthily? God is merciful and quick to forgiveness, but slow to vengeance. Therefore let no man despair of salvation. Peter, the chief and foremost of the Apostles, denied the Lord thrice before a little serving maid; but, moved to repentance, he wept bitterly. His weeping revealed his heartfelt repentance, and for that reason not only did he receive pardon for his denial, but retained his Apostolic prerogative.

(20) Therefore, brethren, having before you many examples of sinners who repented and were saved, be you also earnest in confessing to the Lord, that you may receive pardon for past sins, be made worthy of the heavenly gift, and inherit the kingdom of heaven with all the saints, in Christ, to whom be glory forever and ever. Amen.

---

46 Cf. Dan. 4.31.

CATECHESIS III

On Baptism

*"Do you not know that all we who have been baptized
into Christ Jesus have been baptized into his death? For
we were buried with him by means of Baptism into death,
[in order that, just as Christ has arisen from the dead
through the glory of the Father, so we also may walk in
newness of life]."*[1]

(1) "Rejoice, O ye heavens, and let the earth be glad,"[2]
in honor of those who are to be sprinkled with hyssop, and
cleansed by the spiritual hyssop and by the power of Him
who, in His Passion, was offered drink on a stalk of hyssop.
Let the heavenly powers rejoice, and let the souls who are to
be united with their spiritual Spouse prepare themselves. For
there is "the voice of one crying in the desert: Make ready
the way of the Lord."[3] For this is no slight matter, no ordinary
or common fleshly union, but the election according to faith
by the Spirit who "searches all things."[4] For worldly marriages
and contracts are not always made with judgment, and the
bridegroom is quickly swayed wherever there is wealth or
beauty. But here there is concern not for beauty of body,
but for the blameless conscience of soul; not for the accursed
Mammon, but for the wealth of the soul in piety.
(2) Yield then, O children of justice, to the urging of John,

---

1 Rom. 6.3, 4.
2 Cf. Ps. 95.11; Isa. 49.13.
3 Cf. Isa. 40.3.
4 1 Cor. 2.10.

when he says: "Make ready the way of the Lord."[5] Remove all hindrances and stumbling blocks, that you may hold a straight course unto eternal life. Make ready the vessels of the soul, purifying them by sincere faith, for the receiving of the Holy Spirit. Begin to wash your garments through repentance that, when you are called to the bridal chamber, you may be found clean. For the Bridegroom invites all without distinction, for His grace is bountifully bestowed, and the cry of His loud-voiced heralds draws all together; but He Himself thereafter separates those who have come in.[6] God forbid that any of those enrolled should now hear those words: "Friend, how didst thou come in here without a wedding garment?"[7] Rather, may you all hear: "Well done, good and faithful servant; because thou hast been faithful over a few things, I will place thee over many: enter into the joy of thy master."[8] Up to now you have stood outside the gate, but may all of you be able to say: "The king hath brought me into his storerooms";[9] "Let my soul be joyful in the Lord: for he has clothed me with a garment of salvation and a robe of gladness; like a bridegroom he has adorned me with a diadem; like a bride, bedecked me with jewels."[10] Thus may the souls of all of you be found "not having spot, or wrinkle, or any such thing."[11] I do not mean before you have received the grace (for how could that be true of you who are called for the remission of sins?) but that, the grace given, your conscience, being found blameless, may be suitable for grace.

(3) This is a truly serious matter, my brethren, and you must approach it with great care. Each of you is to stand before God, in the presence of myriads of the angelic host. The Holy Spirit is about to imprint a seal upon your souls.

5 John 1.23.
6 Cf. Matt. 22.9, 10.
7 Matt. 22.12.
8 Matt. 25.23.
9 Cf. Cant. 1.3.
10 Isa. 61.10 (Sept.).
11 Eph. 5.27.

You are to be enlisted in the service of the Great King. Therefore prepare and equip yourselves, not by putting on shining white garments, but piety of soul with a good conscience. Regard not the laver as fresh water, but look to the spiritual grace given with the water. For just as the offerings on the pagan altars, though morally neutral in themselves, become defiled by the invocation of the idols, so contrariwise the plain water, after the invocation of Holy Spirit, and Christ, and Father, acquires a power of sanctification.

(4) For since man's nature is twofold, compounded of soul and body, the purification is also twofold, incorporeal for the incorporeal part, bodily for the body. For as the water purifies the body, so the Spirit seals the soul, that having our hearts sprinkled, and our bodies washed with clean water, we may draw near to God.[12] Therefore when about to enter the water, regard it not as mere water, but look for its saving power by the efficacy of the Holy Spirit, for without both you cannot be made perfect. It is not I who say this, but the Lord Jesus, who has the power in this matter, says: "Unless a man be born again, of water and the Spirit, he cannot enter into the kingdom of God."[13] Neither does he who is baptized, but has not been deemed worthy of the Spirit, possess perfect grace; nor will a man who acts virtuously, but does not receive the seal by water, enter into the kingdom of heaven. This may appear a bold saying, but it is not mine, for it was Jesus who pronounced it. And here is the proof of the statement from inspired Scripture. Cornelius was a just man, deemed worthy of a vision of angels, a man who had set up his prayers and alms as a fair column in the heavens in the sight of God. Peter came, and the Spirit was poured out upon those that believed, and they spoke with divers tongues and they prophesied.[14] And yet after the grace of the Spirit, Scripture says that Peter "ordered them to be

---

12 Cf. Heb. 10.22.
13 John 3.5.
14 Cf. Acts 10.46.

baptized in the name of Jesus Christ,"[15] that after the soul had been regenerated by faith, the body also, by means of the water, might share the grace.

(5) But if any man wishes to know why the grace is given through water instead of some other element, he will find the answer if he takes up the divine Scriptures. For water is a noble thing and the fairest of the four visible elements of the world. Heaven is the dwelling place of angels, but the heavens are from the waters. Earth is the home of men, and the earth is from the waters. And before the whole six days' formation of created things, "The spirit of God was stirring above the waters."[16] With water the world began; the Jordan saw the beginning of the Gospels. The sea was the means of Israel's liberation from Pharao, and freedom for the world from sin comes through the laver of water in the Word of God.[17] Wherever there is a covenant there also is water. After the deluge, a covenant was made with Noe; it was given from Mount Sinai, but "with water and scarlet wool and hyssop."[18] Elias was taken up, but not without water; for first he crosses the Jordan, and only then mounts to heaven in a chariot. The high priest washes himself, then offers incense; for Aaron was first washed, then became high priest. For how could one who had not yet been cleansed by water pray for others? Further, the laver had been set within the tabernacle, as a symbol of baptism.

(6) Baptism marks the end of the Old Testament and the beginning of the New. For its author was John, than whom there was no one greater among those born of women.[19] He marked the end of the Prophets: "For all the prophets and the Law were until John."[20] He likewise marks the beginning

15 Acts 10.48.
16 Gen. 1.2. The opening verses of Genesis seem to refer to water as prime matter. Water is mentioned in Scripture more often than the other three elements.
17 Cf. Eph. 5.26.
18 Heb. 9.19.
19 Cf. Matt. 11.11.
20 Cf. Matt. 11.13; Luke 16.16.

of the things of the Gospel: "The beginning of the gospel of Jesus Christ," and what follows: "There came John in the desert, baptizing."[21] You may mention Elias, who was taken up to heaven, but he is not greater than John. Enoch was transported, but he is not greater than John. Mightiest was Moses the lawgiver, and all the Prophets, but they are not greater than John. It is not I who venture to compare Prophets with Prophets, but their Master and ours who has declared: "Among those born of women, there has not risen a greater than John."[22] He does not say, "among those born of virgins," but, "of women." The comparison is between the great servant and his fellow-servants; but the pre-eminence and the grace of the Son over the household is beyond compare. Do you see how great a man God chose to be the first minister of this grace? He was a man who possessed nothing, a lover of solitude, but no hater of mankind; who ate locusts, and fitted wings to his soul, satisfying his hunger with honey, and speaking words sweeter and more wholesome than honey; clad in a garment of camel's hair, and showing in himself the model of the ascetic life; who was sanctified by the Holy Spirit when still borne in his mother's womb. Jeremia also was sanctified, but he did not prophesy in the womb. Only John leaped for joy when still being carried in the womb.[23] Without seeing Him with the eyes of the body, he recognized his Master by the Spirit. For since the grace of Baptism was a great one, it called for greatness in its author.

(7) John was baptizing in the Jordan and there went out to him all Jerusalem, to have the benefit of the first-fruits of baptism;[24] for the prerogative of all good things is in Jerusalem. But notice, O people of Jerusalem, how those who went out were baptized by him "confessing their sins."[25] First they displayed their wounds; then he applied the remedies,

---

21 Mark 1.1, 4.
22 Matt. 11.11.
23 Cf. Luke 1.44.
24 Cf. Matt. 3.5.
25 *Ibid.* 6.

and to those who believed he granted redemption from eternal fire. And if you wish a proof on this point, that the baptism of John was a redemption from the threat of fire, listen to his own words: "Brood of vipers, who has shown you to flee from the wrath to come?"[26] Be not, then, henceforth a viper, but though you were once of viper's brood, put off, he says, your former sinful nature. For every snake, retreating into a nook, puts off its age, and sloughing off its skin by constriction, henceforth is rejuvenated; so you, too, enter in through the narrow and straitened gate; constrain yourself by fasting, do violence to what threatens your destruction. "Strip off the old man with his deeds,"[27] and say in the words of the Canticles: "I have taken off my robe, how am I then to put it on?"[28]

But perhaps there is some hypocrite among you, who seeks the favor of men and makes a pretense of piety, but does not believe from the heart, who with the hypocrisy of Simon Magus approaches not to share in the grace, but out of meddlesome curiosity concerning what is given. Let him listen to John: "For even now the ax is laid at the root of the trees. Every tree, therefore, that is not bringing forth good fruit is to be cut down, and thrown into the fire."[29] The Judge is inexorable, so cast aside your hypocrisy.

(8) What must be done, then, and what are the fruits of repentance? "Let him who has two tunics share with him who has none."[30] Now the teacher was one worthy of credence, since he had first put his teaching into practice; he was not ashamed to speak, for his tongue was not checked by a bad conscience. "And let him who has food do likewise."[31] While aspiring to the grace of the Holy Spirit for yourself, will you deny bodily food to the poor? Do you seek great things, but share not the small?

---

26 *Ibid.* 7.
27 Col. 3.9.
28 Cant. 3.5.
29 Matt. 3.10.
30 Luke 3.11.
31 *Ibid.*

Though you be a publican or fornicator, yet hope for salvation. "The publicans and harlots are entering the kingdom of God before you."[32] Paul testifies to this when he says: "Neither fornicators nor idolaters," nor the rest, "will possess the kingdom of God. And such were some of you, but you have been washed, and you have been sanctified."[33] He did not say, some of you "are," but some of you "were." The sin committed in ignorance is pardoned, but persistent wickedness is condemned.

(9) You have for the glorification of baptism the Only-begotten Son of God Himself. Why should I speak any further of man? John was great, but what was he compared to the Lord? Loud was his voice, but what compared with the Word? Noble was the herald, but what was he to the King? Glorious was he who baptized with water, but what in comparison to Him who baptizes "with the Holy Spirit and with fire"?[34] The Savior baptized with the Holy Spirit and with fire when: "suddenly there was a sound from heaven as of a violent wind coming, and it filled the whole house where they were sitting. And there appeared to them parted tongues as of fire, which settled upon each of them. And they were all filled with the Holy Spirit."[35]

(10) If a man does not receive baptism he does not attain salvation, excepting only the martyrs, who, even without the water, receive the kingdom. For the Savior who redeemed the world by the Cross, when His side was pierced, poured forth blood and water, that in time of peace men might be baptized in water, but in time of persecution in their own blood. For the Savior could call martyrdom a baptism, saying: "Can you drink the cup of which I drink or be baptized with the baptism with which I am baptized?"[36] For the martyrs, indeed, make their confession of faith, when "made a spectacle

32 Matt. 21.31.
33 1 Cor. 6.9-11.
34 Matt. 3.11.
35 Acts 2.2-4.
36 Mark 10.38.

to the world, and to angels, and to men."[37] In a little while you too shall make your confession. But it is not yet time for you to hear about this.

(11) Jesus sanctified baptism when He Himself was baptized. If the Son of God was baptized, can anyone who scorns baptism pretend to piety? Not that He was baptized to receive the remission of sins—for He was without sin—but being sinless, He was nevertheless baptized, that He might impart grace and dignity to those who receive the sacrament. For, "since the children share in flesh and blood, so he in like manner has shared in these,"[38] that we, sharing His incarnate life, might also share His divine grace. So Jesus was baptized that we, in turn, herein also made partakers with Him, might receive not only salvation, but also the dignity. The dragon, according to Job, was in the water, he who received the Jordan in his maw.[39] When, therefore, it was necessary to crush the heads of the dragon,[40] descending into the water, He bound the strong one, that we might receive the "power to tread upon serpents and scorpions."[41] It was no ordinary beast, but a horrible monster. No fishing ship could last under a single scale of his tail; before him stalked Destruction, ravaging all in her path.[42] But Life came running up, that the maw of Death might be stopped and all we who were saved might say: "O death, where is thy sting? O grave, where is thy victory?"[43] Baptism draws death's sting.

(12) For you go down into the water bearing your sins, but the invocation of grace, placing a seal upon your soul, makes you proof against the dragon's maw. Though dead in sin when you went down, you will come up vivified in justice. For, if you have been planted together in the likeness of the death of the Savior, you shall be counted worthy of His

37 1 Cor. 4.9.
38 Heb. 2.14.
39 Cf. Job 40.18.
40 Cf. Ps. 73.14.
41 Luke 10.19.
42 Cf. Job 40.26 and 41.13 (Sept.).
43 Cf. 1 Cor. 15.55.

Resurrection also.[44] For just as Jesus died, taking upon Himself the sins of the whole world, that by slaying sin He might rise again in righteousness, so you, also, after entering and being as it were buried in the water, as He was in the rock, are raised up again to walk in newness of life.

(13) Then, after you have been vouchsafed the grace, He gives you the strength to struggle with the enemy powers. For just as He was tried for forty days after His baptism—not that He was unable to conquer sooner, but because He wished to accomplish all things in due order and sequence—so do you also, who before your baptism dared not close with your adversaries, from the moment of receiving the grace, trust henceforth in the armor of justice,[45] do battle, and, if you will, preach the Gospel.

(14) Jesus Christ was the Son of God, but before His baptism He did not preach the Gospel. If the Master Himself in all things observed order and due season, can we, His servants, presume to disregard right order? Jesus began to preach from the time when "the Holy Spirit descended upon him in bodily form as a dove."[46] (This was not to permit Jesus to see Him for the first time—for He knew Him even before He came in bodily form—but that John the Baptist might see Him; for he said: "I did not know him. But he who sent me to baptize with water said to me, 'He upon whom thou wilt see the Spirit descending, he it is.' "[47]) Upon you also, if you possess sincere piety, the Holy Spirit will descend, and from above will be heard over you the voice of the Father, saying not: "This is my Son,"[48] but, "This has now become My son." For to Christ alone belongs the "is," since, "In the beginning was the Word, and the Word was with God; and the Word was God."[49] To Him belongs the word

44 Cf. Rom. 6.5.
45 Cf. 2 Cor. 6.7.
46 Luke 3.22.
47 John 1.33.
48 Matt. 3.17.
49 John 1.1.

"is," since He is at all times the Son of God. To you belongs "has now become," since you do not possess the sonship by nature, but receive it by adoption. He is Son eternally, but you receive that grace by advancement.

(15) Therefore, prepare the vessel of your soul, that you may become a son of God, and joint heir, indeed, of God, and joint heir with Christ.[50] That is, if you are preparing actually to receive; if in faith you are coming forward to be confirmed in faith; if of set purpose you are putting off the old man. For all your sins will be forgiven, whether fornication or adultery or any other licentiousness. What sin is greater than crucifying Christ? But baptism can expiate even this, as Peter told the three thousand who had crucified Christ when they came to him and asked him, saying: "Brethren, what shall we do?"[51] For great is our wound. You advised us of our fall, O Peter, when you said: "The author of life you killed."[52] What salve is there for so great a wound? What purification for such foulness? What salvation for such perdition? "Repent," he says, "and be baptized every one of you in the name of Jesus Christ for the forgiveness of your sins; and you will receive the gift of the Holy Spirit."[53] O the ineffable loving-kindness of God! They despair of salvation and yet are deemed worthy of the Holy Spirit. There you see the power of baptism. If any man has crucified Christ by blasphemous words, if any man in ignorance has denied Him before men, if any man by wicked deeds has caused His doctrine to be blasphemed, let him repent and be of good hope. For the same grace is even now at hand.

(16) Take heart, O Jerusalem, the Lord will take away your iniquities.[54] The Lord will wash away the filth of His sons and daughters by the spirit of judgment and the spirit of burning.[55] He will pour upon you clean water and you

---

50 Cf. Rom. 8.17.
51 Acts 2.37.
52 Acts 3.15.
53 Acts 2.38.
54 Cf. Soph. 3.14, 15.
55 Cf. Isa. 4.4.

shall be cleansed from all your sins.[56] Choiring angels shall encircle you, chanting: Who is it that comes up all white and leaning upon her beloved?[57] For the soul that was formerly a slave has now accounted her Lord as her kinsman, and He, acknowledging her sincere purpose, will answer: "Ah, you are beautiful my beloved, ah, you are beautiful! . . . Your teeth are like a flock of ewes to be shorn"[58]—a sincere confession is a spiritual shearing; and further: "all of them big with twins,"[59] signifying the twofold grace, either that perfected by water and the Spirit, or that announced in the Old and in the New Testament.[60] God grant that all of you, your course of fasting finished, mindful of the teaching, fruitful in good works, standing blameless before the spiritual Bridegroom, may obtain the remission of your sins from God, in Christ Jesus our Lord, to whom be the glory forever and ever. Amen.

56 Cf. Ezech. 36.25.
57 Cf. Cant. 8.5.
58 Cant. 4.1, 2.
59 Ibid.
60 Cyril takes every opportunity to stress the agreement of the Old and the New covenants, in opposition to the heretics, particularly Marcion.

CATECHESIS IV

On the Ten Doctrines

"See to it that no man deceive you by philosophy and vain deceit, according to human tradition, according to the elements of the world [and not according to Christ]."[1]

(1) Vice mimics virtue and cockle works to pass for wheat, which it resembles, though a discriminating palate is not thereby deceived. So the devil "disguises himself as an angel of light,"[2] not to mount up again where he was before (with a heart as inflexible as an anvil, his will is forever impenitent), but to envelop in blinding mist and the poisonous air of scepticism those leading an angelic life. Many a wolf goes about in sheep's clothing;[3] their fleece is that of sheep, not so their claws and fangs. Clad in the gentle wool, and beguiling the innocent by their appearance, they pour forth from their fangs the deadly poison of impiety. We have need therefore of divine grace, and a sober mind, and eyes that see clearly, lest, eating cockle for wheat, we take hurt out of our ignorance; or, mistaking the wolf for a sheep, we become his prey, or, supposing the baleful devil to be a good angel, we shall be devoured. For, "as a roaring lion, he goes about seeking whom he may devour," as Scripture says.[4] This is the reason for the Church's admonitions; this is the reason for the present instructions and for the lessons that are read.

(2) True religion consists of these two elements: pious doc-

---

1 Col. 2.8.
2 2 Cor. 11.14.
3 Matt. 7.15.
4 Cf. 1 Peter 5.8.

trines and virtuous actions. Neither does God accept doctrines apart from good works, nor are works, when divorced from godly doctrine, accepted by God. What does it profit a man to be an expert theologian if he is a shameless fornicator; or to be nobly temperate, but an impious blasphemer? The knowledge of doctrines is a precious possession; there is need of a vigilant soul, since many there are who would deceive you by philosophy and vain deceit.[5] The Greeks, indeed, by their smooth tongue lead men astray, for honey drops from the lips of a harlot.[6] Those of the Circumcision deceive their disciples by the divine Scripture, which they twist by false interpretations, though they study them from childhood to old age and grow old in ignorance. The children of heretics "by smooth words and flattery deceive the hearts of the simple,"[7] disguising with the honey of Christ's name the poisoned shafts of their impious doctrines. Concerning all these alike the Lord says: "Take care that no one lead you astray."[8] This is the reason for the teaching of the Faith, and for the expositions of it.

(3) Before delivering to you the Creed, I think it well at this time to present a short compendium of the necessary doctrines, that the multitude of things to be said, and the intervening period of the entire season of holy Lent may not cause forgetfulness in the minds of the more simple among you, but that scattering seeds of doctrines now in summary fashion, we may not forget the same when they are more widely tilled later. But let those present who are of more mature understanding and "have their faculties trained to discern good and evil,"[9] be patient as they listen to an introductory course suited to children, milk for sucklings. In this way, those who need catechetical instruction will profit and

---

5 Cf. Col. 2.8.
6 Cf. Prov. 5.3.
7 Rom. 16.18.
8 Matt. 24.4.
9 Heb. 5.14.

those who have the knowledge will revive the memory of what they already know.

Of God

(4) First, then, let there be laid as a firm foundation in your souls the doctrine concerning God: That God is One alone, unbegotten, without beginning, immutable, unchangeable; neither begotten by another, nor having any successor to His life; who neither began to live in time, nor shall ever have an end. He is both good and just, and so if ever you hear a heretic saying that the just God is one and the good God another, you may at once be warned and recognize the poisoned shaft of heresy. For some have impiously dared to divide the One God in their teaching; and some have said that the Creator and Master of the soul was one, and that of the body another—a doctrine at once absurd and impious.[10] For how could the same man be the servant of two masters, when the Lord says in the Gospel: "No man can serve two masters"?[11] There is, then, One God alone, the Maker of souls and bodies; there is One, the Creator of heaven and earth, the Maker of angels and archangels, who is the Creator of many things, but the Father of One only before all ages, of One only, His Only-begotten Son, our Lord Jesus Christ, through whom He made all things visible and invisible.

(5) This Father of our Lord Jesus Christ is not circumscribed in any place nor is He less than the heavens; but the heavens are the works of His fingers,[12] and the whole earth is held in His palm.[13] He is in all things and about all. Consider not that He is less than the sun or equal to it, for He who fashioned the sun ought Himself, first, be far more sur-

---

10 The heresies referred to seem to be those of Marcion and Mani. Cf. *Cat.* 6.16-32.
11 Matt. 6.24.
12 Cf. Ps. 8.4.
13 Cf. Isa. 40.12.

passing, greater and brighter. He foreknows all future things and is mightier than all. He knows all things and does as He wills, not being subject to any sequence of events or nativity or chance or fate, perfect in all things and possessing in equal measure every form of virtue. He neither diminishes nor increases, but is ever and in every way the same; who has prepared chastisement for sinners and a crown for the just.

(6) Since, then, many have gone astray in divers ways from the One God—and some have deified the sun (so that after sunset, for the space of the night, they are godless); others, the moon, so they have no God during the day; still others, the other parts of the world; some have deified the arts, others food, others pleasures; and some, mad after women, have set up on high the image of a naked woman and, calling it Aphrodite, have bowed down before their passions in visible form. Others, again, dazzled by the splendor of gold, have deified that, and other substances as well. If a man first fixes as a foundation in his heart the doctrine of the One God and firmly believes it, he cuts away at once all the corruption of the evils of idolatry and of the error of the heretics. By faith, therefore, lay as a foundation in your soul this first doctrine of religion.

Of Christ

(7) Believe also in the One and Only Son of God, our Lord Jesus Christ, begotten God of God, begotten Life of Life, begotten Light of Light, like in all things to Him who begot Him; who received not His being in time, but before all ages was eternally and incomprehensibly begotten of the Father; who is the Wisdom and Power of God and co-essential Justice; who before all ages sits at the right hand of the Father. For it was not, as some have held, after His Passion, as though crowned by God for His patient suffering, that He received the throne on God's right hand, but for as long as He has existed—and He is begotten eternally—He has the

kingly dignity, sitting together with the Father, since He is God, and Wisdom and Power, as has been said; reigning together with the Father, and Creator of all things through the Father; lacking nothing for the dignity of Godhead, and knowing Him who begot Him, as He is known by Him.[14] To speak briefly, remember what is written in the Gospels: "No one knows the Son except the Father; nor does anyone know the Father except the Son."[15]

(8) Do not separate the Son from the Father,[16] nor yet by blending them, believe in the Son-Fatherhood, but believe that of One God there is one Only-begotten Son, who is before all the ages God the Word; the Word, not uttered externally and dispersed into the air, nor like words without substance, but the Word, the Son, the Maker of intelligible beings, the Word who listens to the Father and who speaks Himself. And on these points, if God grant it, we will speak more fully at the proper time, for we do not forget our purpose, to give at present only a summary introduction to the Faith.

His Virgin Birth

(9) Believe, too, that this Only-begotten Son of God came down from heaven to earth for our sins, taking on this passible human nature of ours, and being born of the holy Virgin and the Holy Spirit, His incarnation taking place, not in appearance or fantasy but in truth. He did not pass through the Virgin as through a channel,[17] but was truly made flesh from her, and truly nourished with her milk. For, if the Incarnation was a fantasy, salvation is also a fantasy. Christ was twofold in nature: man in what was seen, but God

---

14 Cyril several times refers to the heretical view that Christ was advanced in honor in time, a view held among others by Paul of Samosata (3rd cent.).
15 Matt. 11.27.
16 Sabellius is the most prominent of the heretics holding the views expressed here.
17 The virgin as channel—a doctrine held by the Valentinian heretics.

in what was not seen. As man He ate truly as we do—for He had like feelings of the flesh with us—but as God, He fed the five thousands from five loaves. He died truly as man, but raised him who was four days dead, as God. He truly slept in the ship as man, and walked upon the waters as God.

His Cross

(10) He was truly crucified for our sins. And should you wish to deny this, the visible place itself, this blessed Golgotha,[18] refutes you, where, in the name of Him who was here crucified, we are gathered together. Besides, the whole world has now been filled with pieces of the wood of the Cross. He was crucified not for His own sins, but that we might be freed from ours. He was despised and buffeted by men at that time as man, but was acknowledged as God by creation. For the sun, seeing its Master dishonored, was darkened and trembled, not enduring the sight.

His Burial

(11) He was truly laid as man in a rock tomb, but the rocks were rent for fear because of Him. He descended to the regions beneath the earth, that thence also He might redeem the just.[19] For tell me, would you wish the living to enjoy His grace, and that too when most of them are unholy, and have those who from Adam on had been long imprisoned not at length obtain deliverance? The Prophet Isaia heralded with loud voice so many things concerning Him; would you not wish the King to descend and deliver His herald? David was there, and Samuel, and all the prophets, and John himself, who said by his messengers: "Art thou he who is to

---

18 Here and elsewhere Cyril implies that the lectures were given on the actual site of the crucifixion.
19 The descent into Limbo was not in the Jerusalem creed.

come, or shall we look for another?"[20] Would you not wish Him to descend and deliver such men?

His Resurrection

(12) He who descended to the regions beneath the earth ascended again, and the Jesus who was buried rose again truly on the third day. And if the Jews ever trouble you, meet them at once by thus questioning them: Can it be that Jona came forth from the whale after three days and Christ had not risen from the earth on the third day? If a dead man, by touching the bones of Eliseus, was raised to life, will not the Maker of men be raised far more easily by the power of the Father? He did, then, truly rise, and after He had risen, was seen again by His disciples; and the twelve disciples were witnesses of His resurrection, testifying, not with words meant to please, but contending for the truth of the resurrection even unto torture and death. Further: "On the word of two or three witnesses every word may be confirmed," according to Scripture.[21] There are twelve witnesses to the resurrection of Christ, and do you still disbelieve in the resurrection?

His Ascension

(13) When Jesus had completed the course of His patient endurance and had redeemed men from their sins, He ascended again into heaven, a cloud taking Him up; and angels stood by as He ascended and Apostles looked on. But if any man doubt what we say, let him believe the power of the things seen now. All kings, when they die, lose, along with their life, their power. But Christ, though He was crucified, is worshiped by the whole world. We proclaim the

20 Matt. 11.3.
21 Matt. 18.16.

Crucified and the demons tremble; many at divers times have been crucified, but has the invocation of any other ever put the demons to flight?

(14) Let us not be ashamed of the Cross of Christ. But even though another hide it, do you seal it openly on your brow, that the demons, seeing the royal sign, may tremble and flee far away. Make this sign when eating and drinking, when sitting, lying down, rising, speaking, or walking; in a word, on every occasion. For He who was here crucified is in heaven above. For if, when He had been crucified and buried, He had remained in the tomb, we should perhaps have cause for shame, but He who was crucified here on Golgotha ascended into heaven from the Mount of Olives on the east. For having gone down hence into the nether world, and returned to us again, He ascended again from us into heaven, His Father addressing Him and saying: "Sit at my right hand until I make your enemies your footstool."[22]

Of Judgment to Come

(15) This Jesus Christ who ascended will come again from heaven, not from the earth. And I have said, "not from the earth," because many Antichrists at this time are to come from the earth. For already, as you have seen, many have begun to say: "I am the Christ,"[23] and afterwards there is to come "the abomination of desolation,"[24] assuming for himself the false title of Christ. But do you look for the true Christ, the Only-begotten Son of God, coming henceforth no more from the earth, but from heaven, appearing to all as lightning and splendor of light above all, attended by a guard of angels, that He may judge the living and the dead, reigning over a kingdom, heavenly, eternal, and without end.

---

22 Ps. 109.1.
23 Matt. 24.5.
24 Matt. 24.15.

For on this point also, make yourself sure, I pray you, since there are many who say there is an end to Christ's kingdom.

Of the Holy Spirit[25]

(16) Believe also in the Holy Spirit and cherish the right knowledge concerning Him; since there are many strangers to the Holy Spirit and they teach blasphemous things about Him. Learn then that this Holy Spirit is one and indivisible, His powers manifold; various as are the effects He produces, He is not Himself divided. He knows the mysteries, and "searches all things, even the deep things of God."[26] It is He who descended upon the Lord Jesus Christ in the form of a dove, who wrought in the Law and the Prophets, yes, who even now, at the time of baptism, puts a seal upon your soul; of His holiness every intellectual nature stands in need. If any man dare to blaspheme against Him, "It will not be forgiven him, either in this world or in the world to come";[27] who is ranked in honor of dignity with Father and Son; of whom also Thrones, Dominationes, Principalities, and Powers have need. For there is one God, the Father of Christ, and One Lord Jesus Christ, the Only-begotten Son of the One God, and One Holy Spirit who sanctifies and defies all, who spoke in the Law and the Prophets, both in the Old and the New Testaments.

(17) Keep this seal in mind at all times. I have spoken of it summarily, touching the main points, but if the Lord grant, I shall discuss it more fully later, to the best of my power, with proof from the Scriptures. For in regard to the divine and holy mysteries of the faith, not even a casual statement should be delivered without the Scriptures, and we must not be drawn aside merely by probabilities and artificial argu-

---

25 Cyril alludes in the first sentence to a heresy making the Holy Spirit a mere creature. He deals at great length with the Holy Spirit in *Cat.* 16-17.
26 1 Cor. 2.10.
27 Matt. 12.32.

ments. Do not believe even me merely because I tell you
these things, unless you receive from the inspired Scriptures
the proof of the assertions. For this saving faith of ours
depends not on ingenious reasonings but on proof from the
inspired Scriptures.

Of the Soul

(18) After the knowledge of this august and glorious and
all-holy faith, next know yourself for what you are, that you
are a man, twofold in nature, composed of soul and body,
and that, as was said a short time ago, the same God is the
creator of the soul and the body. Know also that this soul
of yours is free, self-determining, the fairest work of God,
made according to the image of its Creator, immortal because
of God who makes it immortal, a living being, rational, im-
perishable, because of Him who has conferred these gifts;
having power to do as it will. For it is not according to your
nativity that you sin, nor is it according to fortune that you
fornicate, nor, as some foolishly say, do the conjunctions
of the stars compel you to cleave to wantonness. Why, to
avoid confessing your own evil deeds, do you ascribe the
blame to the guiltless stars? Pay no attention henceforth to
astrologers, for concerning them Holy Scripture says: "Let
the astrologers stand forth to save you";[28] and further on:
"Behold they all shall be consumed by fire as stubble and
they shall not deliver their soul from flame."[29]

(19) Learn this also, that before the soul comes into the
world, it has committed no sin; but though we came into
the world sinless, we now of our own choice commit sin.
Listen not, I pray you, to anyone who gives a perverse interpretation of the words: "If I do what I do not wish,"[30]
but remember Him who says: "If you are willing, and obey,

28 Isa. 47.13.
29 Cf. Isa. 47.14 (Sept.).
30 Rom. 7.16.

you shall eat the good things of the land; but if you refuse
and resist, the sword shall consume you";[31] and again: "As
you have yielded your members as slaves of uncleanness and
iniquity unto iniquity, so now yield your members as slaves
of justice, unto sanctification."[32] Remember also the Scripture
which says: "As they have resolved against possessing the
knowledge of God";[33] and: "Seeing that what may be known
about God is manifest to them";[34] and again: "Their eyes
they have closed."[35] Remember also how God again accuses
them and says: "I had planted you, a choice vine of fully
tested stock; how could you turn out obnoxious to me, a
spurious vine?"[36]

(20) The soul is immortal, and all souls are alike, both of
men and women; only their bodily members are differen-
tiated. There is not a class of souls sinning by nature and a
class of souls acting justly by nature. But both act from choice,
since the substance of souls is of one kind and alike in all.
I realize that I am talking at length and much time has
already elapsed; but what is to be put above salvation? Are
you unwilling to take the trouble to receive provision for
the way against the heretics? Are you unwilling to learn the
turnings of the road, to avoid falling down the precipice
through ignorance? If your teachers count it no little gain
for you to learn these things, ought not you, the learner,
gladly receive the multitude of the things that are told you?

(21) The soul possesses freedom; and though the devil
can make suggestions, he has not the power to compel against
the will. He brings to your mind the thought of fornication;
if you will, you accept it; if you will not, you do not accept
it. For, if you committed fornication by necessity, then why
did God prepare Gehenna? If you acted justly by nature and

---

31 Isa. 1.19, 20.
32 Rom. 6.19.
33 Rom. 1.28.
34 *Ibid.* 19.
35 Matt. 13.15.
36 Jer. 2.21.

not by choice, why did God prepare ineffable crowns? The sheep is meek, but it has never been crowned for its meekness; for its meekness comes not from choice but from nature.

Of the Body

(22) You have been taught, beloved, the lore of the soul, as far as time allows at present. Now receive as best you can the doctrine concerning the body also. Let no one tell you that this body of ours is a stranger to God; for those who believe that the body is something alien readily abuse it to fornication. Yet what is it that they complain of in this wonderful body?[37] For what does it lack in comeliness? What is there in its structure that is not wrought skilfully? Ought they not to have considered the brilliant conformation of the eyes? And how the ears are set obliquely to receive the sound without hindrance? And how the sense of smell can distinguish and perceive odorous exhalations? And how the tongue ministers to two things, the sense of taste and the power of speech? And how the lungs, placed out of sight, are equipped for the unceasing respiration of air? Who gave the heart its incessant beating? Who made the division into so many veins and arteries? Who interwove the bones with the sinews so skilfully? Who assigned a part of our food for our substance, and separated a part for seemly excretion, and hid our uncomely members in more fitting places? Who, when the human race was likely to fail, made it perpetual by a simple conjunction?

(23) Tell me not that the body is the cause of sin; for, if the body is the cause of sin, how is it that a corpse does not sin? Put a sword in the right hand of one just dead and no murder takes place. Let beauties of all kinds pass before a young man just dead and no desire of fornication arises.

---

37 The marvelous composition of the body was a commonplace argument for its creation by God.

Why? Because the body of itself does not sin, but the soul through the body. The body is the soul's instrument, its cloak and garment. If then it is given up to fornication by the soul, it becomes unclean; but if it dwells with a holy soul, it becomes a temple of the Holy Spirit. It is not I who say these things, no, it is the Apostle Paul who has said: "Do you not know that your members are the temple of the Holy Spirit, who is in you?"[38] Defile not, then, your flesh in fornication; stain not your fairest garment. But if you have stained it, now cleanse it by repentance; for it is the time for purification.

(24) Let this doctrine of chastity be heeded above all by the order of solitaries and virgins, who are establishing in the world an angelic mode of life, and after them, by the rest of the people of the Church. A great crown is laid up for you, brethren; barter not a great dignity for a petty pleasure. Listen to the Apostle saying: "Lest there be any immoral, or profane person, such as Esau, who for one meal sold his birthright."[39] Once enrolled in the angelic books for your profession of chastity, take care that you are not blotted out thereafter for practicing fornication.

(25) Again, because you practice chastity, do not be puffed up with conceit against those who live in the humbler state of matrimony. "For let marriage be held in honor, and let the marriage bed be undefiled,"[40] as the Apostle says. For have not you who keep your purity been born of married persons? Do not, therefore, because you possess gold, contemn the silver. But let those be of good cheer also, who, being married, use marriage rightfully; who order their marriage according to law, not making it wanton by uncontrolled license; who recognize times of abstinence, that they may give themselves to prayer; who, at the assemblies, bring into the Church clean bodies as well as clean garments; who have entered into

---

38 1 Cor. 6.19.
39 Heb. 12.16.
40 Heb. 13.4.

marriage for the sake of begetting children, not for self-indulgence.

(26) Let not those who have been married only once[41] find fault with those who have indulged in a second marriage. For, while continence is a noble and admirable thing, it is also allowable to enter upon a second marriage, that the weak may not commit fornication. For, "it is good for them if they so remain, even as I," says the Apostle. "But if they do not have self-control, let them marry, for it is better to marry than to burn."[42] But let all other things be put far away, fornication, adultery, and every kind of licentiousness; and let the body be kept pure for the Lord, that the Lord also may respect the body.

(27) Let the body eat to live and be a ready servant; not, however, that it may be given up to luxuries. Concerning food, let these be your ordinances, since with regard to meats many also stumble. For some, without discrimination, partake of the things offered to idols; others, while they practice an ascetic life, condemn those who eat; and so, in various ways, the soul of some is defiled in the question of meats, out of ignorance of the useful reasons for eating or abstaining. For we fast by abstaining from wine and flesh, not because we abhor them as abominations, but because we expect the reward, that by scorning sensible things, we may enjoy a spiritual and invisible table, and that, though we now "sow in tears, we shall reap rejoicing"[43] in the world to come. Do not despise, then, those who eat and take food because of bodily weakness. Do not censure those who "use a little wine for their stomach's sake, and frequent infirmities."[44] And do not condemn them as sinners. Do not abhor flesh meats as something strange; for the Apostle knows some

---

41 Apparently there was considerable prejudice against a second marriage in the early church. It was very strong among the puritan sects like the Montanists.
42 1 Cor. 7.8, 9.
43 Cf. Ps. 125.5.
44 Cf. 1 Tim. 5.23.

such men when he says: "They will forbid marriage, and will enjoin abstinence from foods which God has created to be partaken of with thanksgiving by the faithful."[45] When you abstain from these things, do not, then, abstain from them as though they were abominable, else you receive no reward. Rather, while recognizing that they are good, yet prefer the better, spiritual things set before you.

(28) Safeguard your soul, never eating of the things offered to idols. For, in regard to the meats, not only I, at this time, but before now, the Apostle also, and James, once the Bishop of this Church, have shown concern. For the Apostles and the ancients wrote a Catholic epistle to all the Gentiles that they should abstain first of all from things sacrificed to idols, and then from blood and things strangled. For many men, being of savage nature and living like dogs, lap up the blood after the manner of the fiercest wild beasts, and eat their fill unsparingly of things strangled. But do you, the servant of Christ, see to it that when you eat you eat with reverence. But of meats enough.

Apparel

(29) Let your dress be plain, not serving for adornment, but for necessary covering. The purpose of clothes is not to minister to your vanity, but to keep warm in winter and cover your nakedness. Take care lest, under pretense of hiding your unseemliness, by your extravagant apparel, you fall into another sort of unseemliness.

Of the Resurrection

(30) Treat this body with care, I pray you, and understand that with this body you will rise from the dead to be judged. But, if any thought of doubt should steal into your

---

45 1 Tim. 4.3.

mind, as though the thing were impossible, judge the things unseen from your own experience. For tell me—just think where you were, you, yourself, a hundred or more years ago. From what an extremely small and mean substance have you come to such magnitude of stature and to such dignity of form! Cannot He, who brought what was not into being, raise up again that already in existence which has decayed? Will He, who raises up the corn for us when it dies, year by year, have difficulty in raising up us, for whose sake the corn has been raised? You see how the trees have stood now for so many months without fruit or foliage. But with the passing of winter they return wholly to life again, as though from the dead. Shall not we much more and far more easily live again? The rod of Moses, by the will of God, was transformed into the quite dissimilar nature of a serpent; and shall not man, who has fallen into death, be restored anew?

(31) Attend not to those who say that this body does not rise; for rise it does. Isaia is a witness of this when he says: "The dead shall rise, and those in the tombs shall be raised";[46] and according to Daniel: "Many of those who sleep in the dust of the earth shall awake, some unto life everlasting and some unto shame everlasting."[47] Now, while the resurrection is common to all men, it will not be alike for all; for we shall all, indeed, receive everlasting bodies, but not all like bodies. For the just receive them that through eternity they may join the chorus of angels, but the sinners that they may endure the torment due to their sins forever.

(32) For this reason, the Lord, beforehand in His loving-kindness, has granted us the repentance of the laver of baptism, that, by casting off the chief, nay, rather the whole burden of our sins, and receiving the seal of the Holy Spirit, we may be made heirs of eternal life. But since we have already spoken sufficiently of the laver of baptism, let us proceed to the remaining topics of our introductory teachings.

---

46 Isa. 26.19 (Sept.).
47 Cf. Dan. 12.2 (Sept.).

Of the Holy Scriptures

(33) The teaching you have heard is that of the divinely-inspired Scriptures, both of the Old and the New Testament. For there is One God of the two Testaments, who foretold in the Old Testament the Christ who appeared in the New, and who, through the preparatory school of the Law and the Prophets, led us to Christ. For "before the faith came, we were guarded under the Law";[48] and, "the Law trained us for Christ's school."[49] And so, if ever you hear any heretic blaspheming the Law or the Prophets, quote that saving word against him: Jesus came not to destroy the Law, but to fulfill it.[50] Be eager to learn, and from the Church, what are the books of the Old Testament, what of the New; and I pray you, read none of the apocryphal books. For why should you, when you do not know the books acknowledged by all, trouble yourself needlessly with those whose authenticity is disputed? Read the divine Scriptures, these twenty-two books of the Old Testament translated by the seventy-two interpreters.[51]

(34) When Alexander, king of Macedon, died, his empire was divided into four kingdoms, Babylon and Macedon, Asia and Egypt. One of the Egyptian dynasty, Ptolemy Philadelphus, a great lover of learning, when he became king and was collecting books from every quarter, heard from Demetrius of Phalerum, the curator of his library, of the divine Scriptures of the Law and the Prophets. He judged it far better not to get the books by force from unwilling persons, but rather to win over the possessors with gifts and friendship, since he knew that what is forced from men, because it is given against their will, is often adulterated, while that which is freely offered is given with all sincerity. When he had

---

48 Gal. 2.23.
49 *Ibid.* 24.
50 Cf. Matt. 5.17.
51 The reference is to the Septuagint. In chapter 34 Cyril tells the popular legend of its origin.

sent to Eleazar, the High Priest at that time, very many gifts for the temple here at Jerusalem, he had six men out of each of the twelve tribes of Israel dispatched to him for the work of translation. Then, to prove whether the books were divine or not, and to prevent collusion by the members of the mission, he assigned to each of the interpreters a separate dwelling in the place called Pharus, lying near Alexandria, and committed to each all the Scriptures to translate. When they had completed their task in seventy-two days, the king compared all their translations, which they had made in separate cells without communicating with one another, and found that they exactly agreed, not only in sense, but even in words. For the process did not admit of a naturalistic explanation, nor was it any contrivance of human ingenuity; no, but the translation of the divine Scriptures, spoken by the Holy Spirit, was completed by the Holy Spirit.

(35) Of these, read the twenty-two books, and have nothing to do with the apocryphal writings. Study earnestly only those books which we read openly in Church. For far wiser and more devout than yourself were the Apostles and the ancient bishops, the rulers of the Church, who handed down these books. Therefore, since you are a child of the Church, do not transgress her ordinances. Of the Old Testament, then, as it has been said, study these twenty-two books and, if you are eager to learn, strive to fix them by name in your memory as I enumerate them. For of the Law the books of Moses are the first five, Genesis, Exodus, Leviticus, Numbers, Deuteronomy; then Josue, the son of Nun, and the book of Judges, which, along with Ruth, is numbered the seventh. Of the remaining historical books, the first and second books of Kings are among the Hebrews one book, and the third and fourth one book. Likewise, the first and second books of Paralipomenon make one book, and the first and second books of Esdras are reckoned as one. The book of Esther is the twelfth; and these are the historical books. The books written in verse are five, Job, the book of Psalms, Proverbs, Eccle-

siastes, and the Canticle of Canticles, which is the seventeenth book. There follow the five prophetic books: the one book of the twelve prophets, of Isaia one, of Jeremia with Baruch, the Lamentations and the Epistle one; the Ezechiel, and the book of Daniel, the twenty-second of the Old Testament.

(36) Of the New Testament, there are only four gospels; for the rest are not genuine and are harmful. The Manichaeans also wrote a "Gospel according to Thomas," which, through the spurious odor of sanctity conferred by its title, corrupts simple folk. Receive also the Acts of the Twelve Apostles; and in addition to these, the seven Catholic Epistles of James, Peter, John, and Jude; then, as a seal upon all of them, and the last work of the disciples, the fourteen Epistles of St. Paul.[52] But let all the rest be put in the second rank; and whatever books are not read in the churches read not by yourself, in accordance with what you have been told. Thus far concerning these matters.

(37) Flee every diabolical influence[53] and hearken not to the apostate Serpent, who of his own deliberate choice was transformed from a good nature; who can persuade the willing, but can force no one. Attend not to the fabulous divinations of the Greeks. As for sorcery, incantation, and the wicked practices of necromancy, do not admit them within your hearing. Stand aloof from every form of intemperance, being neither a glutton nor a lover of pleasure, and, above all, from covetousness and usury. Venture not among the assemblies of the heathen spectacles; never use amulets in times of sickness; put aside also the defilement of frequenting taverns. Fall not into the sect of the Samaritans or into Judaism; for henceforth Jesus Christ has redeemed you. Stand aloof from all observation of Sabbaths and speak not of any of the indifferent meats as common or unclean. But abhor especially all the assemblies of the wicked heretics; and in every way

---

52 Note the omission of the Apocalypse form Cyril's Canon.
53 This chapter gives us some idea of the pagan atmosphere in which the Christian had to live.

make your own soul safe, by fasting, prayers, alms, and the reading of the divine oracles, that living in temperance and in the observance of pious doctrines for the rest of your time in the flesh, you may enjoy the one salvation of the laver of baptism, and so, enrolled in the heavenly hosts by God the Father, you may be deemed worthy of the heavenly crowns, in Christ Jesus our Lord, to whom be glory forever and ever. Amen.

CATECHESIS V

On Faith

"Now faith is the substance of things to be hoped for, the evidence of things that are not seen; for by it the men of old had testimony borne to them."[1]

(1) How great a dignity the Lord confers upon you in transferring you from the rank of catechumens to that of the faithful Paul the Apostle indicates when he says: "God is faithful, by him you have been called into fellowship with his Son, Jesus Christ."[2] For, since God is called faithful, you also, in receiving this title, receive a great dignity. For as God is called Good, and Just, and Almighty, and Creator of the universe, so also is He called faithful. Consider then to what a dignity you are being exalted in that you are about to become a sharer of a title of God.

(2) Moreover, it is required that each of you be found faithful in conscience.[3] For, "it is a task to find a faithful man."[4] Not that you should show your conscience to me—for not by man's day are you to be judged[5]—but that you may show the sincerity of your faith to God, "the searcher of reins and hearts,"[6] who "knows the thoughts of men."[7] A great thing is a faithful man, no man is so rich as he. For,

---

1 Heb. 11.1, 2.
2 1 Cor. 1.9.
3 Cf. 1 Cor. 4.2.
4 Prov. 20.6 (Sept.).
5 Cf. 1 Cor. 4.3.
6 Ps. 7.10.
7 Ps. 93.11.

"to the faithful man belongs the whole world of riches,"[8] inasmuch as he disdains wealth and tramples it underfoot. For those who in appearance are rich, though they have many possessions, are yet poor in soul; for the more they amass, the more they pine with longing for what they lack. But the believer, paradoxically, is rich even when poor; for knowing that we have need only of raiment and food, and being content with these, he has trampled riches underfoot.[9]

(3) It is not only among us, who are marked with the name of Christ, that the dignity of faith is great; all the business of the world, even of those outside the Church, is accomplished by faith.[10] By faith, marriage laws join in union persons who are strangers one to another; the spouses, though erstwhile strangers, bestow on each other their bodies and material possessions, because of faith in the marriage contracts. By faith agriculture is sustained; for a man does not endure the toil involved unless he believes that he will reap a harvest. By faith, seafaring men, entrusting themselves to a tiny wooden craft, exchange the solid element of the land for the unstable motion of the waves, surrendering themselves to uncertain hopes and carrying about with them a faith more sure than any anchor. Most of the affairs of men, then, depend on faith; and not only among us does this hold true, but also, as I have said, among those outside the fold. For though they do not accept the Scriptures but advance certain doctrines of their own, yet even these they receive on faith.

(4) The lesson read today likewise calls you to the true faith, as it points out the way by which you must please God; for it says that "without faith it is impossible to please [God]."[11] For when will a man propose to serve God, unless he believes that He is a rewarder?[12] When will a young

---

8 Prov. 17.6 (Sept.).
9 Cf. 1 Tim 6.8.
10 This chapter constitutes an excellent approach to the meaning of faith.
11 Heb. 11.6.
12 Cf. *ibid.*

woman lead the life of a virgin or a young man a life of
self-control, unless they believe that for chastity there is a
never-fading crown? Faith is the eye that enlightens every
conscience and produces understanding; for the Prophet says:
"If you will not believe, you shall not understand."[13] Faith
stops up the mouths of lions,[14] according to Daniel; for
Scripture says of him: "Daniel was removed from the den,
unhurt because he trusted in his God."[15] Is there anything
more terrible than the devil? Yet, even against him, we have
no other armor than faith, a spiritual shield against an invisible enemy. For he discharges manifold arrows, and shoots
in the dark those who are not vigilant;[16] but, though the
enemy is unseen, we have our faith as a strong protection,
according to the saying of the Apostle: "In all things taking
up the shield of faith, with which you may be able to quench
all the fiery darts of the most wicked one."[17] Oftentimes a
fiery dart of desire of base indulgence is discharged by the
devil; but faith, representing to us the Judgment, and cooling
the mind, extinguishes the dart.

(5) Much is to be said about faith, and the whole day
would not suffice for us to discourse fully upon it. For the
present let us be content with Abraham as an example from
the Old Testament, since of him also we have become sons
by faith. He was justified, not by works alone, but by faith.
For he had done many things well, yet he was never called
friend of God but when he believed;[18] and further, every
deed of his was perfected by faith. By faith, he left his
parents; by faith, he left country, district, and home. Just as
he was justified, so you also will be justified. He was dead in
body for the further begetting of children; for he was an old
man, his wife Sara was old also, and there was no hope left

---

13 Isa. 7.9 (Sept.).
14 Cf. Dan. 6.23; Heb. 11.33.
15 Dan. 6.24.
16 Cf. Ps. 10.3.
17 Eph. 6.16.
18 Cf. Gen. 15.6; James 2.23.

of offspring. God promised offspring to the old man; and Abraham was not weak in faith,[19] and considering his own body now dead, he looked not to the weakness of his body, but to the power of Him who promised, believing "that he who had given the promise was faithful,"[20] and so from bodies as good as dead, beyond all expectation, he obtained a son. Then, after begetting a son, when he was commanded to offer him, though he had already heard the words: "In Isaac thy seed shall be called,"[21] he proceeded to offer his only-begotten son to God, "reasoning that God has power to raise up even from the dead."[22] And when he had bound his son and placed him on the wood, in will, indeed, he sacrificed him, but by the goodness of God, who supplied him a lamb in place of his child, he received his son alive. Therefore, because he was faithful, he was sealed unto righteousness, and he received circumcision as the seal of the faith which he had while uncircumcised,[23] having received a promise that he would be "the father of a multitude of nations."[24]

(6) Let us see in what respect Abraham is the father of many nations. Admittedly, he is the father of the Jews, by succession according to the flesh. But if we look only to succession according to the flesh, we shall be forced to say that the oracle is false; for he is no longer father of all of us according to the flesh. But the example of his faith makes us all sons of Abraham. How and in what manner? It is incredible among men that one should rise from the dead; as it is likewise incredible that offspring be born of aged persons as good as dead. But when Christ is preached as having been crucified on the tree, as having died and risen again, we believe it. By the likeness of our faith, therefore, we become the adopted sons of Abraham; and consequent upon our faith,

---

19 Rom. 4.19.
20 Heb. 11.11.
21 Heb. 11.18.
22 Heb. 11.19.
23 Cf. Rom. 4.11.
24 Gen. 17.5.

like him we receive the spiritual seal, being circumcised by the Holy Spirit through the laver of baptism, not in the foreskin of the body, but in the heart, according to the words of Jeremia: "For the sake of the Lord, be circumcised, remove the foreskins of your hearts,"[25] and according to the Apostle: In the "circumcision which is of Christ, buried together with him in baptism," and so forth.[26]

(7) If we guard this faith, we shall be free from condemnation and be adorned with virtues of every kind. For the power of faith is so great that it even buoys up men walking upon the sea. Peter was a man like ourselves, composed of flesh and blood, and living on like foods. But when Jesus said: "Come,"[27] believing, he walked upon the waters, having in his faith a support firmer than any natural ground, and upholding the weight of his body by the buoyancy of his faith. Now as long as he believed, he had firm footing upon the water, but when he doubted, then he began to sink; for as his faith gradually gave way, his body also was drawn down along with it. Realizing his predicament, Jesus, who cures our souls' sicknesses, said: "O thou of little faith, why didst thou doubt?"[28] Then, strengthened by Him who grasped his right hand, as soon as he had recovered his faith, led by the hand of the Master, he walked upon the waters as before. For the Gospel signifies this indirectly in the words: "And when they got into the boat."[29] For it does not say, swimming to the boat, Peter got into it, but it gives us to understand that, after retracing the distance he had traversed in going to Jesus, he re-entered the boat.

(8) Further, faith has such power that not only is the believer saved, but some have been saved through the faith of others. The man sick of the palsy in Capharnaum was not a believer; but those who brought him, and let him down

25 Jer. 4.4.
26 Cf. Col. 2.11, 12.
27 Matt. 14.29.
28 Ibid. 14.31.
29 Ibid. 14.32.

through the tiles, had faith; for the soul of the sick man
shared the sickness of his body. And do not think that I
accuse him rashly. The Gospel itself says: "Jesus seeing," not
his faith but "their faith, he said to the paralytic, Arise."[30]
They who brought him believed and the one sick with the
palsy got the benefit of the cure.

(9) Do you wish to see with more certainty that some are
saved by the faith of others? Lazarus died; one day had passed,
and a second, and a third, and dissolution and putrefaction
were already setting into his body. How could one four days
dead believe and call upon the Redeemer on his own behalf?
But what was lacking in the dead man was supplied by his
sisters. For when the Lord came, one of them fell at His
feet. To His question: "Where have you laid him?"[31] she
answered: "Lord, by this time he is already decayed, for he
is dead four days."[32] Then the Lord said: "If you believe,
you shall behold the glory of God."[33] This was tantamount
to saying: Wake up what is wanting in your dead brother's
faith. And the sisters' faith, in fact, availed to recall the dead
man from the gates of hell. Now if men, believing one for
another, have been able to raise from the dead, will not you,
if you believe sincerely on your own behalf, be profited all
the more? Indeed, even though you be faithless or of little
faith, the Lord is benevolent, and shows indulgence to you
when you repent; only do you, too, say with all sincerity:
"I do believe, Lord; help my unbelief."[34] But if you think
that you are a believer, but have not yet attained the perfection of faith, you too have need of saying with the Apostles:
Lord, "increase our faith."[35] For, while you have some part
from yourself, the greater part you receive from Him.

(10) Though the term "faith" is one, as far as expression

---

30 Matt. 9.2, 6.
31 John 11.34.
32 *Ibid*. 11.39.
33 *Ibid*. 11.40.
34 Mark 9.23.
35 Luke 17.5.

goes, it may mean either of two things. Dogmatic faith involves an assent to some truth; and this truly profits the soul, as the Lord says: "He who hears my words, and believes him who sent me, has life everlasting; and does not come to judgment." And again: "He who believes in the Son is not judged, but has passed from death to life."[36] O the great loving-kindness of God! Now the just, indeed, in many years of service have pleased God; but what they succeeded in gaining by many years of well-pleasing service, this Jesus now bestows on you in a single hour. For, if you believe that Jesus Christ is Lord, and that God raised Him from the dead, you will be saved and translated into paradise by Him who brought the robber into paradise. Doubt not that this is possible; for He who here on holy Golgotha saved the robber after a single hour of faith will save you also when you believe.

(11) There is a second kind of faith, which is bestowed by Christ as a special gift. "To one through the Spirit is given the utterance of wisdom; and to another the utterance of knowledge, according to the same Spirit; to another faith, in the same Spirit; to another the gift of healing."[37] Now this faith, given as a grace by the Spirit, is not only doctrinal, but also effects things beyond man's power. For whoever possesses this faith "will say to this mountain, 'Remove from here,' and it will remove."[38] For whenever anyone shall say this in faith, believing that it will come to pass, "and does not waver in his heart,"[39] then he receives that grace. It is of this grace that the saying stands: "If you have faith like a mustard seed."[40] For just as the mustard seed, tiny as it is, has a fiery power and, narrow though its seed-bed, has a mighty spread of branches, so that when full-grown it affords shelter to the birds of the air, so also faith, in a twinkling, produces mighty effects in the soul. For when it is enlightened by faith,

---

36 John 3.18; 5.24.
37 1 Cor. 12.8, 9.
38 Matt. 17.19.
39 Mark 11.23.
40 Matt. 17.19.

the soul has visions of God, and contemplates God, as far as it may; it ranges over the bounds of the universe, and before the consummation of this world, beholds the judgment and the payment of the promised rewards. Cherish therefore that faith which comes from yourself and is directed towards Him, that you may also receive from Him that faith which accomplishes things beyond man's power.

(12) In learning and professing the faith, embrace and guard that only which is now delivered to you by the Church, and confirmed by all the Scriptures. For since not everyone has both the education and the leisure required to read and know the Scriptures, to prevent the soul perishing from ignorance, we sum up the whole doctrine of the faith in a few lines. This summary I wish you to commit to memory, word for word, and to repeat among yourselves with all zeal, not writing it on paper, but engraving it by memory on the heart. Only take care, in rehearsing it, that no catechumen chance to overhear what has been delivered to you. Keep it as a provision for the way throughout the whole course of your life, and beyond this, never receive any other, even though we ourselves should change and contradict what we now teach; nay, even though an enemy angel, transformed into an angel of light, should try to lead you astray. For "even if we or an angel from heaven should preach a gospel to you other than that which you have now received, let him be anathema."[41] For the present, just listen and memorize the creed as I recite it, and you will receive in due course the proof from Scripture of each of its propositions. For not according to men's pleasure have the articles of faith been composed, but the most important points collected from the Scriptures make up one complete teaching of the faith. And just as the mustard seed in a small grain contains in embryo many future branches, so also the creed embraces in a few words all the religious knowledge in both the Old and the New Testament. Take heed, therefore, brethren, and hold fast to

---

41 Gal. 1.8, 9.

the teachings[42] which are now delivered to you, and "write them on the tablet of your heart."[43]

(13) Guard them with care else by chance the enemy may despoil those who have grown remiss, or some heretic may pervert the traditions entrusted to you. Faith is like opening a deposit account at the bank, as we have now done; but it is God who is the author. "I charge thee," as the Apostle says, "in the sight of God, who gives life to all things, and in the sight of Christ Jesus, who bore witness to that great claim before Pontius Pilate,"[44] that you keep this faith which is delivered unto you, without stain until the coming of our Lord Jesus Christ. A treasure of life has now been committed to you, and the Master will require the deposit at the time of His coming, which "he in his own time will make manifest, who is the blessed and the only sovereign, the King of Kings, and Lord of Lords; who alone has immortality and dwells in light inaccessible, whom no man has seen nor can see";[45] to whom be glory, honor, and power forever and ever. Amen.

---

42 2 Thess. 2.14, 15.
43 Prov. 7.3. The text of the Nicene creed follows this chapter in some manuscripts.
44 1 Tim. 6.13, 14.
45 1 Tim. 6.15, 16.

CATECHESIS VI

On the Unity of God

"Be renewed unto me, you islands. Israel is saved by the Lord, saved forever! They shall never be put to shame or disgraced in future ages."[1]

(1) "Blessed be the God and Father of our Lord Jesus Christ."[2] For, with the thought of God, let the thought of Father be joined, that Father and Son may be perfectly and indivisibly glorified. For the Father does not have one glory and the Son another, but both have one and the same. For as the Father's Only-begotten Son, when the Father is glorified, the Son shares in the glory. For the Son's glory stems from His Father's honor; and when in turn the Son is glorified, the Father of so blessed a Son is greatly honored.

(2) Now while the mind's thought is very swift, the tongue needs words and much intermediary discourse. The eye too takes in at once a great company of stars, but when a man wishes to isolate one in particular to identify the morning star, the evening star, and the other individual stars, he must discourse at length. Similarly, the mind in a twinkling comprehends earth and sea and all the bounds of the world. But that which it perceives in an instant it describes in many words. Now, however impressive the example I have given, it is still weak and feeble. For we say about God not what is due (for this is known to Him alone), but as much as man's nature grasps and our weakness can bear. For we do not declare what God is but we frankly confess that we have no

1 Isa. 45.16, 17 (Sept.).
2 2 Cor. 1.3.

148

exact knowledge concerning Him. On the subject of God, it is great knowledge to confess our ignorance. "Glorify," then, "the Lord with me; and let us together extol his name";[3] all of us in union, for one does not suffice; nay, though all of us join together, it will still be inadequate. Nor do I mean you alone who are present, but even if all the children of the universal Church, present and future, should meet together, they could not sing worthily the praises of our Shepherd.

(3) Great and honorable was Abraham, but great in comparison with men; when he came nigh to God he acknowledged truthfully: "I am but earth and ashes."[4] He did not say "earth" and stop there, to call himself by that great element, but added, "and ashes," that he might represent his own nature, prone to dissolution and corruption. Is there anything, he says, meaner or more insignificant than ashes? For compare, he says, ashes with a house, a house with a city, a city with a province, a province with the Roman Empire, the Roman Empire with the whole earth and all its bounds, and the whole earth with the heaven which encompasses it. The earth, compared to the heaven, is as the hub to the circumference of the wheel (for such is the proportion between earth and heaven); and consider that this first heaven which we see is smaller than the second, and the second smaller than the third; for thus far has Scripture named them,[5] not because there are only so many, but because it was expedient for us to know only so many. When you have perceived all the heavens in the mind's eye, then even these will still be unable to praise God as He is, though they ring with a voice louder than thunder. But if such vast expanses of heavens cannot celebrate God worthily, how will earth and ashes, the smallest and least of substances, ever avail to hymn praises worthy of God, who "sits enthroned above the vaults of the earth, and its inhabitants are like grasshoppers"?[6]

---

3 Ps. 33.4.
4 Cf. Gen. 18.27.
5 Cf. 2 Cor. 12.2. Cyril speaks of three heavens but suggests there may be more. Some early writers mention three heavens, others seven.
6 Isa. 40.22.

(4) If any man undertakes to speak of the attributes of God, let him first describe the bounds of the earth. Though you dwell on the earth you do not know the limit of your dwelling place; how then will you be able to form a worthy concept of its Creator? You see the stars, but their Maker you do not see; first, number the stars, which are seen, and then set forth Him who is not seen; "He tells the number of the stars; he calls each by name."[7] The recent violent rains all but destroyed us; number the drops of rain in this city alone; rather, not in the city, but number the drops which fell upon your own house in a single hour, if you can. But since you cannot, you acknowledge your own weakness. From this learn the power of God. For "he has numbered the rain-drops"[8] poured down upon the whole earth, not only now but through all time. The sun is a work of God, great indeed, but very small compared to the whole heavens. Fix your attention on the sun first, and then inquire assiduously about its Lord. "What is too sublime for you seek not; into things beyond your strength search not. What is committed to you, attend to."[9]

(5) But someone will say: if the Divine Nature is incomprehensible, then why do you discourse about these things? Well then, because I cannot drink up the whole stream, am I not even to take in proportion to my need? Or because I cannot take in all the sunlight owing to the constitution of my eyes, am I not even to gaze upon what is sufficient for my wants? On entering a vast orchard, because I cannot eat all the fruit therein, would you have me go away completely hungry? I praise and glorify Him who made us; for it is a divine command which says: "Let everything that has breath praise the Lord!"[10] I am endeavoring now to glorify the Lord, not to describe Him, though I know that I shall fall short of glorifying Him worthily; still I consider

7 Ps. 146.4.
8 Job 36.27 (Sept.).
9 Ecclus. (Sir.) 3.20, 21.
10 Ps. 150.6.

it a godly work to try all the same. For the Lord Jesus encourages my weakness when He says: "No one has at any time seen God."[11]

(6) But, I shall be told, is it not written: "The angels of the little ones always behold the face of my Father in heaven"?[12] The angels see God, not as He is, but in the measure of their capacity. For it is Jesus Himself who says: "Not that anyone has seen the Father except him who is from God, he has seen the Father."[13] Angels see according to their capacity and the archangels as they are able; and the Thrones and Dominations in a greater measure than the former, but still less than God's real being. Only the Holy Spirit, together with the Son, can behold Him perfectly. For He "searches all things, even the deep things of God";[14] just as even the Only-begotten Son, together with the Holy Spirit, knows the Father perfectly. "Nor does anyone know the Father," He says, "except the Son and him to whom the Son reveals Him."[15] For He beholds Him fully and, through the Holy Spirit, reveals God according to the capacity of each; since the Only-begotten Son, together with the Holy Spirit, is a partaker of the Godhead of the Father. He who was begotten without passion[16] from all eternity knows Him who begot, and He who begot knows Him who is begotten. Since then angels are ignorant (for to each, according to his individual capacity, does the Only-begotten reveal, with and through the Holy Spirit, as we have said), let no man be ashamed to confess his ignorance. I am speaking now, and all do on occasion, yet how we speak we cannot tell; how then can I describe Him who gave the power of speech? How shall I, who have a soul and yet cannot declare its characteristics, set forth its Giver?

11 John 1.18.
12 Cf. Matt. 18.10.
13 John 6.46.
14 1 Cor. 2.10.
15 Matt. 11.27.
16 "Without passion" refers especially to the immutability of God.

(7) This alone will be a sufficient incentive to piety, to know that we have a God, a God who is One, a God who is, who is eternal, who is ever the self-same, with no father, no one mightier than Himself, no successor to drive Him out of His kingdom, who is honored under many names, is all-powerful, and uniform in substance. For although He is called Good, and Just and Omnipotent, and Sabaoth, this does not mean He is diverse;[17] but being One and the same, He fathers the countless operations of the Godhead; not abounding on one side and deficient on another, but being in all things like unto Himself; not great in loving-kindness and little in wisdom, but possessing wisdom and loving-kindness in like measure; not seeing in part and in part deprived of sight, but being all eye and all ear and all mind; not as we, knowing in part and in part ignorant, for such an assertion were blasphemous and unworthy of the Divine Nature. He has foreknowledge of the things that are, and is Holy and Omnipotent, and surpasses all in goodness and greatness and wisdom. Of Him we can declare neither form nor shape. For "you have never heard his voice, nor seen his face,"[18] says Scripture. Therefore, Moses says to the Israelites: "Be strictly on your guard" because "you saw no form at all."[19] For, if it is quite impossible to imagine His likeness, how will thought ever come near His substance?

(8) Many have been the imaginings of many men, but all have failed. Some have thought God to be fire, others like a man with wings, because of the perverse interpretation of a text true in itself: "Hide me in the shadow of your wings."[20] They have forgotten that our Lord Jesus Christ, the Only-begotten, spoke in similar terms concerning Himself to Jerusalem: "How often would I have gathered thy children

---

17 Cyril stresses the various titles and attributes of God not merely to refute the heretics but also to protect the more simple among his hearers.
18 John 5.37.
19 Deut. 4.15.
20 Ps. 16.8.

together, as a hen gathers her young under her wings, but thou wouldst not."[21] For, while His protective power is compared to wings, these men, not understanding, and falling to the level of human things, conceived His unsearchable being in terms of human experience. Others have ventured to say that He has seven eyes, because it is written: ". . . seven . . . eyes of the Lord that range over the whole earth."[22] For, if seven eyes, and no more, encircle Him, then He sees in part only and not perfectly, and to say this is blasphemous. For we must believe that God is perfect in all things, according to the saying of the Savior: "Your heavenly Father is perfect";[23] perfect in sight, perfect in power, perfect in greatness, perfect in foreknowledge, perfect in goodness, perfect in justice, perfect in loving-kindness; not limited by space, but the Creator of space, existing in all things but circumscribed by none. The heaven is His throne, but He who sits thereon is above it; the earth His footstool,[24] but His power extends even to the things beneath the earth.

(9) He is One, everywhere present, seeing all things, understanding all things, fashioning all things through Christ. He is a fountainhead of all good, immense and unfailing, a stream of blessings, light eternal shining unceasingly, power insuperable, condescending to our infirmities; we cannot endure even His name. "Wilt thou find the footstep of God," says Job, "or hast thou attained to the least things which the Almighty hath made?"[25] If the very least of His works are not comprehended, will He who made all things be comprehended? "Eye has not see nor ear heard, nor has it entered into the heart of man, what things God has prepared for those who love him."[26] If the things God has prepared are beyond our comprehension, can we comprehend Him who

---

21 Matt. 23.27.
22 Zach. 4.10.
23 Matt. 5.48.
24 Cf. Acts 7.49.
25 Job 11.7 (Sept.).
26 1 Cor. 2.9.

has prepared them? "Oh, the depth of the riches of the wisdom and of the knowledge of God! How incomprehensible are his judgments and how unsearchable his ways!"[27] If His judgments and ways are incomprehensible, will He Himself be comprehended?

(10) Though God is so great, and even still greater (for if I were to become all tongue, not even then could I speak of Him adequately; nay, more, not even if all angels should gather together, could they speak of Him adequately); though He is so great, in goodness and majesty, man said to the stone he had himself graven: "Thou art my God."[28] O monstrous blindness, to descend from such majesty to such baseness! The tree which God planted and rain increased, and which afterwards is burned and turned into glowing ashes, this is proclaimed God, while the true God is despised. The wickedness of idolatry abounded still more, and cat and dog[29] and wolf were worshiped instead of God; and the man-eating lion was adored instead of the most loving God. Snake and dragon, counterparts of him who caused us to be driven from paradise, were worshiped, while He who planted paradise was scorned. I am ashamed to say it, but say it I will, even onions have been worshiped among some.[30] Wine was given "to gladden men's hearts,"[31] and Dionysus was worshiped in the place of God. God made corn by saying: "Let the earth bring forth vegetation, yielding seed after its kind,"[32] "that bread may fortify man's heart."[33] Why then was Demeter worshiped? Even today we still strike fire from flint; how then was Hephaestus the creator of fire?

(11) Whence arose the polytheistic error of the Greeks? God is incorporeal; whence, then, the charges of adultery against

27 Rom. 11.33.
28 Isa. 44.17.
29 At *Cat.* 13.40 Cyril refers to the cult of cat and dog specifically in Egypt.
30 Cf. Juv., *Sat.* 15.7ff.
31 Ps. 103.15.
32 Gen. 1.11 (Sept.).
33 Cf. Ps. 103.15.

their so-called gods? I say nothing about the changes of Zeus into a swan; I am ashamed to speak of his transformation into a bull, for bellowings are unworthy of a god. The god of the Greeks has been proven an adulterer, but they are not ashamed; yet if he is an adulterer, let him not be called a god. They tell of deaths among their gods, and expulsions and thunderbolts. Do you see from what majesty to what depths they have descended? Was it for nothing, then, that the Son of God came down from heaven to heal so great a wound? Was it for nothing that the Son came that the Father might be acknowledged? You realize what it was that moved the Only-begotten to descend from the throne of God's right hand. The Father was being scorned; it behooved the Son to correct the error; it behooved Him, through whom all things were made, to offer them all to the Lord of all. The wound had to be healed; stones were being given the worship due to God: could man's sickness go further?

(12) But apart from these diabolic onslaughts among the pagans, many also of those "Christians" who misappropriate Christ's sweet name have dared in their impiety to separate God from His own creatures.[34] I am referring to the accursed, irreligious brood of heretics, who, while they pretend to be lovers of Christ, hate Him utterly. For he who speaks ill of the Father of Christ is an enemy of the Son. These men have dared to speak of two godheads, one good and one evil. O monstrous blindness! If a Godhead, it is surely good; if it is not good, why is it called Godhead? For, if goodness belongs to God, if loving-kindness, beneficence, omnipotence, are proper to God, then let them choose one of two things: either let them call Him God and then give Him the reality along with the name; or if they must deny Him the reality, let them not bestow the empty title.

(13) Heretics have dared to speak of two Gods and two primal sources of good and evil, respectively. If both were

---

34 In chapters 12-32 Cyril gives a short history of heresy beginning with Simon Magus. The chapters on Mani (21-32) make fascinating reading.

primal and uncreated, both would be equal, both mighty; but
how is it, then, that the light destroys darkness? Further, are
they in the same place, or apart? They cannot be together,
for "what fellowship has light with darkness?"[35] says the
Apostle. But if they are far from each other, then surely each
has its own place. But if they have their own private places,
then it is obvious that we are in the dominion of the One
God and worship one God. So we must conclude, even if we
give assent to the foolish doctrine of these men, that we must
worship one God. Now let us inquire what they say about
the good God. Is He powerful, or does He lack power? If
He possesses power, how did evil originate against His will?
How does the evil substance intrude itself without His consent? For, if He knows but cannot hinder it, they charge
Him with impotence; but if He can and does not hinder it,
they accuse Him of wantonness. See how illogical they are:
at one time they say that the evil God has nothing in common with the good God in the creation of the world, but at
other times that he has a quarter part. They say also that
the good God is the Father of Christ, whom they identify
with our sun. If, then, our universe, on their theory, was
made by the evil God, and the sun is in the universe, how
does the Son of the good God serve against His will in the
realm of the evil God? Even to speak of these blasphemous
doctrines is a sort of defilement, but speak I must, if I am
to save someone perhaps present from falling, through ignorance, into the mire of heresy. I know I have profaned my
own mouth and your ears, but it is for the best. For it is
far better to listen to others exposing these absurdities, if it
saves you from falling victims to them yourselves out of
ignorance. Better to know the quagmire and hate it than
blindly to plunge into it. The history of godless heresies is a
maze; to stray from the one straight way is to find oneself
faced with precipices at every step.

(14) The inventor of all heresy was Simon Magus; that

35 2 Cor. 6.14.

Simon who, in the Acts of the Apostles,[36] thought he could buy with money the gift of the Holy Spirit, that is beyond price, and who heard these words: "Thou hast no part or lot in this matter," . . .;[37] to whom the text applies: "They have gone forth from us, but they were not of us. For if they had been of us, they would surely have continued with us."[38] After his rejection by the Apostles he came to Rome and, winning over a harlot, Helena, he first dared to say with impious mouth that it was he who had appeared as the Father on Mount Sinai; that afterwards among the Jews, not in the flesh, but in semblance, he had appeared as Christ Jesus; and after this as the Holy Spirit, whom Christ had promised to send as the Advocate. So successfully did he impose upon the inhabitants of the imperial city that Claudius set up his statue, writing beneath it in the Roman tongue: SIMONI DEO SANCTO, that is, "To Simon the Holy God."[39]

(15) But when the deception was gaining ground, that noble pair, Peter and Paul, the champions of the Church, arrived on the scene and saved the day; and the supposed god Simon, as he was displaying his powers, they promptly showed to be no better than a dead man. For when Simon publicly announced that he was to be carried up into the heavens, and was actually borne through the air in a demon's chariot, the servants of Christ, falling on their knees and manifesting that concord of which Jesus said: "If two of you shall agree . . . about anything at all for which they ask, it shall be done for them,"[40] they hurled against Simon the weapon of united prayer and struck him down to earth. And no wonder, though it was wonderful. For Peter was there, the keeper of the keys of heaven.[41] No wonder, too, for Paul was there; he who had been "caught up to the third heaven"

---

36 Cf. Acts 8.18, 19.
37 Acts 8.21.
38 1 John 2.19.
39 Justin Martyr (Apol. 2.69, 94) is the authority for this story, apparently confusing Simon with a Sabine divinity, Semo Sancus.
40 Matt. 18.19.
41 Cf. Matt. 16.19.

and "into paradise, and heard secret words that man may not repeat."[42] They brought down that supposed god from the sky to earth, to be led thence to the realms beneath the earth. This man was the first dragon of wickedness; but when one head had been cut off, the stem of wickedness proved to be many-headed.

(16) The Church was ravaged by Cerinthus, Menander, and Carpocrates; also by the Ebionites and by that mouthpiece of impiety, Marcion. For he who preaches different gods, one the good and another the just, contradicts the Son who says: "Just Father."[43] Again, anyone who differentiates between Father and Creator sets himself against the Son when He says: "But if God so clothes the grass which today is alive in the field and tomorrow is thrown into the oven";[44] and "Who makes his sun to rise on the good and the evil, and sends rain on the just and the unjust."[45] There followed Marcion, a deviser of fresh mischief. He was the first to dare to cut out the Old Testament testimonies cited in the New—for these brought him to naught—and to leave the preaching of the word without witness. He fancied he had disposed of God with a pair of scissors, and hoped thus to corrupt the faith of the Church—as if there were no kerygmatic tradition to be reckoned with.[46]

(17) Still another succeeded him, Basilides, of evil name, a formidable customer, a preacher of licentiousness.[47] Valentinus vied in iniquity with his doctrine of thirty deities.[48] The Greeks do not name so many but Valentinus, a Christian in name only, brought the tally up to thirty. According to him Bythos, the Abyss (for it was fitting that he who is the abyss

---

42 2 Cor. 12.2-4.
43 John 17.25.
44 Luke 12.28.
45 Matt. 5.45.
46 Marcion denied the Gospels, except that of St. Luke, which he mutilated. He represented the Old and New Testaments as revelations of two different gods.
47 On Basilides, cf. Irenaeus, *Adv. haer.* 1.24.3ff.
48 On Valentinus, cf. *ibid.* 1.1.1.

of iniquity should base his doctrine on the Abyss), begot
Silence, and of Silence begot the Word. This Bythos was
worse than the Greeks' Zeus who was united to his sister,
for Silence was said to be the daughter of Bythos. There you
have absurdity cloaked with a semblance of Christianity. In a
moment you will be filled with loathing at his impiety. For
he says that there were begotten of this Bythos eight Aeons,
and of these ten more, and of these still another twelve, male
and female. What proof does he offer of these things? Recognize their nonsense from the arguments they invent. Your
proof of the thirty Aeons? It is Holy Writ that Jesus was
baptized when He was thirty years of age.[49] But what argument is there from the thirty years, even if we grant that He
was baptized when He was thirty? Are there five gods because
He broke five loaves among five thousand? Or because He
had twelve disciples, must there be also twelve gods?

(18) This however is mere trifling compared to the rest of
his impieties. For he says that the last of the deities, which
he dares to say is a hermaphrodite, is Wisdom. O what impiety! For Christ is "the wisdom of God,"[50] His Only-begotten
Son. But Valentinus in his doctrine reduced the Wisdom of
God to the female sex, and a thirtieth element, and a last
creation. He adds that Wisdom attempted to look upon the
first God and, not being able to endure His brightness, fell
from the heavens and was cast out of the thirtieth place; then
she groaned and of her groans begot the devil; and she wept
over her fall and by her tears she produced the sea. Is not that
plain impiety? For how is the devil begotten of wisdom?
and wickedness of prudence? or darkness of light? He adds
that the devil begot others who made the world; and that
Christ came to lead men in rebellion against the Creator of
the world.

(19) Now let me tell you what account they give of Christ,
that you may loathe them all the more. For they teach that

49 Cf. Luke 3.23.
50 1 Cor. 1.24.

after Wisdom fell, that the number of the thirty might not be incomplete, the twenty-nine Aeons, each contributing a small element, produced the Christ; and He too, they say, is hermaphrodite. Could anything be more impious? anything more pitiful? I am detailing their error to you that you may loathe them the more. Therefore, shun such impiety; you are not to salute such people, that you may "have no fellowship with the unfruitful works of darkness";[51] do not be over curious nor wish to enter into conversation with them.

(20) Abhor all heretics, but especially him who has the manic name, who arose not long ago under the Emperor Probus. It is a matter of seventy years since the error originated, and there are men living today who saw Mani with their own eyes. But it is not simply because he lived so recently that you are to abhor the scoundrel; no, but for his impious doctrines, this vessel of all uncleanness, this garbage-bin of all the heresies. For, conceiving the ambition to be pre-eminent in evils, combining all into a single heresy brimful of blasphemies and all iniquity, he proceeded to ravage the Church, or rather, those outside the Church, like a lion going about and devouring.[52] Heed not their fair speaking or their mock humility; for they are serpents, a "brood of vipers."[53] Remember that when Judas said, "Hail, Rabbi,"[54] the salutation was an act of betrayal. Don't be deceived by the kiss, but beware of the venom.

(21) To avoid giving the impression of groundless accusations, allow me to digress in order to explain who this Mani is and to give an account, however incomplete, of his doctrines. For all time could not adequately describe all his foul teaching. You must store up in your memory, to be a help at need, the instruction imparted to former classes and now to be repeated to you; so what I shall say by way of

---

51 Eph. 5.11.
52 Cf. 1 Peter 5.8.
53 Matt. 3.7.
54 Matt. 26.49.

instructing the uninformed will serve also to refresh the memory of the instructed. Mani is not of Christian origin, God forbid! Nor was he, like Simon Magus, cast out of the Church, neither he, nor the teachers before him; for he is a plagiarist of bad authors, and makes their wickedness his own. But how and in what manner, you must hear.

(22) There was in Egypt a certain Scythianus, a Saracen by race, having nothing in common with Judaism or Christianity. Having settled at Alexandria, where he emulated the life of Aristotle, Scythianus composed four books. One he styled a *Gospel,* although, in spite of the title, it did not contain the acts of Christ; another he called *Chapters,* and a third *Mysteries,* and a fourth still being hawked about, the *Treasure.* This man had a disciple named Terebinthus. Scythianus had determined to come into Judaea and to ravage the region, but the Lord, causing his death by disease, put an end to the plague.

(23) Terebinthus, his disciple in wickedness, being the heir of his gold, his books, and his heresy, came to Palestine, but, on being recognized and condemned in Judaea, he decided to cross over into Persia. To prevent his name betraying him there too, he called himself Buddas. But in Persia also he found adversaries in the ministers of Mithras. Worsted in many arguments and discussions, and at last hard pressed, he sought refuge with a certain widow. Going up on to the roof of her house, and calling upon the demons of the air, which even to this day the Manichaeans invoke over their abominable ceremony of the fig, he was struck by God, cast down from the roof, and gave up the ghost. Thus was the second wild beast cut off.

(24) But the books, the records of his impiety, remained, and the widow became heir to these and to his money. Without relatives and being, indeed, alone in the world, she determined to purchase a boy named Cubricus with the money. Adopting him, she instructed him as a son in the lore of the

Persians and thus sharpened a deadly weapon against mankind. Cubricus, the poor house slave, made a brilliant debut in learned circles. Upon the widow's death he inherited her property, including the library. Then, to escape the reproach of his slave name, Cubricus, he changed it to Mani, which in Persian means "discourse." For, since he had some reputation as a dialectician, he styled himself Mani, as one might say, "prince of talkers." But although his efforts thus secured for him a great name (at least in Persian), Providence so contrived it that he unwittingly pronounced sentence upon himself; for his fancy Persian name proclaimed him, in Greek-speaking countries, a maniac.

(25) He dared to say that he was the Advocate, though it is written: "Whoever blasphemes against the Holy Spirit never has forgiveness."[55] He blasphemed, then, in saying he was the Holy Spirit. Let the man who associates with such heretics see what company he is joining. The servant boy shook the world, since, "Under three things the earth trembles, yes, and under a fourth it cannot bear up: under a slave, when be becomes king . . ."[56] Once launched on a public career, Mani pretended to superhuman powers. The son of the king of the Persians was sick, and throngs of physicians were in constant attendance; but Mani promised, as a man of piety, to restore him by prayer. The physicians departed, and with them the life of the child. The impious character of the man was detected, and our fine philosopher was put in chains and cast into prison, not for reproving the king concerning truth, not for shattering the idols, but for the lying promise to save the king's son, or rather, if the truth be told, for committing murder. For, when the child might have been saved by medical treatment, be became his murderer by sending away the physicians, since by denying him medical care, he caused his death.

(26) In this catalog of crimes remember, first, his blas-

55 Mark 3.29.
56 Prov. 30.21, 22.

phemy; second, his slavery—not that slavery is a disgrace, but it is wicked for a slave to pretend he is free; third, his lying promise; fourth, the child's murder; fifth, the disgrace of imprisonment. Beside the disgrace, there was the flight from the prison. For the self-styled "Advocate" and champion of the truth ran away. He was no successor of Jesus, who went eagerly to the cross, but the very opposite, a runaway. Then, the king of the Persians ordered the guards of the prison to be executed. Mani, by his arrogance, was responsible for the death of the child and, by his flight, for the death of his jailers. Ought an accessory to murder be worshiped? Should he not have imitated Jesus and said: "If, therefore, you seek me, let these go their way."[57] Should he not have said, like Jona: "Pick me up and throw me into the sea," for "it is because of me that this violent storm has come upon you."[58]

(27) Escaping from prison, Mani went to Mesopotamia. But there, he encountered a shield of justice in the person of Bishop Archelaus, who convened a gathering of Gentiles and arraigned him before a jury of philosophers, for he saw that the verdict of Christians might savor of bias. "Tell us what you preach," said Archelaus to Mani. But he whose "throat was an open grave,"[59] began first with blasphemy against the Creator, saying: "The God of the Old Testament is the inventor of evils, saying of Himself: I, God, am 'a consuming fire.' "[60] Then the wise Archelaus refuted the blasphemy with these words: "If the God of the Old Testament, as you say, calls Himself fire, whose Son is He who says: 'I have come to cast fire upon the earth'?[61] If you find fault with Him who says: 'The Lord killeth and maketh alive,'[62] why do you honor Peter, who raised up Tabitha, but visited death upon

---

57 John 18.8.
58 Jona 1.12.
59 Cf. Ps. 5.10.
60 Deut. 4.24.
61 Luke 12.49.
62 1 Kings 2.6.

Sapphira?[63] If, again, you find fault because He invented fire, why do you not find fault with Him who says: 'Depart from me . . . into the everlasting fire'?[64] If you find fault with Him who says: 'I (am God who) make well-being and create woe,'[65] explain how Jesus says: 'I have come to bring a sword, not peace.'[66] Since both speak alike, take your choice: either both are good because of their agreement, or if Jesus, in saying these things, is free from blame, why do you censure Him who in the Old Testament speaks in like manner?''

(28) Mani returned to the charge, saying: "What sort of God is it who causes blindness? For it is Paul who says: 'In their case the god of this world has blinded their unbelieving minds, that they should not see the light of the gospel.' ''[67] But Archelaus made a good rejoinder: "Go back a little, to the verse, 'And if our gospel also is veiled, it is veiled only to those who are perishing.'[68] It is in the case of the perishing, you see, that it is veiled. For holy things must not be given to dogs.[69] Besides, is it only the God of the Old Testament who blinded the minds of unbelievers? Did not Jesus Himself say: 'This is why I speak to them in parables, in order that seeing they may not see'?[70] Was it out of hate that He wished them not to see? Or because of the impropriety, when they had closed their own eyes?[71] For where there is deliberate wickedness, there is also a withholding of grace: 'For to everyone that hath shall be given'; 'but from him who does not have, even that which he seems to have shall be taken away.' ''[72]

---

63 Cf. Acts 9.36; 5.10.
64 Matt. 25.41.
65 Isa. 45.7.
66 Matt. 10.34.
67 2 Cor. 4.4.
68 *Ibid.* 4.3.
69 Cf. Matt. 7.6.
70 Cf. Matt. 13.13; Luke 13.10.
71 Matt. 13.15.
72 Matt. 25.29.

(29) Possibly we should take the passage, as some laudably interpret it, thus: Though He has blinded their unbelieving minds, He has blinded them for a good purpose, that they may look to what is good. Paul did not say: He blinded their soul, but "their unbelieving minds." The verse will then mean: "Blind the lustful thoughts of the lustful man, and he is saved; blind the tendency of the robber to plunder and steal, and the man is saved." You will not understand it so? Then there is yet another interpretation. The sun blinds people suffering from poor sight, and those with weak eyes are distressed and blinded by its light; not that the sun of its nature is blinding, but because the human eye cannot look upon it. Similarly, unbelievers, whose sickness is of the heart, cannot look upon the splendor of the Godhead. He did not say: He blinded their minds that they should not hear the gospel, but "that they should not see the light of the glory of the gospel of our Lord Jesus Christ."[73] For all may hear the Gospel, but the glory of the Gospel is reserved for those only who are truly Christ's. We find the Lord speaking in parables to them who could not hear, but to His disciples in private He explained the parables. What the enlightened see as a radiant glory dazzles and blinds the unbeliever.

These mysteries which the Church now explains to you who are passing from the ranks of the catechumens are not customarily explained to heathens. For, not before heathens do we declare the mysteries concerning Father, Son, and Holy Spirit, nor do we speak openly of the mysteries before the catechumens. But many things we often speak of covertly, that the faithful who know may understand, but those who do not know may suffer no harm.

(30) By these and many similar arguments was the serpent worsted. Such were the contests in which Archelaus wrestled with Mani and threw him. Our prison-breaker and runaway

---

73 Cf. 2 Cor. 4.4.

now took to his heels again and, giving his adversary the slip, came to an obscure hamlet, like the serpent in paradise when he left Adam and approached Eve. But the good shepherd, Archelaus, in his provident care for his flock, when he heard of his flight, at once started in hot pursuit of the wolf. Catching sight of his opponent, Mani in a flash was up and off once more—but on his last flight from justice. For the royal guards, raising a hue and cry, caught the runaway, and he met at their hands the fate which by rights should have been his at Archelaus' tribunal. Mani, the venerable object of his disciples' worship, was seized and conducted to the king. The king upbraided him for lying and running away, mocked his slavish condition, exacted vengeance for the murder of his son, and held him guilty of the blood of the jailers. He ordered Mani to be flayed in the Persian fashion. While the rest of his body was given over to be food for wild beasts, his skin, the tenement of that vile spirit, was hung up before the gates like a sack. He who called himself the "Advocate" and professed a knowledge of the future, did not foresee his own flight and capture.

(31) Mani had three disciples, Thomas and Baddas and Hermas. Let none read the gospel according to Thomas, for it is the work, not of one of the twelve Apostles, but of one of Mani's three wicked disciples. Let no man attach himself to the soul-destroying Manichaeans, who affect the austerity of fasting on bran and water, and, while they malign the Creator of meats, gorge themselves with the daintiest; who teach that he who plucks this or that plant is changed into it. If the man who cuts herbs or any vegetable is transformed into the same, into how many different plants will farmers and gardeners be changed? We daily see the gardener using his sickle on a great variety of such plants; into which will he be transformed? The doctrine is obviously ludicrous, shameful, self-condemned. Suppose a shepherd successively sacrifices a sheep and kills a wolf; into which, tell me, is he changed?

Many men have netted fish and snared birds; into which of
their victims are the hunters changed?

(32) Manichaeans, those scions of sloth, who will not work
themselves yet eat up the fruits of those who do, receive with
smiling countenances those who bring them food, and repay
them with curses instead of blessings. For when some simple
soul offers them anything, the Manichaean says: "Stand off
a little, and I will bless you." Then, taking the loaf in his
hands (as converts from the sect have confessed), he says: "I
did not make you"; next, he heaps maledictions upon the
Most High, curses the Maker of the bread, and finally eats it.
If you hate the food, why did you look with smiling countenance upon the bearer? If you are grateful, why do you
blaspheme God, who made and created it? Next, "I did not
sow you," he says, "may he be sown who sowed you! I did
not reap you with sickle; let him be reaped who reaped you!
I did not bake you; may he be baked who baked you!" A
fine thanksgiving indeed!

(33) These are great evils, but small compared with the
rest. I dare not describe their baptism before men and women.
I do not dare say in what they dip the fig they give to their
wretched communicants. I can indicate it only indirectly; let
men think of the delusive dreams of the night, and women
of the menses. In truth, we defile our lips in speaking of
such things. Are Greeks more detestable than they? Are
Samaritans more impious? Are Jews more profane? Are
fornicators more impure? For the fornicator satisfies his
lust in an hour, but soon condemns his deeds, realizing that,
as one defiled, he is in need of washing, and he acknowledges
the foulness of his action. But the Manichaean puts his
macabre offering in the middle of the "altar," and defiles
his lips and his tongue. Who would accept instruction from
such lips? Who would, under any circumstances, kiss him on
meeting? Quite apart from the sin against religion that that
would involve, will you not shun the defilement and men

worse than profligates, and more abominable than any prostitute?

(34) This is the Church's traditional instruction; she touches the mire to save you from defilement. She speaks of the wounds to save you from actual wounds. For you the knowledge is enough; avoid the experience. God thunders and we all tremble, but they blaspheme. God hurls lightnings and we fall to the ground, but they utter maledictions about heaven. Jesus says of His Father: "Who makes his sun to rise on the good and the evil, and sends rain on the just and unjust."[74] But they say the rains arise from erotic passion; and they dare to say that there is a beautiful maiden with a beautiful youth in heaven; and in the way of the camel and the wolf, they have seasons of base desire, so that, in the winter time, the youth rushes furiously after the maiden, while she flees; he pursues her and, in pursuing her, sweats, and from his sweat comes the rain. These things are written in the books of the Manichaeans. We have read them there ourselves, not believing those who told us of them; for your safety we have made a thorough examination of their pernicious doctrines.

(35) May the Lord save you from such error, and may a hatred of the serpent be granted you that, as they lie in wait for your heel, you may crush their head.[75] Be mindful of my words. What agreement can there be between your affairs and theirs? What fellowship has light with darkness,[76] or the majesty of the Church with the abomination of the Manichaeans? Here is order, here is discipline, here is majesty, here is purity, here it is a sin to look upon a woman with lust;[77] here is the high holiness of marriage, here steadfast continence, and the angelic dignity of virginity; here men give thanks when they eat, showing courtesy to the Creator

---

74 Cf. Matt. 5.45.
75 Cf. Gen. 3.15.
76 Cf. 2 Cor. 6.14.
77 Cf. Matt. 5.28.

of all things. Here the Father of Christ is worshiped; here are inculcated fear and trembling of Him who sends the rain; here we sing the praises of Him who causes thunder and lightning.

(36) Abide with the flock; flee from the wolves; depart not from the Church. Shun too those suspected of such things, and unless you are satisfied of their lasting repentance, do not be hasty in trusting yourself to them. The truth of the Unity of God has been delivered to you; distinguish the pastures of doctrines one from another. Be a sound banker, holding fast that which is good, and abstaining from every kind of evil.[78] If at any time you were such as they, now that you have acknowledged your error, abhor it. There is a way of salvation if you spew forth the vomit, if you hate it from the heart, if you turn away from them, not only with your lips, but with your soul; if you worship the Father of Christ, the God of the Law and the Prophets; if you acknowledge the Good and the Just to be one and the same God. May He keep all of you, protecting you from falling and stumbling, firm in the Faith, in Christ Jesus our Lord, to whom be glory forever and ever. Amen.

---

78 Cf. 1 Thess. 5.21, 22.

CATECHESIS VII

On the Father

"For this reason I bend my knees to the Father . . . from whom all fatherhood in heaven and on earth receives its name."[1]

(1) On the Unity of God we spoke at sufficient length yesterday; I mean sufficient, not according to the dignity of the subject (for that is quite impossible for human nature), but as far as it has been granted to our weakness. I detailed the deviations in the manifold errors of the impious heretics. Shaking off their filth and their soul-poisoning doctrines, yet remembering what concerns them (not that we may suffer harm, but that we may loathe them all the more), let us now return to ourselves and take up the saving doctrines of the true faith, joining to the dignity of the Unity of God that of the Fatherhood, and believing in One God, Father. For not only should we believe in One God, but also devoutly accept that He is Father of the Only-begotten, our Lord Jesus Christ.

(2) For thus our thought will rise to a higher plane than that of the Jews, who, while they teach that God is One (though they have often denied this by idolatry), do not admit that He is also the Father of our Lord Jesus Christ. In this they run counter to their own prophets, according to the Scriptures: "The Lord said to me, 'You are my son; this day I have begotten you.' "[2] Even to this day, they rage and

---

1 Eph. 3.14, 15.
2 Ps. 2.7.

170

"conspire together against the Lord and against his anointed,"[3] presuming that they can gain the friendship of the Father without devotion to the Son, not knowing that "no one comes to the Father but through the Son,"[4] who says: "I am the door,"[5] and "I am the way."[6] How will he, who rejects the Way that leads to the Father and denies the Door, be deemed worthy of entrance unto God? They contradict, too, the words of the eighty-eighth Psalm: "He shall say of me, 'You are my father, my God, the Rock, my savior.' And I will make him the first-born, highest of the kings of the earth."[7] For, if they argue that these words were spoken concerning David or Solomon or any of their successors, let them show how the throne of him they deem to be the object of the prophecy is "as the days of heaven,"[8] and "like the sun before me; like the moon, which remains forever."[9] How is it they are not put to shame by that which is written: "from the womb before the daystar I have begotten you";[10] and: "He shall endure as long as the sun, and like the moon through all generations"?[11] To refer these things to a man is to show a complete and utter lack of sense.

(3) But let the Jews, since they will it thus, suffer their wonted sickness of unbelief in the case of these and similar statements of Scripture. For our part, we receive the devout teaching of the faith, worshiping one God, the Father of Christ. For to rob Him, who grants all the prerogative of parents,[12] of like dignity, would be impious. We believe in One God, the Father, in order that even before our fuller discussion of the teachings concerning Christ, the belief in

---

3 Ps. 2.2.
4 John 14.6.
5 John 10.9.
6 John 14.6.
7 Ps. 88.27, 28.
8 Ibid. 88.30.
9 Ibid. 88.37, 38.
10 Cf. Ps. 109.3.
11 Cf. Ps. 71.5.
12 Cf. Isa. 66.9.

the Only-begotten may be fixed in the soul of the hearers, to remain quite intact through the intervening discourses on the Father.

(4) The very mention of the name of the Father suggests the thought of the Son, just as, in turn, the mention of Son implies the thought of the Father. For, if He is a Father, He is surely Father of a Son. Thus we say: "In One God, Father Almighty, Creator of heaven and earth, of all things visible and invisible"; and add: "And in one Lord Jesus Christ."[13] That no one may irreverently suppose that the Only-begotten is second in rank to heaven and earth, before naming these we named God Father, that the thought of Father might suggest the Son; for between Son and Father there is no being whatsoever.[14]

(5) Though God, improperly speaking, is Father of many things, by nature and in truth He is Father of One only, the Only-begotten Son, our Lord Jesus Christ. He did not attain Fatherhood in the course of time,[15] but He is eternally Father of the Only-begotten. Not that He was Sonless before and afterwards became a Father by a change of purpose, but before all substance and all intelligence, before times and all the ages, God has the prerogative of Father, exalting Himself in this dignity before all others. He did not become a Father by passion, or from union, or in ignorance,[16] or by emanation, or diminution or alteration; for "every good gift and every perfect gift is from above, coming down from the Father of Lights, with whom there is no change, nor shadow of alteration."[17] A perfect Father, He begot a perfect Son, delivering all things to Him whom He begot; for He

---

13 From the Creed.
14 Perhaps aimed at the Gnostics and Valentinians. See *Cat.* 11.7-8 for a further development of this idea.
15 Cyril is refuting Arius, quoted by Athanasius as saying: *non semper deus fuit pater.*
16 Men in generating are ignorant of the issue. They beget not whom they will, but whom God grants. To say that God does not know whom He begets is impiety.
17 James 1.17.

says: "All things have been delivered to me by my Father."[18] And the Father is honored by the Only-begotten: "But I honor my Father,"[19] says the Son; and again: "As I also have kept my Father's commandments, and abide in his love."[20] Therefore we too say with the Apostle: "Blessed be the God and Father of our Lord Jesus Christ, the Father of mercies, and the God of all comfort";[21] and: "I bend my knees to the Father . . . from whom all fatherhood in heaven and on earth receives its name,"[22] glorifying Him with the Only-begotten; for he who denies the Father, denies the Son also, and again: "He who confesses the Son, has the Father also,"[23] knowing that "the Lord Jesus Christ is in the glory of God the Father."[24]

(6) Therefore we worship the Father of Christ, the Creator of heaven and earth, the God of Abraham, Isaac, and Jacob, in whose honor the former temple also, opposite us here,[25] was built. For we will not endure the heretics who sever the Old Testament from the New,[26] but we will heed Christ who says of the temple: "Did you not know, that I must be about my Father's business?"[27] and again: "Take these things hence, and do not make the house of my Father a house of business."[28] By these words He clearly confessed that the former temple in Jerusalem was the house of His Father. But if any man, because of unbelief, desires still further proofs that the Father of Christ is one with the Creator of the world, let him hearken to Him saying: "Are not two sparrows sold for a farthing? And yet not one of them will fall to the

18 Matt. 11.27.
19 John 8.49.
20 John 15.10.
21 2 Cor. 1.3.
22 Eph. 3.14, 15.
23 Cf. 1 John 2.22, 23.
24 Phil. 2.11.
25 There were still extensive remains of the ruined temple.
26 He refers especially to Marcion, to the Gnostics, and to the Valentinians.
27 Luke 2.49.
28 John 2.16.

ground without my Father,"[29] who is in heaven; and: "Look at the birds of the air: they do not sow, or reap, or gather into barns; yet your heavenly Father feeds them";[30] and also: "My Father works even until now, and I work."[31]

(7) That no one, out of simplicity or perverseness, may suppose that Christ is equal in honor to just men, because He says: "I ascend to my Father and to your Father,"[32] it may be well to say by way of preface that though the name of Father is one, the power of His operation is manifold. Christ, recognizing this very thing, was careful to say: "I go to my Father, and your Father"; He did not say: "to our Father," but, making a distinction, He first said what was proper to Himself: "to my Father," that is, by nature; then He added: "and your Father," that is, by adoption. For though we have been granted the privilege of saying in our prayers: "Our Father who art in heaven,"[33] this proceeds from His loving-kindness. For we do not call Him Father as though we were natural sons of our Father who is in heaven; but, having been translated from servitude to adoption as sons, by the grace of the Father, through Son and Holy Spirit, by His ineffable loving-kindness we are privileged to speak thus.

(8) If any man wishes to learn how we call God Father, let him listen to that excellent tutor Moses: "Is not he your Father who creates you? Has he not made you and established you?"[34] And the Prophet Isaia: "Yet, O Lord, you are our father; we are the clay . . . we are all the work of your hands."[35] For the inspired utterance of the Prophet has made it most clear that it is not according to nature, but by grace and by adoption that we call Him Father.

(9) To perceive more exactly that it is not the natural

---

29 Matt. 10.29.
30 Matt. 6.26.
31 John 5.17.
32 John 20.17.
33 Matt. 6.9.
34 Deut. 32.6.
35 Isa. 64.7.

father only that is called father in the Holy Scriptures, listen to the words of Paul: "For although you have ten thousand tutors in Christ, yet you have not many fathers. For in Christ Jesus, through the gospel, did I beget you."[36] For it was not because of fleshly procreation, but because of teaching and spiritual generation that Paul was the father of the Corinthians. Listen also to Job: "I was a father to the needy."[37] For he called himself father, not for having begotten them, but for caring for them. The Only-begotten Son of God, when He was nailed to the cross in the flesh at the time of His crucifixion, seeing Mary, His own mother according to the flesh, and John, the most beloved disciple, said to him: "Behold thy mother";[38] and to Mary: "Behold thy son,"[39] teaching her the affection due to him thereafter, and indirectly explaining what is said in Luke: "And his father and mother were marvelling";[40] this text the heretics seize upon,[41] saying that He was begotten of a man and a woman. Just as Mary is called the mother of John because of her parental affection for him, not because of having begotten him, so Joseph was called the father of Christ, not by reason of begetting Him (for "he did not know her till she brought forth her firstborn son,"[42] according to the Gospel), but by reason of the care bestowed on His nurture.

(10) Consider what has been said by way of digression as a reminder. But let me add another testimony that God is called the Father of men in an improper sense. When in Isaia God is addressed: "For you are our father, and Abraham has not known us";[43] and: "Sara has not given us birth,"[44] must we inquire still further on this point? But if the Psalmist

36 1 Cor. 4.15.
37 Job 29.16.
38 John 19.27.
39 *Ibid.* 19.26.
40 Luke 2.33.
41 Sc. Carpocrates, Cerinthus, Ebion. .
42 Matt. 1.25.
43 Cf. Isa. 63.16.
44 Cf. Isa. 51.2.

says: "They shall be troubled at his presence, the father of orphans and the defender of widows,"[45] is it not manifest that when God is called the father of the orphans who recently lost their own fathers, He is so named, not for having begotten them of Himself, but for caring and shielding them? He is Father of man, then, in an improper sense. But of Christ only is God Father by nature and not by adoption;[46] and He is Father of men in time, but of Christ before all time, as He Himself says: "And now do thou, Father, glorify me with the glory that I had before the world existed."[47]

(11) We believe, then, in One God, Father, the Unsearchable and Ineffable: whom no man has seen and whom the Only-begotten alone has declared.[48] For He "who is from God, he has seen God,"[49] whose face the angels in heaven see always;[50] but they see each according to the measure of his own rank. The sheer vision of the Father is reserved in its perfection for the Son with the Holy Spirit.

(12) At this point in my discourse I am reminded of the passages mentioned a short time ago, in which God was called the Father of men, and I am greatly amazed at the insensibility of men. For God, with ineffable loving-kindness, deigned to be called Father of men—He in heaven, they upon earth, He the Maker of eternity, they living in time, He, who holds the earth "in the hollow of his hand,"[51] they upon the earth "like grasshoppers."[52] Yet man, forsaking his heavenly Father, said to the stock: "You are my father";[53] and to the stone: "You gave me birth."[54] This is why, I think, the Psalm says to mankind: "Forget your people and your

---

45 Cf. Ps. 67.5, 6.
46 Referring especially to the Arians, who maintain Christ was created in time and was son by adoption and grace.
47 John 17.5.
48 Cf. John 1.18.
49 John 6.46.
50 Cf. Matt. 18.10.
51 Cf. Isa. 40.12.
52 *Ibid.* 40.22.
53 Jer. 2.27.
54 *Ibid.*

father's house,"[55] that is, the father you have chosen and drawn to yourself for your own destruction.

(13) Some have chosen for their father not only stocks and stones, but even Satan himself, the destroyer of souls. To them the Lord in reproof said: "You are doing the work of your father";[56] since Satan is the father of men not by nature, but by deceit. For just as Paul for his devout teaching was called father of the Corinthians, so too the devil is called father of those who deliberately "keep pace with him."[57] For we will not tolerate those who perversely interpret the text: "In this we know the children of God and the children of the devil,"[58] as though there were by nature among men some to be saved and some to be lost. For it is not of necessity but of choice that we come into such holy sonship; nor was it by nature that the traitor Judas was the son of the devil and perdition: otherwise, he would not at first cast out devils in Christ's name; for Satan does not cast out Satan;[59] nor again, would Paul have been transformed from a persecutor to a herald of the Gospel. But the adoption is voluntary, as John says: "But to as many as received him, he gave power of becoming sons of God, to those who believe in his name."[60] For not before faith, but by faith, they were deemed worthy, of their own choice, to be made sons of God.

(14) Recognizing this, therefore, let us live spiritually, that we may be deemed worthy of God's adoption: "For whoever are led by the Spirit of God, they are the sons of God."[61] For it will profit us nothing to have gained the title of Christians unless the works also follow, else it may be said to us also: If you were the children of Abraham, you would do the works of Abraham.[62] For, if we invoke as Father Him who, without

---

55 Ps. 44.11.
56 John 8.41.
57 Ps. 49.18.
58 Cf. 1 John 3.10.
59 Cf. Mark 3.23.
60 John 1.12.
61 Rom. 8.14.
62 Cf. John 8.39.

respect of persons, judges according to each one's work, let us conduct ourselves with fear during our sojourn here,[63] loving "not the world or the things that are in the world"; for, "if anyone loves the world, the love of the Father is not in him."[64] Therefore, my beloved children, let us offer glory to our Father in heaven by our works, that men may see our good works, and glorify our Father in heaven.[65] Let us cast all our care upon Him, "for our Father knows what we need."[66]

(15) But while honoring our heavenly Father, let us also honor the "fathers of our flesh,"[67] since the Lord in the Law and the Prophets has clearly laid this down, saying: "Honor your mother and your father, that it may be well with you, and that you may have a long life in the land."[68] Let those present who have mothers and fathers give heed to this command. "Children, obey your parents in all things, for this is pleasing to the Lord."[69] For our Lord did not say: "He who loves father or mother is not worthy of me,"[70] else what was well written you might interpret falsely out of ignorance, but He added [loves father or mother] "more than me."[71] When our fathers on earth are contrary-minded to our Father in heaven, then we must obey His word; but when, though they hinder not our piety, we are carried away by ingratitude and, forgetting their benefits to us, despise them, then that saying will hold true: "whoever curses his father or mother shall be put to death."[72]

(16) Among Christians the first virtue of piety is to honor one's parents, to requite the toils of those who begot us, and with all our power to provide for their comfort (for though

---

63 Cf. 1 Peter 1.17.
64 1 John 2.15.
65 Cf. Matt. 5.16.
66 Cf. 1 Peter 5.7; Matt. 6.8.
67 Heb. 12.9.
68 Cf. Exod. 20.12; Deut. 5.16.
69 Col. 3.20.
70 Matt. 10.37.
71 Ibid.
72 Exod. 21.17.

we make the greatest possible return, we will never be able to repay them for the gift of life); that enjoying the ease we afford them, they may confirm us in those blessings which Jacob the supplanter prudently seized; and that our heavenly Father, approving our good purpose, may deem us worthy, with the just, to "shine forth like the sun in the kingdom of our Father,"[73] to whom be glory with the Only-begotten, our Savior Jesus Christ, and with the Holy and life-giving Spirit, now and always and for all eternity. Amen.

---

73 Matt. 13.43.

CATECHESIS VIII

On the Omnipotence of God

"The great God and the mighty Lord, great in counsel, and mighty in works, the Lord omnipotent, of great name...."[1]

(1) By belief "in One God," we cut off all polytheistic error, arming ourselves against the Greeks and all opposition on the part of heretics. By adding "in One God, Father," we combat the Jews who deny the Only-begotten Son of God. For, as I said yesterday, even before explaining the doctrines concerning our Lord Jesus Christ, by the very mention of "Father" we have already implied that He is Father of a Son; that just as we understand that God is, so we may understand that He has a Son. Now to these attributes we add that He is also "Almighty," and this we assert because of Greeks and Jews and all heretics.

(2) Of the Greeks, some have said that God is the soul of the world; others that His power does not extend to earth, but only to heaven. Some, laboring under a similar delusion, pervert the text: "And your faithfulness to the skies,"[2] and have dared to circumscribe the providence of God by skies and heaven and to alienate from God the things on earth, forgetting the Psalm which says: "If I go up to the heavens, you are there; if I sink to the nether world, you are present there."[3] For, if there is nothing higher than heaven, and

1 Jer. 32.18, 19 (Sept.).
2 Ps. 107.5.
3 Ps. 138.8.

the nether world is deeper than the earth, He who rules the lower regions reaches the earth also.

(3) But heretics,[4] as we said before, do not acknowledge One Almighty God. For He is Almighty who rules over all things and exercises authority over all. They who say that there is one Lord of the soul and another of the body affirm that neither of these is perfect, in that each lacks what the other has. For how is he almighty who has power over the soul, but not over the body? And how is he almighty who has dominion over bodies, but not over spirits? But the Lord confutes them when He says: "Rather be afraid of him who is able to destroy both soul and body in hell."[5] For, unless he has power over both, how does the Father of our Lord Jesus Christ subject both to punishment? For how will He be able to take a body that belongs to another and cast it into hell, "unless He first binds the strong man"[6] and plunders his goods?

(4) The Holy Scripture and the true doctrine know but One God, who has dominion over all things, yet tolerates many things because He so wills. For He rules over idolaters, but out of forbearance endures them; He rules over the heretics also, who reject Him, but puts up with them patiently. He rules over the devil, but tolerates him in His long-suffering; but it is not for want of power, as though defeated, that he endures him, for "he is the beginning of the Lord's creation, made to be mocked,"[7] not by Himself, for that would be beneath His dignity, but "by the angels"[8] who were made by Him. He has allowed the devil to live for two reasons, that he might suffer greater shame by defeat, and that men might be crowned with victory. O all-wise providence of God which takes wicked purpose as a basis of salvation for

---

4 Here Cyril is refuting the Manichaeans and those who followed their errors.
5 Matt. 10.28.
6 Matt. 12.29.
7 Job 40.19 (Sept.).
8 *Ibid.*

the faithful! For He made use of the unbrotherly purpose of Joseph's brethren to carry out His own dispensation, and allowed them to sell their brother out of hatred, to take thence the occasion to make him king whom He wished. In like fashion He has permitted the devil to wrestle with men, that they who conquer him might be crowned, and after the victory, the devil might suffer greater shame for being defeated by inferiors, while men might gain great glory for having triumphed over him who was once an archangel.

(5) Nothing, therefore, is excluded from the dominion of God, for Scripture says of Him: "All things serve you."[9] All things indeed are His servants; but one, His Only Son, and one, His Holy Spirit, are outside all these; and all things that serve Him serve their Lord through the One Son in the Holy Spirit. God, then, rules over all things, and in His forbearance endures even murderers and robbers and fornicators, having determined a fixed time for requiting each, that they who, granted a long reprieve, remain impenitent may suffer the greater condemnation. There are kings of men who reign upon the earth, yet not without power from on high. This, of old, Nabuchodonosor knew from experience when he said: "His kingdom is an everlasting kingdom, and his dominion endures through all generations."[10]

(6) Riches, gold and silver, are not the devil's, as some think, for "the whole world of riches is for the faithful man, but for the unfaithful not a farthing."[11] But nothing is more faithless than the devil. God through the Prophet says plainly: "Mine is the silver and mine the gold."[12] Only use it well and there is nothing blameworthy in silver; but when you abuse a good thing and are then unwilling to blame your own conduct, you impiously put the blame on the Creator. One can even be justified by money. "I was hungry, and

---

9 Ps. 118.91.
10 Dan. 3.100.
11 Prov. 17.6 (Sept.).
12 Ag. 2.9.

you gave me to eat,"[13]—undoubtedly by the use of money; "I was naked and you covered me,"[14]—assuredly by the use of money. Consider too that money can be a door to the heavenly kingdom. "Sell," He says, "what thou hast, and give to the poor, and thou shalt have treasure in heaven."[15]

(7) I have said these things because of the heretics who condemn possessions and money and men's bodies. For I wish you neither to be the slaves of riches, nor yet to regard as enemies the things God has given to serve you. Therefore, never say that money is the devil's. For though he says: "To thee will I give all . . . for to me they have been delivered,"[16] one can reject his words, for one need not believe a liar. But perhaps, compelled by the power of Christ's presence, he spoke the truth. For he did not say: "To thee will I give all because they are mine," but because "to me they have been delivered." He did not seize the dominion of them, but he confessed that they had been committed to him, and their disposition, up to a certain point, entrusted to him. Let the exegetes ponder at a suitable time whether his statement is true or false.

(8) There is, then, One God the Father, the Almighty, whom the heretics have dared to flout; for they have dared to flout the Lord Sabaoth, "with his throne upon the cherubim."[17] They have dared to blaspheme the Lord Adonai; they have dared to blaspheme Him who is in the prophets the Almighty God. But for your part worship One, the Almighty God, the Father of our Lord Jesus Christ, shunning polytheism and all heresy, saying with Job: "I will call upon the Lord Almighty, who does great things and inscrutable, glorious things and marvelous without number";[18]

---

13 Matt. 25.35.
14 *Ibid.* 25.36.
15 Matt. 19.21.
16 Luke 4.6.
17 Cf. Ps. 79.2.
18 Job 5.8, 9 (Sept.).

and: "For all these things there is honor from the Almighty,"[19]
to whom be glory now and forever and ever. Amen.

---

19 Cf. Job 37.22, 23 (Sept.).

CATECHESIS IX

On God the Creator

"Who is this that conceals counsel from me, and keeps words in his heart and thinks to hide from me?"[1]

(1) It is impossible to see God with the eyes of the flesh, for what is incorporeal cannot fall under bodily sight. The Only-begotten Son of God bears witness to this when He says: "No one has at any time seen God."[2] One might gather from a passage in Ezechiel that Ezechiel saw him, but what does Scripture actually say? He saw "the likeness of the glory of the Lord";[3] not the Lord Himself, but the "likeness of His glory" merely, not the glory itself as it really is. Yet, on beholding the likeness of His glory, and not the glory itself, he fell to the earth in fear. But if the vision of the likeness of the glory inspired the prophets with fear and trepidation, any man attempting to look upon God Himself would surely lose his life, according to the text: "No man shall see my face and live."[4] Therefore, God in His great loving-kindness has spread the heavens as a veil before His own Godhead, that we might not perish. This assertion is not mine, but the prophet's: "If you shall rend the heavens, trembling will seize the mountains before you, and they shall melt away."[5] But why wonder that Ezechiel fell down on seeing the likeness of the glory? For when Gabriel, the

1 Job 38.2, 3 (Sept.).
2 John 1.18.
3 Ezech. 1.28.
4 Exod. 33.20 (Sept.).
5 Isa. 63.19.

185

servant of God, appeared to Daniel,[6] Daniel was struck with fear at once and fell on his face; and the prophet did not dare to speak until the angel had taken a form like a man. Now, if the sight of Gabriel caused the prophet to tremble, if God had been seen as He is, would not all have perished?

(2) It is impossible, then, to perceive the Divine Nature with bodily eyes; but from His divine works we may gain some impression of His power, according to the words of Solomon: "For from the greatness and the beauty of created things their original author, by analogy, is seen."[7] Now he did not say that from created things the creator is seen, but he added "by analogy." For so much the greater does God seem to each man, as the man achieves a loftier concept of creatures; and when by deeper contemplation he has elevated his heart, he gains a loftier concept of God.

(3) Learn, then, that it is impossible to comprehend God's nature. The three children in the fiery furnace, singing the praises of God, say: "Blessed are you who look into the depths from your throne upon the cherubim."[8] Tell me what is the nature of the cherubim, and then consider Him who has His throne upon them. But Ezechiel the prophet has produced a description of them, as far as that is possible, saying that every one has four faces,[9] one of a man, another of a lion, a third of an eagle, and a fourth of a calf; and that each one has six wings and eyes on every side; and that beneath each is a wheel of four parts. Yet, after this description of the prophet, we still cannot comprehend as we read. But, if we cannot comprehend the throne which he has described, how will we be able to comprehend Him who sits thereon, the invisible and ineffable God? It is impossible to examine closely into the nature of God; but, for His works which we see, we can offer Him praise and glory.

---

6 Cf. Dan. 10.5-18.
7 Wisd. 13.5.
8 Dan. 3.55.
9 Cf. Ezech. 1.6ff.

(4) I say these things to you because of the sequence of the Creed, and because we say: "We believe in One God, Father Almighty, Creator of heaven and earth, of all things visible and invisible"; that we may remember that He who is the Father of our Lord Jesus Christ is the very same who made heaven and earth;[10] that we may be made secure against the aberrations of the impious heretics, who have dared to speak ill of the All-wise Artificer of all this world; they see with eyes of flesh, but the eyes of their understanding are blinded.

(5) For what have they to blame in this vast creation of God? They ought to have been struck with wonder on contemplating the vaulted expanses of the heavens, and to have worshiped Him who established the sky as a dome, who from naturally fluid waters formed the stable substance of the heavens. For God said: "Let there be a firmament in the midst of the waters."[11] God spoke once and it stands and does not fall. The heaven is water, but the bodies fixed therein, sun, moon, and the stars, are of fire. How do the fiery bodies run in the water? If any man has doubts because of the contrary natures of fire and water, let him remember the fire which in Moses' time in Egypt flamed in the hail.[12] Let him consider also the all-wise disposition of God in creation. Since there was to be need of water for the tilling of the soil, He prepared the watery heavens above, that when the region of the earth should need showers to irrigate it, the heavens of their nature would be ready for this very purpose.

(6) What then? Should not a man marvel as he contemplates the sun's structure? For though it appears a small body, it encompasses tremendous power, appearing in the east and sending forth its light even to the west. Its morning rising the Psalmist describes: [the sun] "which comes forth

---

10 These words are directed against the old heretics who asserted the world was created by angels, or a demiurge, or by the devil.
11 Gen. 1.6.
12 Cf. Exod. 9.23, 24.

like the groom from his bridal chamber."[13] This is a description of its gently beaming and temperate state as it first appears to men, for we often flee its fiery heat when it rides at high noon. But at its rising it is a delight to all, as a bridegroom to look upon. Consider the apt disposition of the sun, or rather of Him whose ordering determined its course; how in summer it is higher in the heavens and makes the days longer, thereby giving men good time for their works, while in winter it contracts its course, that the cold season might not be too long and that the nights, becoming longer, might serve as the repose of men and for the fruitfulness of the earth's products. See too how the days give way to each other in due order, lengthening in summer, growing shorter in winter, but in spring and autumn affording mutually equal intervals; and the nights likewise, so that the Psalmist says: "Day pours out the word to day, and night to night imparts knowledge."[14] For to the heretics, who have no ears, they all but shout, and by their good order they say that there is no other God save their Creator, who fixed their bounds and laid out the universe.

(7) Let no man tolerate those who say that the Creator of light is one, but that of darkness another; for let him remember Isaia saying: "I am the God who made the light, and created the darkness."[15] Why be vexed at this? Why take ill the time given for your rest? A servant would receive no rest from his masters did not the darkness bring a necessary respite. How often, when wearied from the toil of the day, are we refreshed in the night, and he who was yesterday toilworn comes forth vigorous in the morning because of the night's rest. What is more conducive to wisdom than the night, during which we often ponder the things of God, and devote ourselves to the reading and contemplation of the

---

13 Ps. 18.6.
14 *Ibid.* 18.3. Some of the arguments would hardly appeal to those not living in temperate climates.
15 Cf. Isa. 45.7.

sacred Scriptures? When does our mind tend more towards psalmody and prayer? Is this not at night? When do we come oftener to the remembrance of our own sins? Is it not at night? Therefore let us not perversely entertain the thought that God is not the author of darkness; for experience shows that this too is good and most useful.

(8) Men ought to have been astonished and amazed, not only at the structure of the sun and moon, but also at the well-ordered movements of the stars and their unfettered courses, and the timely risings of each of them; how some are signs of summer, others of winter; how some indicate the time for sowing, others the beginning of navigation; and man, sitting in his ship and sailing amid the boundless waves, guides his ship by observing the stars. For concerning these things Scripture well says: "Let them serve as signs and for the fixing of seasons, days, and years,"[16] not for astrological fables of birth. Again, notice how kind God has been to us in gradually increasing the light of day; for we do not see the sun rising at once, but a little light runs up beforehand, that the pupil of the eye by previous trial may be able to look upon its stronger rays. Consider also how He has cheered the darkness of the night by the bright rays of the moon.

(9) "Has the rain a father; or who has begotten the drops of dew?"[17] Who has condensed the air into clouds and bid them support the waters of the rain showers, sometimes bringing the gleaming golden clouds from the north, sometimes making them uniform in appearance, and again changing them into various types of circles and other shapes? "Who can count the clouds in his wisdom?"[18] Therefore Job says of Him: "He knows the differences of the clouds,"[19] "and has bent the heaven to earth";[20] and "who counts the clouds in

16 Gen. 1.15.
17 Job 38.28.
18 Cf. *Ibid.* 38.37.
19 Job 37.16 (Sept.).
20 Job 38.37 (Sept.).

his wisdom,"[21] and "the cloud is not rent beneath him."[22] For though so many measures of water rest upon the clouds, they are not rent, but with all due order they come down upon the earth. Who is He who brings forth the winds from their stores?[23] Who is He, as we said above, "who has begotten the drops of dew"? "Out of whose womb comes the ice?"[24] For though its substance is watery, it has the property of stone. Sometimes the water becomes "snow like wool";[25] sometimes it serves Him who "strews frost like ashes";[26] sometimes it is changed into a stony substance, since "He governs the water as he will."[27] In nature it is uniform, but in operation manifold. Water in vines becomes wine, that gladdens men's hearts;[28] and in the olives, oil, which causes the face of man to shine; it is transformed also into bread which "fortifies the hearts of men,"[29] and into all kinds of created fruits.

(10) What should have followed from these marvels? That the Creator be blasphemed or rather that He be worshiped? And so far I have not spoken of the secrets of His wisdom. Just consider the spring, and the various kinds of flowers, so like and yet so diverse, the deep red of the rose and the pure white of the lily. Yet these come from the same rain and the same earth; who makes them differ? Who forms them? Just observe the neat precision: from the one substance of the tree, there is a part for shelter and a part for divers fruits, and the Artificer is One. A part of the vine is for burning, another for shoots, another for foliage, another for tendrils, another, finally, for clusters. Marvel too at the thickness of the knots that circle the reed, the work of the Artificer.

---

21 *Ibid.*
22 Job 26.8 (Sept.).
23 Cf. Ps. 134.7.
24 Job 38.29.
25 Ps. 147.16.
26 Cf. *Ibid.*
27 Job 37.10 (Sept.).
28 Cf. Ps. 103.15.
29 *Ibid.*

From the same earth come forth creeping things, wild beasts, cattle, trees, food, gold, silver, brass, iron, stone. From the one nature of the waters comes the substance of swimming things and of birds, and as the fish swim in the waters so the birds fly in the air.

(11) "This great and wide sea; in it there are creeping things without number."[30] Who can describe the beauty of the fishes therein? Who can describe the greatness of the whales and the nature of the amphibious animals, how they live on the dry land and in the waters? Who can describe the depth and breadth of the sea or the shock of its tumultuous waves? The sea stays within its confines because of Him who said: "This far shall you come but no farther, and here shall your proud waves be stilled!"[31] It clearly reveals the decree imposed upon it, when running out it leaves on the sands a distinct line marked by its waves, as though to signify to those who see it that it has not transgressed its appointed bounds.

(12) Who can explore the nature of the birds of the air, how some are equipped with melodious song, how others have varicolored wings; and others, flying aloft into mid-air, like the hawk stay motionless? For by the Divine command: "The hawk spreading his wings, stays motionless, looking down towards the south."[32] What man can observe the eagle's lofty flight? But if you cannot comprehend the flight of the most senseless of the birds, how will you comprehend the Maker of all things?

(13) What man knows even the names of all wild beasts? Who can discern the nature of each of them? But if we do not know the mere names of the wild beasts, how shall we comprehend their Maker? God's command was but one which said: "Let the earth bring forth all kinds of living creatures: cattle, crawling creatures and wild animals";[33] and different

30 Ps. 103.25 (Sept.).
31 Job 38.11.
32 Job 39.26 (Sept.).
33 Gen. 1.24.

natures of animals sprang forth from the one earth at a single command—the gentle sheep and the carnivorous lion—and the various tendencies of irrational animals that resemble various human characteristics. Thus the fox typifies the craftiness of men, the snake the venomous treachery of friends, and the neighing horse the wanton young man. There is the busy ant to rouse the indolent and sluggish; for when a man spends an idle youth, then he is instructed by the irrational creatures, being chided by the sacred Scripture which says: "Go to the ant, O sluggard, and considering her ways, emulate her and become wiser than she."[34] For when you observe her treasuring up food for herself in good season, imitate her, and treasure up for yourself the fruits of good works for the world to come. And again: "Go to the bee and learn how industrious she is";[35] how, hovering about flowers of all kinds, she gathers the honey for your use, that you also, by ranging over the sacred Scriptures, may lay hold of salvation for yourself, and, sated with the Scriptures, you may say: "How sweet to my palate are your promises, sweeter than honey to my mouth!"[36]

(14) Does not, then, the Artificer deserve rather to be glorified? Granted you do not know the nature of all things, are the created things thereby useless? Can you know the efficacy of all herbs, or the benefit coming from every animal? Already even from poisonous vipers have come antidotes for the safety of men. But you will say: "The snake is terrible"; fear the Lord and he will not be able to harm you. "A scorpion has power to sting"; fear the Lord and it will not sting you. "A lion is bloodthirsty"; fear the Lord and he will lie down beside you, as by Daniel.[37] Yet the powers of the animals are truly wonderful; some, like the scorpion, have their attack in their sting; the strength of others is in their

---

34 Prov. 6.6 (Sept.).
35 *Ibid.* 6.8 (Sept.).
36 Ps. 118.103.
37 Cf. Dan. 6.18 (Sept.).

fangs; still others fight with their claws, and the might of the basilisk is in its aspect. From the variety of His workmanship, therefore, learn the power of the Creator.

(15) But perhaps you do not know these things; you have nothing in common with the creatures outside of you. Then enter into yourself, and gain knowledge of the Creator from your own nature. What is there to blame in the constitution of your body? Be master of yourself and no evil proceeds from your members. From the beginning Adam was unclothed in paradise with Eve; but it was not because of his members that he deserved to be cast out. Therefore, the members are not the cause of sin, but they who abuse their members; and the Maker of the members is wise. Who prepared the recesses of the womb for child-bearing? Who gave life to the lifeless thing within it? "Who has knit us together with sinews and bones, and clothed us with skin and flesh"[38] and as soon as the child is born brings forth fountains of milk from the breasts? How does the babe grow into a boy, and the boy into a youth, and then into a man, and being the same, pass into an old man, though no one perceives the precise change from day to day? How is our food partly changed into blood, partly separated into waste matter, partly transformed into flesh? Who causes the heart to beat incessantly? Who so wisely guarded the soft eyes with the covering of eyelids? Regarding the intricate and marvelous structure of the eyes, the voluminous books of physicians hardly give an adequate explanation. Who imparts one and the same breath to the whole body? You see, then, the Artificer; you see the wise Creator.

(16) My discourse has dwelt at length on these points (passing over many, indeed countless, other matters, especially things incorporeal and invisible), that you may loathe those who blaspheme the wise and good Artificer; and further, from what has been said and read and from what you can

---

38 Cf. Job 11.11.

discover and ponder, that by analogy from the greatness and the beauty of created things,[39] you may have a concept of the Creator; and devoutly bending the knee before the Maker of the universe, of things sensible and intelligible, visible and invisible, with grateful and pious tongue, with unwearied lips you may praise God, saying: "How manifold are your works, O Lord! In wisdom you have wrought them all":[40] for to Thee is due honor, glory, and majesty, now and forever and ever. Amen.

---

39 Cf. Wisd. 13.5.
40 Ps. 103.24.

CATECHESIS X

On One Lord, Jesus Christ

"For even if there are what are called gods, whether in heaven or earth ... yet for us there is only one God, the Father from whom are all things, and we unto him; and one Lord, Jesus Christ, through whom are all things and we through him."[1]

(1) Those who have been taught to believe in One God Father Almighty ought to believe also in His Only-begotten Son. For he that denies the Son has not the Father.[2] "I am the door,"[3] Jesus says; "no one comes to the Father, but through me."[4] If you deny the Door, the knowledge of the Father is closed to you. "No one knows the Father, except the Son, and him to whom the Son chooses to reveal him."[5] If you deny Him who reveals, you remain in ignorance. Then there is the Gospel text: "He who is unbelieving towards the Son shall not see life, but the wrath of God rests upon him."[6] For the Father is wrathful when His Only-begotten Son is disregarded. The dishonorable treatment of a mere soldier is a grievous matter for his king; when a nobler attendant or friend is treated dishonorably, then his anger becomes still greater; but if anyone should treat with contumely the king's only-begotten son, who will appease the father's ensuing indignation?

---

1 1 Cor. 8.5, 6.
2 Cf. 1 John 2.23.
3 John 10.9.
4 John 14.6.
5 Cf. Matt. 11.27.
6 John 3.36.

(2) If anyone wishes to serve God piously, let him worship the Son; otherwise, the Father will not accept his service. The Father spoke aloud from heaven, saying: "This is my beloved Son, in whom I am well pleased."[7] The Father was well pleased in His Son; unless you also are well pleased, you will not have life. Do not be led astray by the Jews who say guilefully: "There is one God alone." But with the knowledge that God is One, know that there is also an Only-begotten Son of God. I am not the first to say this, but the Psalmist in the person of the Son says: "The Lord said to me, 'You are my son.' "[8] Therefore attend not to what the Jews say, but to what the Prophets say. Are you surprised if they who stoned and killed the Prophets disregard the words of the Prophets?

(3) Believe in One Lord Jesus Christ, the Only-begotten Son of God.[9] We say, "One Lord Jesus Christ," that His Sonship may be "Only-begotten"; we say "One," that you may not suppose another; we say "One," that you may not impiously distribute among many sons the many names of His power. For He is called a Door; regard this not as meaning a wooden door, but rather a spiritual, living Door, distinguishing those who enter. He is called a Way,[10] but not that trodden by men's feet, but one which leads to the Father in heaven. He is called a Sheep;[11] not a senseless one, but that which cleanses the world from sin by its precious blood, and when led before its shearer knows when to be silent. This Sheep again is called a Shepherd, who says: "I am the [good] shepherd";[12] a Sheep because of His human nature, a Shepherd because of the loving-kindness of His Godhead. Know

---

7 Matt. 3.17.
8 Ps. 2.7.
9 Cyril stresses the oneness of Christ under His many titles not only to combat heretics but to strengthen the faith of his hearers. He explains that Christ is not divided in any way, but that His many titles reflect our needs.
10 John 14.6.
11 Acts 8.32; Isa. 53.7.
12 Cf. John 10.11.

too that there are spiritual sheep, for He says to the Apostles: "Behold I am sending you forth like sheep in the midst of wolves."[13] Again, He is called a Lion;[14] not a devourer of men, but, as it were, showing by this title His kingly, strong, and resolute nature. Then too, He is called a Lion in opposition to the lion, our adversary, who roars and devours those who have been deceived.[15] For the Savior came, not having changed His own gentle nature, and yet as the mighty lion of the tribe of Juda, saving them that believe, but trampling upon the adversary. He is called a Stone;[16] not a lifeless one, cut out by human hands, but the "chief corner stone" in whom he who will believe " shall not be put to shame."[17]

(4) He is called Christ;[18] not as having been anointed by human hands, but anointed eternally by the Father to His High-Priesthood over men. He is called Dead;[19] not as abiding among the dead, as all in the nether world, but alone "free among the dead."[20] He is called Son of Man;[21] not as having had His generation from the earth, as each one of us, but as "coming upon the clouds of heaven"[22] to judge the living and the dead. He is called Lord;[23] not improperly, as those among men are so called. He is fittingly called Jesus,[24] having the title from His salutary healing. He is called Son,[25] not as having been advanced by adoption, but naturally begotten. Many, therefore, are the titles of our Savior. That His many titles may not cause you to think of many sons, and that you may meet the errors of the heretics, who say that Christ is one,

---

13 Matt. 10.16.
14 Gen. 49.9.
15 Cf. 1 Peter 5.8.
16 1 Peter 2.4.
17 Cf. *Ibid.* 6.
18 Matt. 1.16.
19 Apoc. 1.18.
20 Cf. Ps. 87.6.
21 Matt. 16.13.
22 Matt. 24.30.
23 Luke 2.11.
24 Matt. 1.21.
25 Matt. 3.17.

Jesus another,[26] the Door another, and so on, the faith fore-arms you, saying well: "in One Lord Jesus Christ." For though the titles are many, their subject is one.

(5) The Savior comes in various forms to each man for his profit. For to those who lack joy, He becomes a Vine;[27] to those who wish to enter in, He is a Door;[28] for those who must offer prayers, He is a mediating High-Priest.[29] Again, to those in sin, He becomes a Sheep, to be sacrificed on their behalf. He becomes "all things to all men,"[30] remaining in His own nature what He is. For so remaining, and possessing the truly unchangeable dignity of the Sonship, as the best of physicians and a sympathetic teacher, He adapts Himself to our infirmities. He is Lord in truth, not having advanced to the Lordship, but possessing that dignity by nature. He is called Lord, not improperly as we are, but in very truth He is Lord, since by the decree of the Father He has the Lordship over His own works. Our lordship is over those equal in honor and subject to the same affections, often even over our elders, and often a youth is the master of aged servants. But in our Lord, Jesus Christ, the Lordship is not of this kind, but first He is Maker, then Lord; first, by the will of the Father, He made all things; then He assumed the Lordship over the things made.

(6) Christ the Lord was born in the city of David.[31] Know, too, that Christ is Lord with the Father even before His incarnation, and hence accept what is said, not only by faith, but also with proof from the Old Testament. Go to the first book, Genesis. God says: "Let us make mankind," not "in My image," but "in our image."[32] And, after Adam was

---

26 Valentinians and others distinguished between Jesus and Christ (Iren. 3.16.8).
27 John 15.1.
28 John 10.7.
29 1 Tim. 2.5; Heb. 7.26.
30 1 Cor. 9.22.
31 Luke 2.11.
32 Gen. 1.26.

made, Scripture says: "God created man. . . . In the image of God he created him."[33] For He did not restrict the dignity of the Godhead to the Father alone, but included the Son also; that it might be shown that man is not the work of God alone, but of our Lord Jesus Christ also. This Lord who cooperates with the Father worked with Him also in the case of Sodom, according to the Scripture: "The Lord poured down on Sodom and Gomorrah sulphur from the Lord out of heaven."[34] This Lord afterwards appeared to Moses, insofar as he could behold Him.[35] For the Lord is kind, ever adapting Himself to our infirmities.

(7) To realize that it is He who appeared[36] to Moses take the testimony of Paul: "For they drank from the spiritual rock that followed them, but the rock was Christ";[37] and again: "By faith he left Egypt";[38] and thereafter: "Esteeming the reproach of Christ greater riches than the treasures of the Egyptians."[39] Moses says to Him: "Show me yourself."[40] You see that then also the prophets saw Christ, that is, in the measure each was able. "Show me yourself, that I may see you clearly."[41] But He said: "No one sees me and still lives."[42] Therefore, because no one could see the face of the Godhead and live, He assumed the face of human nature, that seeing this we might live. Yet, when He wished to show even this with a little majesty, at the time when "his face

---

33 *Ibid.* 27.
34 Gen. 19.24.
35 Exod. 3.2, 6; 34.5, 6.
36 The various divine apparitions recorded in the Old Testament at an early date were attributed to the Son of God by way of anticipation of the incarnation, but always "under the likeness of his glory" (cf. *Cat.* 9.1). Cyril wishes to supply arguments to his candidates against the Jews.
37 1 Cor. 10.4.
38 Heb. 11.27.
39. *Ibid.* 26.
40 Exod. 33.13 (Sept.).
41 *Ibid.*
42 *Ibid.* 20.

shone as the sun,"[43] the disciples fell to the earth terrified.[44] Now if His bodily countenance, shining not according to the full power of Him who wrought, but in the measure the disciples could bear, terrified them and even thus they could not bear it, how could anyone gaze upon the majesty of the Godhead? It is a great thing you desire, O Moses, the Lord says; and I approve your insatiable longing and "this word will I do"[45] for you, but according to your capacity. "Behold I will set you in the hollow of the rock";[46] for as you are small, you will lodge in a small place.

(8) Now here please note carefully what I am to say, because of the Jews. For it is our purpose to demonstrate that the Lord, Jesus Christ, was with the Father. The Lord then said to Moses: "I will make all my beauty pass before you, and in your presence I will pronounce my name, 'Lord.' "[47] Being Himself the Lord, what Lord does He proclaim? You see how in a veiled manner He was teaching the holy doctrine of Father and Son. Again, in what follows, it is written in express terms: "Having come down in a cloud, the Lord stood with him there and proclaimed his name, 'Lord.' Thus the Lord passed before him and cried out, 'The Lord, the Lord, merciful and gracious, slow to anger and rich in kindness and fidelity, and guarding justice and continuing his kindness for a thousand generations, and forgiving wickedness and crime and sin.' "[48] And thereafter: "Moses at once bowed down to the ground in worship"[49] before the Lord proclaiming the Father, and said: "O Lord, do come along in our company."[50]

(9) This is the first proof, and now for a second clear

43 Matt. 17.2.
44 Cf. ibid. 6.
45 Exod. 33.17.
46 Ibid. 22.
47 Ibid. 19 (Sept.).
48 Cf. Exod. 34.5-7.
49 Ibid. 8.
50 Ibid. 9.

proof: "The Lord said to my Lord: 'Sit at my right hand.' "[51]
The Lord says this to the Lord, not to a servant, but to the
Lord of all things and His own Son, to whom He has subjected all things.[52] "But when He says all things are subject
to him, undoubtedly he is excepted, who has subjected all
things to him":[53] "that God may be all in all."[54] The Only-
begotten Son is Lord of all things, yet is the obedient Son
of the Father, for He did not seize the Lordship but received
it by nature, of the Father's own will. For neither did the
Son seize it, nor the Father begrudge imparting it. He it is
who says: "All things have been delivered to me by my
Father,"[55] delivered to Me not as though I lacked them
before; and I keep them well, not despoiling Him who has
given them.

(10) The Son of God is the Lord, the Lord who was born
in Bethlehem of Judaea, according to the words of the angel
to the shepherds: "I bring you good news of great joy . . .
for there has been born to you today in the town of David
Christ the Lord."[56] Of Him an Apostle elsewhere says: "He
sent his word to the children of Israel, preaching peace
through Jesus Christ who is Lord of all."[57] When he says
"of all," exclude nothing from His lordship, for whether they
be angels or archangels "or dominations or principalities,"[58]
or any other created thing named by the Apostles, all are
subjected to the lordship of the Son. He is Lord of angels, as
you have it in the Gospel: "Then the devil left him; and
behold, angels came and ministered to him."[59] For Scripture
does not say that they helped Him, but that they ministered
to Him, a function belonging to servants. When He was

---

51 Ps. 109.1.
52 Heb. 2.8.
53 1 Cor. 15.27.
54 *Ibid.* 28.
55 Matt 11.27.
56 Luke 2.10, 11.
57 Acts 10.36.
58 Col. 1.16.
59 Matt. 4.11.

born of a virgin Gabriel served Him, having received his service as his own special privilege.[60] When He was about to go into Egypt, that He might destroy the idols of Egypt,[61] again, "an angel appeared in a dream to Joseph."[62] When He rose again after His crucifixion, an angel proclaimed the good tidings, and as a good servant said to the women: "Go quickly and tell his disciples that he has risen; and behold, he goes before you into Galilee; . . . Behold, I have foretold it to you."[63] As though he were to say: I have not disobeyed my command; I bear witness to the fact that I have told you; that if you disregard it, the blame may not be on me, but on those who have disregarded it. This, then, is the one Lord Jesus Christ, of whom the passage just read says: "For even if there are what are called gods, whether in heaven or on earth," and so on, "yet for us there is only one God, the Father from whom are all things, and we unto him; and one Lord Jesus Christ, through whom are all things, and we through him."[64]

(11) He is called by two names, Jesus Christ; Jesus because He is a Savior, Christ because He is a Priest. With this in mind the divinely inspired prophet Moses gave these two titles to two men eminent above all, changing the name of his own successor in the sovereignty, Auses, to Jesus,[65] and giving to his own brother, Aaron, the surname Christ,[66] that through these two chosen men he might represent at once the High Priesthood and the Kingship of the One Jesus Christ who was to come. For Christ is a High Priest, like Aaron, since He "did not glorify himself with the high priesthood, but he who spoke to Him, 'Thou art a priest forever, according to the order of Melchisedec.' "[67] But

---

60 Luke 1.16.
61 Cf. Isa. 19.1.
62 Matt. 2.13.
63 Matt. 28.7.
64 1 Cor. 8.5, 6.
65 Num. 13.17.
66 Cf. Lev. 4.5 (Sept.).
67 Heb. 5.5, 6.

Jesus, son of Nave, was a type of Him in many things; for when he began to rule the people, he began from the Jordan;[68] thence also did Christ begin to preach the Gospel after He was baptized.[69] The son of Nave appoints the twelve to divide the inheritance;[70] and Jesus sends forth the twelve Apostles, heralds of truth, into the whole world.[71] He who was the type saved Rahab, the harlot, who had believed;[72] the True Jesus on the other hand says: Behold: "the publicans and the harlots are entering the kingdom of God before you."[73] With but a shout, the walls of Jericho collapsed in the time of the type;[74] and because of these words of Jesus: "There will not be left here one stone upon another,"[75] the temple of the Jews just opposite us is fallen; not that this sentence was the cause of its ruin, but rather the sin of the transgressors.

(12) There is One Lord Jesus Christ, a wonderful name, proclaimed beforehand indirectly by the prophets. For Isaia the prophet says: "Your savior comes! Here is his reward with him."[76] Among the Hebrews, "Jesus" is interpreted Savior; for the prophetic gift, foreseeing the spirit of the Jews bent upon the slaying of the Lord, veiled His name, that they might not know it clearly beforehand and plot against Him more readily. He was openly called Jesus, not by men, but by an angel, coming not of his own authority, but by the power of God, and saying to Joseph: "Do not be afraid to take to thee Mary thy wife, for that which is begotten in her is of the Holy Spirit. And she shall bring forth a son, and thou shalt call his name Jesus";[77] and giving the

---

68 Jos. 3.1.
69 Matt. 3.13.
70 Jos. 14.1.
71 Matt. 10.5.
72 Jos. 6.25; Heb. 11.31.
73 Matt. 21.31.
74 Jos. 6.20.
75 Matt. 24.2.
76 Isa. 62.11.
77 Matt. 1.20, 21.

reason for this name, he straightway adds: "For he shall save his people from their sins."[78] Consider how He who was not yet born could have a people, unless He were in being before He was born. This the prophet says in His person: "From my mother's womb he gave me my name";[79] because the angel foretold that He would be called Jesus. Again, concerning the plots of Herod, he says: "He . . . concealed me in the shadow of his arm."[80]

(13) Therefore, according to the Hebrews, Jesus means Savior, but in the Greek tongue, "the Healer"; inasmuch as He is both healer of bodies and physician of spirits, curing the blind of body and bringing light to minds; healing those visibly lame and guiding the steps of sinners to repentance, He says to the paralytic: "Sin no more,"[81] and: "Take up thy pallet and walk."[82] Because the body was palsied through the sin of the soul, He first healed the soul, that He might then extend the healing to the body also. Therefore, if anyone is sick in soul because of sin, he has a Physician; if any man here be of little faith, let him say to Him: "Help my belief."[83] If any man is beset with bodily ailments, let him not be diffident but rather draw near—for He heals these ills also—and know that Jesus is the Christ.

(14) For the Jews grant that He is Jesus, but deny that He is also Christ. For this reason, the Apostle says: "Who is the liar but he who denies that Jesus is the Christ?"[84] But Christ is a High Priest, having "an everlasting priesthood";[85] neither having begun His priesthood in time, nor having any successor in His High Priesthood, as you have heard in Church on the Lord's day when we were discoursing on the

---

78 *Ibid.*
79 Isa. 49.1.
80 *Ibid.* 2.
81 John 5.14.
82 *Ibid.* 8.
83 Mark 9.23.
84 1 John 2.22.
85 Heb. 7.24.

words "according to the order of Melchisedec."[86] He did not receive the High Priesthood through bodily succession, nor was he anointed with man-prepared oil, but before all ages by the Father; and He so far surpasses the others as He is made a priest with an oath. "Others indeed were made priests without an oath, but he with an oath through him who said unto him: The Lord hath sworn and will not repent."[87] The will of the Father in itself was sufficient assurance, but as a double measure of assurance, with the will there follows also the oath: "That by two unchangeable things, in which it is impossible for God to deceive, we may have the strongest comfort"[88] for our faith, who receive Christ Jesus the Son of God.

(15) This Christ, when He came, the Jews denied,[89] though the devils confessed Him.[90] His forefather David was not ignorant of Him when he said: "I will place a lamp for my anointed."[91] Some have interpreted "lamp" as the splendor of prophecy; others have understood by the lamp the flesh He assumed of the Virgin, according to the words of the Apostle: "But we carry this treasure in vessels of clay."[92] The Prophet was not ignorant of Him when he said: "And declaring his Christ to men."[93] Moses also knew Him, and Isaia and Jeremia as well; none of the prophets was ignorant of Him. Even the devils acknowledged Him, for He rebuked them and Scripture adds: "Because they knew that he was the Christ."[94] The Chief Priests did not know Him, and the devils confessed Him; the Chief Priests did not know Him, and the Samaritan woman proclaimed Him, saying: "Come

---

86 Ps. 109.4.
87 Heb. 7.20, 21.
88 Heb. 6.18.
89 John 19.5.
90 Luke 4.41.
91 Ps. 131.17.
92 2 Cor. 4.7.
93 Amos 4.13 (Sept.).
94 Luke 4.41.

and see a man who has told me all that I have ever done.
Is he not the Christ?"[95]

(16) This is Jesus Christ who came "as high priest of the
good things to come,"[96] who, in the lavishness of His Godhead,
imparted His own title to all of us. For kings among men
possess the royal title unshared with others, but Christ Jesus,
being the Son of God, has vouchsafed that we be called
"Christians." But someone will say: the name "Christians"
is new and unheard of until now, and new things are often
objected to because of their strangeness. The Prophet anticipated this objection when he said: "But my servants shall be
called by a new name, which shall be blessed upon the
earth."[97] Let us ask the Jews: Do you serve the Lord, or not?
Show me, therefore, your new name; for you were called
"Jews" and "Israelites" in the time of Moses and the other
prophets, and after the return from Babylon, and up to the
present day; where, then, is your new name? But we, since we
serve the Lord, have that new name, new indeed, but the new
name "which shall be blessed upon the earth."[98] This name
has taken hold of the world; for while the Jews are within
the bounds of a certain region, the Christians reach to the
ends of the earth; for what is proclaimed is the Name of the
Only-begotten Son of God.

(17) Rest assured that the Apostles knew and preached the
Name of Christ, or rather, they had Christ Himself within
them. Paul says to his hearers: "Do you seek a proof of
the Christ who speaks in me?"[99] Paul proclaims Christ. Now
who is this? It is His former persecutor. O mighty wonder!
He who formerly persecuted Him, himself preaches Christ.
Why? Was it that he was won over by bribery? But there
was no one to persuade him thus. Was it that he saw Him

---

95 John 4.29.
96 Heb. 9.11.
97 Isa. 65.15, 16 (Sept.).
98 *Ibid.*
99 2 Cor. 13.3.

present on earth and was moved by shame? He had already ascended into heaven. He went forth to persecute and, after three days, the persecutor is a preacher in Damascus. By what power? Others call upon friends to testify for friends; I have offered you a witness who was once an enemy, and do you still doubt? Great, indeed, is the testimony of Peter and John, yet open to suspicion, because they were His friends. But when he who was formerly His enemy afterwards dies for His sake, who can entertain doubts about the truth?

(18) At this point in my discourse I confess my amazement at the wise dispensation of the Holy Spirit, in limiting the Epistles of the others to a small number, but granting the grace to Paul, the former persecutor, to write fourteen. For it was not as though Peter or John were less than Paul that He withheld the gift in their case—God forbid!—but that His doctrine might be beyond question, He gave the grace to the former enemy and persecutor to write more, that thus we might all be confirmed in our faith. Indeed, all were astonished at Paul and said: "Is not this he who used to make havoc" aforetime "and who has come here for the purpose of taking us in bonds to Jerusalem?"[100] Do not be astonished, Paul says; "I know that 'it is hard' for me 'to kick against the goad.'[101] I know that 'I am not worthy to be called an apostle, because I persecuted the Church of God,'[102] but 'I acted ignorantly.'[103] For I considered the preaching of Christ to be the destruction of the Law, for I did not know that He came 'to fulfill the Law, not to destroy it.'[104] But 'the grace of our Lord has abounded beyond measure'[105] in me."

(19) There are many true testimonies, my dear brethren, concerning Christ. The Father from heaven bears witness

---

100 Acts 9.21.
101 *Ibid.* 5.
102 1 Cor. 15.9.
103 1 Tim. 1.13.
104 Matt. 5.17.
105 1 Tim. 1.14.

concerning the Son;[106] the Holy Spirit, descending in a bodily shape, in the form of a dove;[107] the Archangel Gabriel, announcing the good tidings to Mary.[108] The Virgin Mother of God is His witness;[109] the blessed place of the manger is His witness.[110] Egypt bears witness to Him, having received Him when still young in body.[111] Simeon is a witness, who took Him in his arms and said: "Now thou dost dismiss thy servant, O Lord, according to thy word, in peace; because my eyes have seen thy salvation."[112] Anna, a prophetess, a most religious widow of austere life, bears witness to Him.[113] A witness also is John the Baptist, the greatest of the prophets and the inaugurator of the New Testament, and, in a way, linking in himself the Old and the New Testaments.[114] Among rivers, the Jordan bears witness;[115] among seas, the Sea of Tiberias.[116] The blind, the lame, the dead brought back to life bear witness to Him;[117] the devils also, saying: "What have we to do with thee, Jesus?" We "know who thou art, the Holy One of God."[118] The winds, calmed at His command, bear witness;[119] the five loaves, multiplied for five thousand.[120] His witness is the holy wood of the cross, seen among us even to this day, and by those who have taken portions thereof, from hence filling almost the whole world. His witness is the palm tree in the valley which supplied

---

106 Mark 3.17; 17.5.
107 Luke 3.22.
108 Luke 1.27-38.
109 *Ibid.* 27. "The Virgin Mother of God": the Greek *theotokos,* defined against Nestorius at Chalcedon.
110 Luke 2.7.
111 Matt. 2.14.
112 Luke 2.38-41.
113 *Ibid.* 36-38.
114 John 1.15.
115 Matt. 3.13.
116 John 6.1.
117 Matt. 11.5.
118 Mark 1.24.
119 Matt. 8.26, 27.
120 Matt. 14.16-21.

branches to the children who shouted His praises.[121] Geth-
semane is His witness, all but showing Judas still, to those
who understand. This holy mount of Golgotha, conspicuous
in its elevation, bears witness to Him.[122] The Holy Sepulchre
bears witness, and the stone which lies there even to this
day.[123] A witness to Him is the sun now shining, which, at
the time of our Savior's Passion, suffered eclipse;[124] and the
darkness, which then lasted from the sixth to the ninth
hour;[125] and the light, which shone from the ninth hour
until evening. The Holy Mount of Olives, from which He
ascended to the Father, bears witness.[126] The rain-bearing
clouds which received their Lord bear witness;[127] and the
heavenly gates, of which the Psalmist says: "Lift up, O gates,
your lintels; reach up, you ancient portals, that the king of
glory may come in!"[128] His former enemies bear witness, one
of whom is blessed Paul, who, though His enemy for a while,
served Him for a long time. The twelve Apostles are His
witnesses, who preached the truth not only in words, but by
their own torments and deaths. The shadow of Peter is a
witness, healing the sick in the name of Christ;[129] and the
handkerchiefs and aprons, which of old worked cures through
Paul by the power of Christ.[130] The Persians and Goths and
all the gentile converts bear witness, by dying for the sake
of Him whom they did not see with the eyes of the flesh.
The devils, who even to this day are driven out by the faithful, bear witness to Him.

(20) So many and diverse, and still more than these, are
the witnesses of Christ; can it be that faith in Christ, thus

121 John 12.13.
122 Matt. 27.33.
123 Ibid. 60.
124 Cf. Luke 23.45.
125 Cf. Matt. 27.45.
126 Cf. Acts 1.12.
127 Ibid. 9.
128 Ps. 23.7.
129 Cf. Acts 5.15.
130 Cf. Acts 19.12.

witnessed, will be hereafter denied? Therefore, if any man did not believe before, let him now believe; but if any man believed before, let him receive a greater increase of faith, believing in our Lord Jesus Christ; and let him realize whose name he bears. You are called a Christian; be careful of that name; let not our Lord Jesus Christ be blasphemed through you; but rather, let your good works shine before men, that they who see them may glorify in Christ Jesus our Lord the Father who is in heaven,[131] to whom be glory, now and forever and ever. Amen.

---

131 Cf. Matt. 5.16.

CATECHESIS XI

On the Only-begotten Son of God, Born of the Father before all Ages, True God, through whom All Things Were Made

"God, who at sundry times and in divers manners spoke in times past to the fathers in the prophets, last of all in these days has spoken to us in his Son."[1]

(1) In yesterday's discourse we gave adequate expression, as far as we could, to the hope we have in Jesus Christ. Yet we must not simply believe in Jesus Christ nor accept Him as one of many who are improperly called Christs. Though there were figurative Christs, He is the true Christ, not raised to the priesthood by advancement among men, but possessing the dignity of the priesthood eternally from the Father. For this reason the Faith, guarding against our supposing Him to be one of the ordinary Christs, adds to the creed we profess the words: "in One Lord Jesus Christ, the Only-begotten Son of God."

(2) Again, when you hear "Son," do not think of Him as an adopted Son, but a Son by nature, an Only-begotten Son, having no brother. He is called Only-begotten because, in the dignity of the Godhead and His generation from the Father, He has no brother. We call Him Son of God not of ourselves, but because the Father Himself named Christ His Son. For the name given to their children by fathers is a true one.

(3) Our Lord Jesus Christ put on man's nature, but He was not known by the many. Wishing to teach what was not

1 Heb. 1.1, 2.

211

known, He gathered His disciples together and asked: "Who do men say the Son of Man is?"[2] He was not seeking vain glory, but wished to show them the truth, that they, living with God, the Only-begotten Son of God, might not look down upon Him as a mere man. When they said that some said Elias and others Jeremia,[3] He said to them: "They who know not are excusable; but you, My Apostles, who in My Name cleanse the lepers, cast out devils, and raise the dead to life, you ought not to be ignorant of Him, by whom you work these wonders." When all were silent (for this lesson was beyond man's powers), Peter, the leader of the Apostles and chief herald of the Church, inventing no words, nor following human reasoning, but enlightened in mind by the Father, said to Him: "Thou art the Christ"; and not that merely, but: "the Son of the living God."[4] At once a blessing follows his declaration (for truly it was above man), and upon what he said was put this seal, that it was the Father who had revealed it to him. For our Savior said: "Blessed art thou, Simon Bar-Jona, for flesh and blood has not revealed this to thee, but my Father in heaven."[5] Therefore, he who acknowledges our Lord Jesus Christ as the Son of God shares this blessing; but he who denies the Son of God is a wretched and miserable man.

(4) Again, when you hear "Son," do not think of it in an improper sense, but in a true sense, that is, a Son by nature, without beginning, not raised from bondage to the rank of adoption, but a Son begotten from all eternity by an inscrutable and incomprehensible generation. Similarly, when you hear "first-born," do not think of this in human fashion; for among men the first-born have other brothers; and it is somewhere written: "Israel is my son, my first-born";[6] but like Reuben, Israel was a rejected first-born; for Reuben went

---

2 Matt. 16.13.
3 *Ibid*. 14.
4 *Ibid*. 16.
5 *Ibid*. 17.
6 Exod. 4.22.

up to his father's bed,[7] and Israel cast the Son of the Father out of the vineyard[8] and crucified Him. To others also Scripture says: "You are children of the Lord your God";[9] and elsewhere: "I said, You are gods; all of you sons of the Most High."[10] Note "I said," not "I begot." They, from the fact that God said it, received the adoption which they did not have; but He was not begotten to be other than He was before; rather He was begotten Son from the beginning, Son of the Father, like in all things to His Genitor, begotten Life of Life, Light of Light, Truth of Truth, Wisdom of Wisdom, King of King, God of God, Power of Power.

(5) Therefore, when you hear the words of the Gospel: "The book of the origin of Jesus Christ, the Son of David, the Son of Abraham,"[11] understand this "according to the flesh." For He is Son of David "at the end of the ages,"[12] but the Son of God before all ages. That which He had not, He did receive, but that which He has, He has eternally, as begotten of the Father. He has two fathers: one, David, according to the flesh, and one, God the Father, according to the Godhead. As the son of David, He is subject to time, and He is palpable and His descent is reckoned; but in His Godhead He is subject neither to time nor place nor genealogical reckoning. For "who shall declare his generation?"[13] "God is spirit";[14] He who is spirit begot spiritually, being incorporeal, by an unsearchable and incomprehensible generation. For the Son Himself says of the Father: "The Lord said to me, 'You are my son; this day I have begotten you.' "[15] Now "this day" is not recent, but eternal; "this day" is timeless, before all ages.

---

7 Gen. 49.4.
8 Cf. Matt. 21.19.
9 Deut. 14.1.
10 Ps. 81.6.
11 Matt. 1.1.
12 Heb. 9.26.
13 Isa. 53.8 (Douay).
14 John 4.24.
15 Ps. 2.7.

"From the womb before the daystar I have begotten you."[16]

(6) Believe, then, in Jesus Christ, Son of the living God; and that Son, Only-begotten, according to the Gospel which says: "For God so loved the world that he gave his only-begotten Son, that those who believe in him may not perish, but may have life everlasting."[17] And again: "He who believes in him is not judged,"[18] "but has passed from death to life."[19] But "he who is unbelieving towards the Son, shall not see life, but the wrath of God rests upon him";[20] because he has not believed in the Only-begotten Son of God.[21] Bearing witness to Him John said: "And we saw his glory—the glory as of the only-begotten of the Father—full of grace and of truth."[22] Before Him the devils trembled and said: "Let us be! What have we to do with thee, Jesus, Son of the living God?"[23]

(7) He is, then, Son of God by nature, not by adoption, begotten of the Father. "And the one who loves him who begot, loves also the one begotten of him";[24] but he who despises Him who is begotten insults in turn Him who begot. When then you hear of God begetting, think not of bodily function, nor suppose corruptible generation, that you may not fall into impiety. "God is spirit,"[25] and His generation is spiritual; for bodies beget bodies, and for the generation of bodies an interval of time is necessary; but there is no intervening time in the generation of Son from Father. In natural generation what is begotten is begotten imperfect; but the Son of God was begotten perfect; for what He now is, this He was begotten from the beginning. We are so begotten that

---

16 Cf. Ps. 109.3.
17 John 3.16.
18 *Ibid.* 18.
19 John 5.24.
20 John 3.36.
21 *Ibid.* 18.
22 John 1.14.
23 Cf. Luke 4.34; Mark 5.7.
24 1 John 5.1.
25 John 4.24.

we pass from the ignorance of infancy to the use of reason; our generation as men is imperfect, for our growth comes by progression. Do not think this is so in His case, nor charge with infirmity Him who begot; for if He begot what was imperfect, though it acquired perfection in the course of time, you impute infirmity to Him who begot; since what time afterwards bestowed, this, in your view, the Father did not bestow from the beginning.[26]

(8) Therefore, do not consider this generation as human or as Abraham begot Isaac. For when Abraham begot Isaac, he begot not what he would, but what another bestowed on him. But when God the Father begets, there is neither ignorance nor intervening deliberation; for to say that He did not know what was begotten is the greatest impiety, and to say that He became a Father after deliberating in time is like impiety.[27] For He was not first God without a Son, but afterwards, in time, became a Father; but He has the Son eternally, having begot Him not as men beget men, but as He Himself alone knows who begot Him before all ages, Very God.

(9) Since the Father is Very God He begot the Son like to Himself, Very God; not as teachers beget disciples, nor as Paul says to some: "For in Christ Jesus, through the gospel, did I beget you."[28] For in this case, he who was not a son by nature became a son by instruction; but in the case of Christ, He is a natural Son, a true Son. Not as you, who are beginning enlightened, now become sons of God; for you also become sons, but by adoption through grace, as it is written: "But to as many as received him he gave the power of becoming the sons of God; to those who believe in his name: who were born not of blood, nor of the will of the flesh, nor of the will of man, but of God."[29] We, indeed, are

---

26 The argument of Cyril against the advancement of the Son in time is logical and sound.
27 Cyril is again arguing against the Arians; cf. *Cat.* 7.5, note.
28 1 Cor. 4.15.
29 John 1.12, 13.

begotten of water and the Spirit,[30] but not thus was Christ
begotten of the Father; for at the time of His baptism, addressing Him and saying: "This is my Son,"[31] He did not
say: This has now become my son, but, "This is my Son,"
that He might show that even before the act of baptism He
was His Son.

(10) Nor did the Father beget the Son as among men
mind begets word. For the mind in us is subsistent, but the
word, when uttered, is dispersed through the air and is lost.
But we know that Christ was begotten, not as a word pronounced, but a Word subsisting and living; not uttered by the
lips and dispersed, but eternally and ineffably begotten of the
Father in substance. For, "In the beginning was the Word,"[32]
sitting at His right hand,[33] the Word, understanding the will
of the Father, and creating all things at His bidding; the
Word, who descended and ascended;[34] for the spoken word,
once uttered, neither ascends nor descends; the Word speaking
and saying: "I speak what I have seen with the Father";[35] the
Word full of power and reigning over all things; for the
Father delivered all things to the Son.[36]

(11) Therefore, the Father begot in a manner no man
would understand, but as He Himself only knows. For we
do not claim to declare how He begot Him, but we merely
affirm that it was not in this way or that. Nor are we alone
ignorant of the generation of the Son from the Father, but
so is all created nature. "Speak to the earth if it will answer
thee";[37] and even if you question carefully all things upon the
earth they will not be able to tell you; for the earth cannot
tell of the substance of its own potter and fashioner. Not only

---

30 Cf. John 3.5.
31 Matt. 3.17; 17.5.
32 John 1.1.
33 Cf. Ps. 109.1.
34 Cf. Eph. 4.10.
35 John 8.38.
36 Cf. Matt. 11.27.
37 Job 12.8 (Sept.).

the earth, but even the sun does not know; for the sun was created on the fourth day, without knowledge of the thing made the three preceding days, and what does not know these things cannot declare the Creator Himself. Heaven will not relate it, for at the bidding of the Father "the heaven also like smoke was established,"[38] by Christ. Neither the heavens of heavens nor the water above the heavens[39] will declare this. Why then should men be distressed at not knowing what even the heavens do not know? Not only the heavens, but the whole angelic nature also are ignorant of this generation. For if anyone (supposing this were possible) mounted to the first heaven, and approached the ranks of angels perceived there, and asked how God begot His Son, they would perhaps answer: "We have above us beings greater and higher; ask them." Ascend to the second and third heaven; reach, if possible, Thrones and Dominations, and Principalities and Powers; even if you could reach them, a thing impossible, they would also decline the telling, for they do not know.

(12) I myself have always been amazed at the curiosity of rash men who, through what they consider reverence, fall into impiety. For though they know nothing about Thrones and Dominations, Principalities and Powers, the works of Christ, they venture to inquire curiously about the Creator Himself.[40] Let these rash men tell me first how a Throne differs from a Domination, and then inquire into what concerns Christ. Tell me, what is a Principality and what a Power, what a Virtue and what an Angel; and then busy yourself with the Creator; for "all things were made through Him."[41] You will not question Thrones or Dominations, or rather you cannot; what other is there who knows "the deep

---

38 Cf. Isa. 51.6 (Sept.).
39 Cf. Ps. 148.4.
40 Cyril here testifies to the current enthusiasm for disputation, and that too, on the most technical theological questions.
41 John 1.3.

things of God"[42] but only the Holy Spirit who spoke the
Divine Scriptures? But even the Holy Spirit has said nothing
in Scripture of the generation of the Son from the Father.
Why then do you busy yourself about things which even
the Holy Spirit has not written of in the Scriptures? Though
you understand not what is written, are you curious about
what is not written? There are many questions in the Divine
Scriptures; if we do not understand what is written, why
weary ourselves about what is not written? It is enough to
know that God begot One Only Son.

(13) Do not be ashamed to confess your ignorance, since
you share it with angels. Only He who begot knows Him who
was begotten; and He who is begotten of Him knows Him
who begot. He who begot knows what He begot, and the
Scriptures testify that He who was begotten is God. "For as
the Father has life in himself, even so he has given to the
Son also to have life in himself";[43] and, "that all men may
honor the Son, even as they honor the Father";[44] and as the
Father gives life to whom He will, "even so the Son also gives
life to whom he will."[45] Neither did He who begot suffer
any loss, nor is there anything lacking to Him who was
begotten. (I know that I have said these things many times,
but it is for your safety that I have repeated them so much.)
Neither does He who begot have a father, nor He who was
begotten a brother; nor did He who begot change into the
Son, nor did He who was begotten become the Father. Of
One Only Father, there is One Only-begotten Son; neither
are there two unbegotten, nor two only-begotten, but there
is one Father, Unbegotten (for He is Unbegotten who has
no father); and One Son begotten eternally of the Father,
not begotten in time, but before all ages; not increased by
advancement, but begotten that which He now is.

---

42 1 Cor. 2.10.
43 John 5.26.
44 *Ibid.* 23.
45 *Ibid.* 21.

(14) We believe then in the Only-begotten Son of God, begotten of the Father Very God. For the true God does not beget a false god, as we have said, nor did He deliberate and afterwards beget Him, but He begot Him eternally, and far more swiftly than our words and thoughts. For in our case, when we speak in time, we consume time; but when there is question of Divine Power, the generation is timeless. As we have often said, He did not bring the Son from non-being into being, nor receive by adoption into sonship him who was not; but the Father, being eternal, eternally and ineffably begot One Only Son, who has no brother. Nor are there two first principles; but the Father is the head of the Son;[46] the beginning is One. For the Father begot the Son Very God, called Emmanuel;[47] but Emmanuel is interpreted "God with us."[48]

(15) You must know that He who was begotten of the Father and afterwards became man is God. Hearken to the Prophet: "Such is our God; no other is to be compared to him; he has traced out all the way of understanding, and has given her to Jacob, his servant, to Israel, his beloved son. Afterwards he was seen upon earth, and conversed with men."[49] Do you see God become man, after the law-giving of Moses? Here is a second testimony to the Godhead of Christ, from what was just read: "Your throne, O God, stands forever and ever";[50] for, that He might not be thought, because of His presence here in the flesh, to have advanced in time to the dignity of the Godhead, Scripture says plainly: "Therefore God, your God, has anointed you with the oil of gladness above your fellow kings."[51] Here you see Christ as God, anointed by God the Father.

(16) For still a third testimony of the divinity of Christ

---

46 Cf. 1 Cor. 11.3.
47 Cf. Isa. 7.14.
48 Matt. 1.23.
49 Bar. 3.36-38 (Douay).
50 Ps. 44.7.
51 *Ibid.* 8.

listen to Isaia: "The earnings of Egypt, the gain of Ethiopia,"[52] and a little further on: "And they shall make supplication to you: 'With you only is God and there is no God beside you. For you are God and we knew it not, the God of Israel, the savior.' "[53] You see the Son is God, having God the Father in Himself, all but saying the very thing He has said in the Gospels: "The Father in me, and I in the Father."[54] He did not say: "I and the Father am one," but "I and the Father are one";[55] that we might neither separate them nor confuse the identities of Son and Father. They are one in the dignity of their Godhead, since God begot God; one in the prerogative of their kingdom; for the Father does not reign over some and the Son over others, setting Himself up against His Father, like Absalom; but over what the Father reigns, the Son also reigns. They are one, because there is no discord or division between them; for the Father does not will some things, and the Son others. They are One, because there are not some things created by Christ and others by the Father; for one is the creation of all things, the Father having created them through the Son: "For he spoke, and they were made; he commanded, and they were created,"[56] says the Psalmist; for He who speaks, speaks to a hearer; and He who commands, commands one who is present.

(17) Therefore, the Son is Very God, having the Father in Himself, not changed into the Father; for the Father did not put on man's nature, but the Son. For let the truth be spoken freely. The Father did not suffer for us, but the Father sent Him who suffered for us. Never let us say: There was a time when the Son was not; nor let us accept the identification of Son with Father. Let us rather proceed on the royal road and turn aside neither to the left nor to the right. Let us

---

52 Isa. 45.14.
53 *Ibid.* 45.14, 15 (Sept.).
54 John 14.11.
55 John 10.30.
56 Ps. 148.5.

not, thinking to honor the Son, call Him Father, nor, thinking to honor the Father, suppose the Son to be but one of His creatures. But let One Father be worshiped through the One Son, and let not their worship be separated. Let One Son be proclaimed, sitting at the right hand of the Father before all ages, not having received this dignity in time by advancement after His passion, but possessing it eternally.

(18) "He who has seen the Son, has seen the Father";[57] for the Son is like in all things to Him who begot Him, begotten Life of Life, Power of Power, God of God. The characteristics of Godhead in the Son are unchangeable, and he who is deigned worthy to behold the Godhead of the Son comes to the enjoyment of the Father. It is not I say this, but the Only-begotten: "Have I been so long a time with you, and you have not known me, Philip. He who sees me sees also the Father."[58] And to speak more briefly, let us neither separate nor confuse Father and Son; and never say that the Son is alien to the Father, nor receive those who say that the Father is at one time Father and at another Son; for such expressions are strange and impious and not the teachings of the Church. But the Father, having begotten the Son, remained Father, and He is not changed. He begot Wisdom, but did not Himself become devoid of wisdom; He begot Power, but He did not become weak; He begot God, but He was not deprived of His own Godhead; neither did He lose anything by way of decrease or change, nor did He who was begotten have any defect. Perfect is He who begot, perfect that which was begotten; He who begot is God, God He who was begotten, God, indeed, of all things, but calling the Father His own God; for He is not ashamed to say: "I ascend to my Father and your Father, to my God and your God."[59]

(19) But that you might not think that He is in a like sense

---

57 John 14.9.
58 *Ibid.*
59 John 20.17.

Father of the Son and the creatures, Christ, in what follows, indicated a distinction. For He did not say: "I ascend to our Father," else a fellowship of creatures with the Only-begotten might be supposed, but He said: "my Father and your Father";[60] in one sense Mine, by nature; in another yours, by adoption. Again: "to my God and your God";[61] in one sense Mine, as His true and Only-begotten Son, and in another sense yours, as His workmanship. The Son of God is, therefore, Very God, ineffably begotten before all ages; for I say the same things to you often, that it may be imprinted on your mind. That God has a Son believe, but how, do not eagerly search out; for seeking you will not find. Do not exalt yourself, that you may not fall; "what is committed to you, attend to."[62] Tell me first who He is who begot, and then learn what He begot. But if you cannot comprehend the nature of Him who begot, busy not yourself with how He begot.

(20) It is enough for piety for you to know, as we have said, that God has One Only Son, One naturally begotten; who did not begin to be when He was born in Bethlehem, but is before all ages. For listen to the Prophet Michea: "And you, Bethlehem, house of Ephratha, are little to be among the thousands of Juda: from you shall come forth for me a leader who shall feed my people Israel; and his goings forth are from the beginning, from the days of eternity."[63] Therefore do not fix your attention on Him as coming from Bethlehem simply, but worship Him as begotten eternally of the Father. Admit no one who speaks of a beginning of the Son in time, but acknowledge His timeless Beginning, the Father. For the Father is the Beginning of the Son, timeless, incomprehensible, without beginning; the Father, the fountain of the streams of justice, even of the Only-begotten;

---

60 *Ibid.*
61 *Ibid.*
62 Ecclus. (Sir). 3.22.
63 Cf. Mich. 5.2; cf. Matt. 2.6.

who begot Him as He Himself only knows. But that you may know that our Lord Jesus Christ is also Eternal King, listen to His words: "Abraham . . . rejoiced that he was to see my day. He saw it and was glad."[64] Then, when the Jews received this obdurately, He said something still harder for them: "Before Abraham came to be, I am."[65] Again, He says to the Father: "And now do thou, Father, glorify me with thyself, with the glory that I had with thee before the world existed."[66] For He has said plainly: "Before the world was, I had glory with thee." Again: "Because thou hast loved me before the creation of the world,"[67] He clearly says: "I have eternal glory with Thee."

(21) Therefore, let us believe in One Lord, Jesus Christ, the Only-begotten Son of God, begotten of the Father before all ages, Very God, through whom "all things were made."[68] "Whether Thrones, or Dominations, or Principalities, or Powers, all things have been created through him";[69] and no created thing has been exempted from His power. Silenced be every heresy that introduces different creators and makers of the world; silenced be that which blasphemes Christ the Son of God; silenced be they who assert that the sun is Christ; for He, not the sun we see, is the Maker of the sun. Let them be silent who say that the world is the workmanship of angels, and who wish to rob the Only-begotten of dignity. For whether visible or invisible, or Thrones or Domination, or anything that is named,[70] all things were made by Christ. He reigns over the things made by Him, not having seized booty of another, but ruling over His own workmanship, as the Evangelist John has said: "All things were made through

64 John 8.56.
65 Ibid. 58.
66 John 17.5.
67 Ibid. 24.
68 John 1.3.
69 Col. 1.16.
70 Cf. Eph. 1.21.

Him, and without Him was made nothing";[71] all things were made through Him, the Father working through the Son.

(22) I wish to bring in an illustration of what I am saying, but I realize that it is feeble; for there can be no exact illustration of the Divine Power in visible things. But still, feeble though it be, let it be spoken by the feeble to the feeble. For consider that a king, having a son a king, and wishing to establish a city, would propose the form of the city to the son who shared his rule, and the son in turn, taking the design, would bring the planned work to completion. In like manner, when the Father wished to form all things, the Son, at the bidding of the Father, created all things, that the Father's bidding might secure for Him His absolute authority, yet the Son might have authority over His own workmanship; thus neither is the Father alienated from the dominion over His own works, nor does the Son reign over things created by others, but by Himself. For, as I have said, the angels did not create the world, but the Only-begotten Son, begotten, to repeat, before all ages; through whom all things were made, nothing being excepted from His creation. Thus far my words, by the grace of Christ.

(23) But returning to our exposition of the faith, let us conclude our discourse for the present. Christ made all things, whether you mention Angels, or Archangels, or Dominations, or Thrones. Not that the Father lacked power to create the works Himself, but because He wished the Son to reign over His own workmanship, furnishing Him the design of the things to be made; for the Only-begotten, honoring His Father, says: "The Son can do nothing of himself, but only what He sees the Father doing. For whatever he does, this the Son does in like manner."[72] Again: "My Father works even until now, and I work";[73] there being no opposition in those who work, for "all things that are mine are thine, and thine

71 John 1.3.
72 John 5.19.
73 *Ibid.* 17.

are mine,"[74] the Lord says in the Gospels. We may know this clearly from the Old as well as from the New Testament. For He who said: "Let us make man in our image and likeness,"[75] was certainly addressing someone present. But most clear are the Psalmist's words: "For he spoke, and they were made; he commanded, and they were created";[76] as if the Father commanded and spoke, and the Son at the Father's bidding created all things. Job also has said this mystically: "He alone stretches out the heavens and treads upon the crests of the sea,"[77] signifying to those who understand that He, who during His presence here walked upon the sea, is He who before had created the heavens. Again, the Lord says: "Or have you taken the slime of the earth and fashioned a living thing?"[78] Then, subsequently: "Have the gates of death been opened to you with fear?"[79] signifying that He who in His loving-kindness descended to hell is He who in the beginning created man out of slime.

(24) Therefore Christ is the Only-begotten Son of God and Maker of the world, for: "He was in the world, and the world was made through him,"[80] and: "He came unto His own,"[81] as the Gospel teaches us. But Christ is the Maker, at the bidding of the Father, not only of things visible, but also things invisible. For, according to the Apostle: "In him were created all things in the heavens and on the earth, things visible and things invisible, whether Thrones, or Dominations, or Principalities, or Powers. All things have been created through him and unto him, and he is before all creatures, and in him all things hold together."[82] Though

---

74 John 17.10.
75 Gen. 1.26.
76 Ps. 148.5 (Douay).
77 Job 9.8.
78 Job 38.14 (Sept.).
79 *Ibid.* 17 (Sept.).
80 John 1.10.
81 *Ibid.* 11.
82 Col. 1.16, 17.

you mention the worlds, Jesus Christ, at the bidding of the Father, is Maker of these, too. For: "last of all in these days, he has spoken to us in his Son, whom he appointed heir of all things, by whom also he made the world";[83] to whom be glory, honor, power, now and always, forever and ever. Amen.

---

83 Heb. 1.1, 2.

CATECHESIS XII

On the Incarnation

"Again the Lord spoke to Achaz: Ask for a sign from the Lord . . . the virgin shall be with child, and bear a son, and they shall name him Emmanuel."[1]

(1) Children of purity and disciples of chastity, let us celebrate the praises of the Virgin-born God with lips all-pure. Being counted worthy to partake of the flesh of the spiritual Lamb, let us take the head with the feet,[2] understanding the head as the Divinity, and the feet as the Humanity. We who listen to the Holy Gospels should give heed to John the divine; for he who said: "In the beginning was the Word, and the Word was with God; and the Word was God,"[3] thereafter added: "And the Word was made flesh."[4] For it is neither holy to worship the mere man, nor pious to speak of Him as God only, apart from His manhood. For if Christ is God, as He truly is, but did not assume manhood, then we are strangers to salvation. Let us, therefore, adore Him as God, but believe that He became man also; for it is neither profitable to speak of Him as man without the Godhead, nor salutary to fail to confess the manhood together with the Godhead. Let us confess the presence of the King and Physician. For Jesus the King, when about to become our Physician, girded Himself with the linen towel of humanity, and cared for that which was sick. The perfect

---

1 Isa. 7.10, 14.
2 Exod. 12.9.
3 John 1.1.
4 *Ibid.* 14.

Teacher of children became Himself a child among children, that He might instruct the unwise. The Bread of heaven came down to earth to feed the hungry.

(2) But the Jews, while they reject Him who has come, and look for him who is to come in wickedness, have repudiated the True Christ, and being deceived themselves, await the deceiver. And so the Savior is again proved true, who said: "I have come in the name of my Father, and you do not receive me. If another come in his own name, him you will receive."[5] Here is a good question for the Jews: "Is the Prophet Isaia, when he says that Emmanuel will be born of a virgin, true or false?" If they accuse him as false, it is not surprising; for it is their custom not only to accuse their prophets as liars, but even to stone them. But if the Prophet is true, point out Emmanuel. Further, is he who is to come, whom you await, to be born of a virgin or not? For if he is not to be born of a virgin, you charge the Prophet with falsehood; but if you expect this in him who is to come, why do you reject that which has already come to pass?

(3) Now let the Jews, since they so will, be led astray; but let the Church of God be glorified. For we receive God the Word made Man in truth, not of the will of man and woman, as heretics say, but according to the Gospel, of the Virgin and the Holy Spirit, made Man, not in appearance, but in reality. That He became man of a virgin will be taught in good time, and you will receive the proofs; for the error of the heretics is manifold.[6] Some have denied altogether that He was born of a virgin; others assert that He was born, not of a virgin, but of a woman dwelling with a husband. Others assert that Christ is not God made man, but a man made God; for they have dared to say that it was not the

---

5 John 5.43.
6 Cyril seems to have in mind three types of heretics, those who denied that Christ was born at all (or admitted he was a man but not born of men); secondly, those who maintain that Christ was born as other men, i.e., not from a virgin; thirdly, those who asserted that Christ was deified from mere man.

pre-existing Word that became man, but that a certain man was crowned by advancement.

(4) But remember the things that were said yesterday regarding His Godhead. Believe that the very same Only-begotten Son of God was Himself again begotten of a virgin. Heed John the Evangelist, when he says: "And the Word was made flesh, and dwelt among us."[7] For the Word is indeed Eternal, begotten of the Father before all ages, but took the flesh recently, in our behalf. But many gainsay this and declare: "What cause was there so great that God should come down to man's level? Again, is it God's nature at all to live among men? Besides, is it possible for a virgin to bear, without man?" Since there is much controversy, and the strife is manifold, let us proceed to resolve each point, by the grace of Christ and the prayers of those present.

(5) First, let us inquire why Jesus came down to earth. Now do not fix your attention on any skill of language on my part, for perhaps you may be deceived; unless you get the testimony of the prophets on each point, do not believe what is said. Unless you learn from the Holy Scriptures regarding the Virgin, the place, the time, the manner,[8] "do not receive the witness of man."[9] For one who is now present and teaches may be open to suspicion; but what man of sense will suspect him who prophesied a thousand years ago and more? If then you seek the reason for Christ's coming, go back to the first book of the Scriptures. God made the world in six days; but the world was made for man. The sun, however bright its shining rays, was yet made to give light to man. In fact, all the living things were created to serve us. Plants and trees were created for our enjoyment. All created things were good, but none of them was the image of God save man alone. The sun was fashioned by a mere command, but man by God's

---

7 John 1.14.
8 Cf. Bar. 3.38.
9 John 5.34.

hands. "Let us make man in our image and likeness."[10] A wooden image of an earthly king is honored; how much more a rational image of God. But the envy of the devil cast out this greatest of God's works, when it was making merry in Paradise. The enemy exulted over the fall of him whom he had envied; would you have wished the devil to continue to rejoice? He did not dare approach the man because of his strength, but approached the woman, as being weaker, when she was still a virgin; for it was after his expulsion from Paradise that "Adam knew Eve his wife."[11]

(6) Cain and Abel followed next in the generation of mankind; and Cain was the first murderer. Afterwards a deluge engulfed the earth because of the exceeding wickedness of men. Fire came down from heaven upon the people of Sodom because of their corruption. Subsequently God chose out Israel; but even Israel became perverse and the chosen race was wounded. For while Moses stood on the mountain before God, the people worshiped a calf in place of God. In the days of their lawgiver Moses, who said: "Thou shalt not commit adultery," a man dared to enter a brothel and be wanton. After Moses, prophets were sent to heal Israel; but in their exercise of healing they deplored the fact that they could not overcome evil, so that one of them says: Alas, "The faithful are gone from the earth, among men the upright are no more!";[12] and again: "All alike have gone astray; they have become perverse; there is not one who does good, not even one."[13] And again: "Cursing, and theft, and adultery, and killing have overflowed"[14] upon the land. "They sacrificed their sons and daughters to demons."[15] They engaged themselves in auguries, and enchantments, and divinations;

---

10 Gen. 1.26.
11 Gen. 4.1.
12 Mich. 7.2.
13 Ps. 13.3.
14 Cf. Osee 4.2.
15 Ps. 105.37.

and again: "They fastened their garments with cords and hung veils next to the altar."[16]

(7) Grievous was the wound of mankind. "From the sole of the foot to the head there was no sound spot; there was no place to apply ointment or oil or bandages."[17] Then, lamenting and in distress the prophets said: "Oh, that out of Sion would come the salvation of Israel!"[18] And again: "May your help be with the man of your right hand, with the son of man whom you yourself made strong. And we will no more withdraw from you."[19] Another prophet made supplication thus: "Incline your heavens, O Lord, and come down."[20] The wounds of mankind are beyond our healing. "They have slain thy prophets, they have thrown down thy altars."[21] The evil cannot be repaired by us; you must repair it.

(8) The Lord heard the prayer of the prophets. The Father did not despise our race which was perishing; He sent from heaven His own Son the Lord as our Physician. One of the prophets says: "The Lord whom you seek, cometh; and He shall come suddenly."[22] Whither? "The Lord shall come to his temple,"[23] where you took up stones against Him.[24] Another of the prophets, on hearing this, says to him: "In speaking of God's salvation, do you speak softly? In announcing the good tidings of God's coming for salvation, do you speak in secret?" "Go up onto a high mountain, Sion, herald of glad tidings; say to the cities of Juda";—what shall I say?—"Here is your God! Here comes with power the Lord God."[25] Again the Lord Himself has said: "Behold I come,

---

16 Amos 2.8 (Sept.).
17 Isa. 1.6 (Sept.).
18 Ps. 13.7.
19 Ps. 79.18, 19.
20 Ps. 143.5.
21 3 Kings 19.10.
22 Cf. Mal. 3.1 (Sept.).
23 *Ibid.*
24 Cf. John 8.59.
25 Isa. 40.9, 10.

and I will dwell in the midst of thee, saith the Lord. And many nations shall be joined to the Lord."[26] The Israelites rejected salvation through Me; "I come to gather nations of every language";[27] for, "he came unto his own, and his own received him not."[28] You come, and what do you bestow upon the nations? "I come to gather nations of every language; . . . I will set a sign among them."[29] For from My conflict on the cross I will give to each of My soldiers a royal sign to bear upon his forehead. Still another prophet said: "He inclined the heavens and came down, with dark clouds under his feet."[30] For His coming down from heaven was unknown to men.

(9) Afterwards Solomon, hearing his father David say these things, and having built a wondrous house, and foreseeing Him who would come to it, says in astonishment: "Is it then to be thought that God should indeed dwell upon earth?"[31] Yes, says David in anticipation in the psalm inscribed "For Solomon," wherein it is said: "He shall be like rain coming down on the fleece";[32] "rain" because of His heavenly origin; but "on the fleece" because of His manhood. For rain, falling upon fleece, falls noiselessly; so that, the mystery of His birth being unknown, the wise men said: "Where is he that is born king of the Jews?" And Herod, being troubled, inquired concerning Him who had been born, and said: "Where is the Christ born?"[33]

(10) Who is this who comes down? He says in what follows: "May he endure as long as the sun, and like the moon through all generations."[34] Again another of the prophets says: "Rejoice heartily, O daughter Sion, shout for joy, O

---

26 Zach. 2.10, 11 (Douay).
27 Isa. 66.18.
28 John 1.11.
29 Isa. 66.18, 19 (Sept.).
30 Ps. 17.10.
31 3 Kings 8.27.
32 Ps. 71.6 (Douay).
33 Matt. 2.2, 4.
34 Ps. 71.5.

daughter Jerusalem! See, your king shall come to you; a just savior is he."[35] There are many kings; explain to us which one you mean, O Prophet. Give us a sign which other kings do not have. If you say, a king clad in purple, the dignity of such vesture has been anticipated. If you say he is guarded by spearmen, and sitting on a golden chariot, this too has been anticipated by others. Give us a sign peculiar to the King whose coming you announce. The prophet answers and says: "See your king shall come to you; a just savior is he, meek, and riding on an ass, on a colt, the foal of an ass,"[36] not upon a chariot. You have a unique sign of the King who came. Alone of kings, Jesus sat upon a foal untried in the yoke, entering Jerusalem with acclamations as a king. What does this King do on entering? "Thou also by the blood of thy testament hast sent forth thy prisoners out of the pit, wherein is no water."[37]

(11) But it might happen that He should sit upon a foal; give us rather a sign where the king who enters will stand. Give us a sign not far from the city, that it may not be unknown to us; give us a sign nearby and clearly visible, that being in the city[38] we may behold the place. Again the prophet answers, saying: "That day his feet shall rest upon the Mount of Olives, which is opposite Jerusalem to the east."[39] Is it possible for anyone standing within the city not to behold the place?

(12) We have two signs, and wish to learn a third; tell us what the Lord shall do on coming. Another prophet says: "Here is your God," and thereafter, "he comes to save you. Then will the eyes of the blind be opened, the ears of the deaf be cleared; then will the lame leap like the stag; then

---

35 Zach. 9.9.
36 *Ibid.*
37 *Ibid.* (Douay).
38 Cyril was preaching on Mt. Golgotha, which was outside the gate of the old Jerusalem, but inside the walls of the later city. The Mount of Olives was easily visible from Calvary.
39 Zach. 14.4.

the tongue of the dumb will sing."[40] But let yet another testimony be told us. You speak, O Prophet, of the Lord coming and doing signs such as never had been done.[41] What other clear signs do you mention? "The Lord enters into judgment with his people's elders and princes."[42] An extraordinary sign: the Master judged by elder servants, and enduring it.

(13) These things the Jews read, but heed not; they have stopped up the ears of their heart, that they may not hear. But for our part, let us believe in Jesus Christ, who came in the flesh and was made man; for we could not receive Him otherwise. For since we could not behold or enjoy Him as He is, He became what we are, that we might be allowed to enjoy him. For if we cannot look full upon the sun, which was made on the fourth day, could we behold God, its Maker? The Lord came down in fire on Mount Sinai and the people could not bear it, but said to Moses: "You speak to us, and we will listen; but let not God speak to us, or we shall die."[43] Again: "What mortal has heard the voice of the living God speaking from the midst of fire, and shall live?"[44] If to hear the voice of God speaking is a cause of death, how will the sight of God not cause death? And why wonder? Even Moses himself says: "I am greatly terrified and trembling."[45]

(14) What then? Would you that He who came for our salvation become a minister of destruction because men could not bear Him? Or rather, that He should temper His grace to our measure? Daniel could not bear the vision of an angel; could you bear the sight of the Lord of angels? Gabriel appeared and Daniel fell down. Of what nature and in what form did he appear? "His face shone like lightning," not as the sun; "his eyes were like fiery torches," not as a

---

40 Isa. 35.4-6.
41 Cf. John 15.24.
42 Isa. 3.14.
43 Exod. 20.19.
44 Deut. 5.26.
45 Heb. 12.21.

furnace of fire; "and the voice sounded like the roar of a
multitude,"[46] not "as of twelve legions of angels."[47] Yet the
Prophet fell down. The angel approached him and said:
"Fear not, Daniel: stand upright, take courage, thy words
have been heard."[48] And Daniel says: "I stood up trembling";[49] yet even so he did not answer, until the likeness of
a man's hand touched him. After the vision changed and
seemed like a man, then Daniel began to speak; and his
words? "My Lord, I was seized with pangs at the vision and
I was powerless. . . . No strength or even breath it left in
me."[50] If the vision of an angel took away the Prophet's voice
and strength, would the sight of God Himself have allowed
him to breathe? Until "the one who looked like a man
touched me,"[51] says the Scripture, Daniel did not take courage.
A proof of our weakness having been shown then, the Lord
took on Himself that which man required. For, since man
sought to hear from one like himself, the Savior put on the
same nature, that men might be taught more easily.

(15) Here is another reason. Christ came that He might be
baptized and might sanctify baptism; He came that He might
work wonders, walking upon the waters of the sea. Therefore,
since before His coming in the flesh, "the sea beheld and
fled; Jordan turned back,"[52] the Lord assumed His body, that
the sea might endure the sight, and Jordan receive Him
without fear. This is one reason, but there is a second also.
Through Eve, yet a virgin, came death; there was need that
through a virgin, or rather from a virgin, that life should
appear; that as the serpent deceived the one, so Gabriel
should bring the good news to the other. Men, having abandoned God, fashioned images like men. Since, therefore, the

46 Dan. 10.6.
47 Cf. Matt. 26.53.
48 Cf. Dan. 10.12-19.
49 *Ibid.* 11 (Sept.).
50 *Ibid.* 16, 17 (Sept.).
51 *Ibid.* 18.
52 Ps. 113.3.

image of man was falsely worshiped as God, God became truly man, that the falsehood might be destroyed. The devil had made use of the flesh as an instrument against us; and knowing this Paul says: "But I see another law in my members, warring against the law of my mind and making me prisoner,"[53] and what follows. We have been saved by the very weapons which the devil used to conquer us. The Lord took from us our likeness, that through human nature, we might be saved. He assumed our likeness that He might bestow the greater grace on that which was lacking, that sinful human nature might be made partaker of God. For: "Where the offense has abounded, grace has abounded yet more."[54] It behooved the Lord to suffer on our behalf; but the devil would not have dared to approach, if he had known Him: "For had they known it, they would never have crucified the Lord of glory."[55] His body, therefore, was made a bait to death, that the dragon, when hoping to devour it, might disgorge those also whom he had already devoured. For: "Death having waxed mighty, devoured";[56] and again: "God wiped away the tears from all faces."[57]

(16) Did Christ become man in vain? Are our doctrines merely clever inventions and human sophistries? Are not the Holy Scriptures our salvation? Are not the predictions of the prophets? Therefore, keep this deposit unshaken, I pray you, and let no one disturb you: believe that God became man. Now it has been proved that this was possible; but if the Jews still refuse to believe, let us propose this to them: "What strange thing do we announce when we say that God became man, when you yourselves say that Abraham received the Lord as a guest? What strange thing do we announce, when Jacob says: 'I have seen a heavenly being face to face, yet

---

53 Rom 7.23.
54 Rom. 5.20.
55 1 Cor. 2.8.
56 Isa. 25.8 (Sept.).
57 *Ibid.*

my life has been spared'?[58] The same Lord who ate with Abraham ate also with us. Therefore, what strange thing do we announce? Further, we present two witnesses who stood before the Lord on Mount Sinai; Moses was 'in the hollow of the rock';[59] and Elias was once in the hollow of the rock.[60] They, being present at His Transfiguration on Mount Tabor, spoke to His disciples 'of his death which he was about to fulfill in Jerusalem.' "[61] That it was possible for Him to be made man has been shown, as I said above; the rest of the proofs may be left for the studious to gather.

(17) But in my discourse above I promised to declare both the time and the place of the coming of the Savior; and I must not depart convicted of falsehood, but rather send away the Church's novices well assured. Therefore, let us inquire the time when the Lord came, since His coming is recent and disputed; and since "Jesus Christ is the same yesterday and today, yes, and forever,"[62] Moses the Prophet says: "A prophet like unto me will the Lord, your God, raise up for you from among your own kinsmen."[63] Let the phrase "like unto me," be reserved awhile, to be examined in its proper place. But when does this expected prophet come? Go back, he says, to what has been written by me; scrutinize the prophecy of Jacob spoken to Juda: "Juda, your brothers shall praise you,"[64] and what follows, not to quote the whole; "A prince shall not fail out of Juda, nor a ruler from his thigh, till he come, for whom it is reserved, and he shall be the expectation," not of the Jews, but "of nations."[65] He gave as a sign of the coming of Christ the cessation of Jewish rule. If they are not now under the sway of the Romans, Christ is not yet come.

---

58 Gen. 32.30.
59 Exod. 33.22.
60 Cf. 3 Kings 19.13.
61 Luke 9.30, 31.
62 Heb. 13.8.
63 Deut. 18.15.
64 Gen. 49.8.
65 *Ibid.* 10 (Sept.).

If they still have a prince of the race of Juda and David, the expected One has not yet come. For I am ashamed to mention their recent doings concerning those who are nowadays called "patriarchs" among them, and what their recent descent is and who their mother; but I leave it to those who know. But He who comes "the expectation of nations," what further sign has He? In the next verse Jacob says: "tying his colt to his vine";[66] you recognize that colt clearly announced by Zacharia.

(18) But again you seek still another testimony of the time. "The Lord said to me, 'You are my son; this day I have begotten you' ";[67] and a little further on: "You shall rule them with an iron rod."[68] I have already said that the rule of the Romans is clearly called "an iron rod"; but what is still wanting concerning this point let us call to mind from Daniel. For in declaring and interpreting the image of the statue of Nabuchodonosor, he tells also his whole vision concerning it; and that "a stone hewn from a mountain without a hand being put to it,"[69] that is to say, not produced by man's contrivance, would overpower the whole world. He speaks most clearly thus: "In the lifetime of those kings the God of heaven will set up a kingdom that shall never be destroyed or delivered up to another people."[70]

(19) But we seek a clearer proof of the time of His coming; for man, being slow to believe, unless he can calculate the very years exactly, does not believe what is said. What were the circumstances and the nature of the time? When the kings out of Juda fail, and a foreigner, Herod, rules. Therefore the angel, speaking to Daniel, says (now mark, I pray you, what is said): "Know and understand this: From the utterance of the word that Jerusalem was to be rebuilt unto

---

66 Cf. *Ibid.* 11.
67 Ps. 2.7.
68 *Ibid.* 9.
69 Dan. 2.34.
70 *Ibid.* 44.

Christ the prince, there shall be seven weeks, and sixty-two weeks."[71] Now sixty-nine weeks of years makes four hundred and eighty-three years. Therefore he declared that four hundred and eighty-three years after the building of Jerusalem, the rulers out of Juda failing, there was to come a certain foreign king, in whose reign Christ was to be born. Darius the Mede built the city in the sixth year of his own reign, in the first year of the sixty-sixth Olympiad. Among the Greeks "Olympiad" is the term given the games occurring every four years, because of the day made up, in every four years of the sun's courses, of the three hours over in each year. Now Herod was king in the fourth year of the one hundred and eighty-sixth Olympiad. Between the sixty-sixth and the one hundred and eighty-sixth Olympiads there are one hundred and twenty Olympiads plus. Now one hundred and twenty Olympiads make up four hundred and eighty years; the three other years remaining are accounted for in the interval between the first and the fourth years. So, therefore, you have the proof from Scripture: "From the utterance of the word that Jerusalem was to be rebuilt unto Christ the prince, there shall be seven weeks, and sixty-two weeks."[72] For the present, then, you have this proof of the time, though the weeks of years foretold in Daniel are interpreted variously.

(20) Listen now to the place of the promise. Michea says: "But you, Bethlehem-Ephratha, are not the least to be among the thousands of Juda: for from you shall come forth for me a leader that is to be the ruler in Israel: and his goings forth are from the beginning, from the days of eternity."[73] Now regarding the place, as an inhabitant of Jerusalem, you already know beforehand what is written in the one hundred and thirty-first psalm: "Behold, we heard of it in Ephratha; we found it in the fields of the wood."[74] For, a few

---

71 Cf. Dan. 9.25.
72 *Ibid.*
73 Cf. Mich. 5.2 (Sept.).
74 Ps. 131.6.

years ago, the place was woody. Again, you have heard Habacuc saying to the Lord: "When the years draw nigh, you shall be known; when the time comes, you shall be shown."[75] What is the sign, O Prophet, of the coming of the Lord? He says next: "In the midst of two lives you shall be known,"[76] saying this plainly to the Lord: "Coming in the flesh, you shall live and die, and rising from the dead you shall live again." From what part of the region about Jerusalem is He to come? From East, or West, or North, or South? Tell us exactly. He answers most clearly and says: "God shall come from Theman (now Theman is interpreted "South"), and the Holy One from Pharan, shady, woody";[77] in agreement with this the Psalmist said: "We found it in the fields of the wood."[78]

(21) We ask further of whom and how He will come. This Isaia tells us: "The virgin shall be with child, and bear a son, and shall name him Emmanuel."[79] The Jews gainsay this; for it has long been their custom to resist the truth perversely; they say the text is not "the virgin," but "the damsel." Even accepting their assertion, I find the truth. For we must ask them: "If a virgin is assaulted, when does she cry out and call for help, before or after the outrage?" If then the Scripture says elsewhere: "The damsel cried, and there was no one to come to her aid,"[80] does it not speak of a virgin? To learn more clearly that even a virgin is called a damsel in the Holy Scripture, hear the Book of Kings, saying of Abisag the Sunamitess: "And the damsel was exceeding beautiful";[81] that she was chosen as a virgin and brought to David is admitted.

(22) But the Jews say again: "This was said to Achaz con-

---

75 Hab. 3.2 (Sept.).
76 Ibid.
77 Ibid. 3 (Sept.).
78 Cf. Ps. 131.6.
79 Isa. 7.14.
80 Cf. Deut. 22.27.
81 3 Kings 1.4.

cerning Ezechia." Therefore, let us read the Scripture: "Ask for a sign from the Lord, your God; let it be deep as the nether world, or high as the sky!"[82] The sign surely ought to be something extraordinary. For the water from the rock[83] was a sign, the dividing of the sea,[84] the turning back of the sun,[85] and the like. What I am about to say contains a clearer refutation of the Jews. (I realize I am speaking at length and that my hearers are wearied. But endure the fullness of my discourse, since it is for Christ's sake that these things are discussed, and they concern no ordinary matters.) Since Isaia spoke these things in the reign of Achaz, and Achaz was king for only sixteen years, during which the prophecy was made, the fact that his successor, King Ezechia, the son of Achaz, was twenty-five years old when be began to reign, refutes the objection of the Jews. For since the prophecy was confined within sixteen years, he must have been begotten at least nine years before the prophecy. Why was it necessary to utter the prophecy about one already born? For he did not say "was with child," but "the virgin shall be with child," speaking as with foreknowledge.

(23) But that the Lord was to be born of a virgin we know clearly; now we must show of what stock the Virgin was. "The Lord swore to David a firm promise from which he will not withdraw: 'Your own offspring I will set upon your throne.' "[86] Again: "I will make his posterity endure forever and his throne as the days of heaven."[87] Then: "Once by my holiness I have sworn; I will not be false to David: his posterity shall continue forever, and his throne shall be like the sun before me; like the moon, which remains forever."[88] You see that the words concern Christ, not Solomon, for

---

82 Isa. 7.11.
83 Exod. 17.6.
84 Exod. 14.21.
85 4 Kings 20.11.
86 Ps. 131.11.
87 Ps. 88.30.
88 *Ibid.* 36-38.

Solomon's throne did not endure as the sun. But if anyone should object that Christ did not sit upon the wooden throne of David, let us produce that saying: "The Scribes and the Pharisees have sat on the chair of Moses."[89] For this signifies, not the chair of wood, but the authority of his teaching. In like manner, in looking for the throne of David, seek not the throne of wood, but the kingly power itself. Take as witnesses the children who cried out: "Hosanna to the Son of David: blessed . . . is the king of Israel."[90] The blind men also say: "Son of David, have mercy on us!"[91] Again, Gabriel bears witness plainly in saying to Mary: "And the Lord God will give him the throne of David his father."[92] Paul, too, says: "Remember that Jesus Christ rose from the dead and was descended from David; this is my gospel."[93] In the beginning of the Epistle to the Romans, he says: "who was born of the seed of David according to the flesh."[94] Therefore, receive Him who was born of David, and heed the prophecy which says: "On that day there shall be a root of Jesse, and he that shall rise to rule over the nations: in him shall the nations trust."[95]

(24) But the Jews are sorely troubled at these things. This also Isaia foreknew when he said: "And they shall desire that they were burnt by fire. For a child is born to us," (not to them) "a son is given us."[96] Note too that He was first the Son of God, then was given to us. A little further on he says: "And of his peace there is no end."[97] The Romans have their limits; but there is no limit of the kingdom of the Son of God. The Persians and the Medes have their limits, but the Son of God has none. Then follows: "Upon the throne

89 Matt. 23.2.
90 Matt. 21.9; John 12.13.
91 Matt. 20.30.
92 Luke 1.32.
93 2 Tim 2.8.
94 Rom. 1.3.
95 Isa. 11.10 (Sept.).
96 Isa. 9.5, 6 (Sept.).
97 Ibid. 7.

of David, and upon his kingdom, to establish it."⁹⁸ The holy
Virgin, then, was sprung from David.

(25) It was fitting that He, most pure and a Teacher of
purity, should issue from a pure bride-chamber. For if one
who fulfills well the priestly office abstains from women, how
was Jesus Himself to be born of man and woman? "For thou
art he," He says in the Psalms, "that hast drawn me out of
the womb."⁹⁹ Mark that carefully, "that hast drawn me out
of the womb," since this signifies that He was born without
man, being drawn from the womb and flesh of a virgin; for
the manner is different for those born in the ordinary course
of marriage.

(26) But He is not ashamed to take flesh from such members, when He framed these very members. Who tells us
this? The Lord says to Jeremia: "Before I formed you in the
womb I knew you, before you were born I dedicated you."¹⁰⁰
If in fashioning men, therefore, He touched them and was
not ashamed, was He ashamed in forming for Himself the
holy flesh, the veil of His Godhead? It is God who even now
creates the babes in the womb, as it is written in Job: "Did
you not pour me out as milk, and thicken me like cheese.
With skin and flesh you clothed me, with bones and sinews
knit me together."¹⁰¹ There is nothing corrupt in man's
frame unless he defiles it with adulteries and wantonness. He
who formed Adam formed Eve also; and both male and female
were fashioned by the Divine hands. None of the members
of the body as fashioned from the beginning is corrupt. Let
all heretics be silent who slander their bodies, or rather Him
who formed them. But let us be mindful of Paul's words:
"Do you not know that your members are the temple of
the Holy Spirit, who is in you?"¹⁰² Again, the Prophet has

98 Ibid.
99 Ps. 21.10 (Douay).
100 Jer. 1.5.
101 Job 10.10, 11.
102 1 Cor. 6.19.

foretold in the person of Jesus: "My flesh is from them."[103] Elsewhere it is written: "Therefore the Lord will give them up, until the time that she brings forth."[104] What is the sign? There follows: "She shall bring forth, and the remnant of their brethren shall be converted."[105] What are the nuptial pledges of the Virgin, the holy bride? "I will espouse you to me in faith";[106] and Elizabeth, speaking to her, says in like manner: "And blessed is she who has believed, because the things promised her by the Lord shall be accomplished."[107]

(27) But both Greeks and Jews deride us and say that it was impossible for Christ to be born of a virgin. Let us silence the Greeks from their own fables. For how can you, who speak of stones being cast and changed into men, assert that birth from a virgin is impossible? When your legends declare that a daughter[108] was born from the brain, how can you assert that a son could not have been born from a virgin's womb? You tell the false story of the birth of Dionysus from the thigh of your Zeus;[109] how can you set at naught our truth? I know I am speaking of what is unworthy of the hearers present, but that you, at the proper time, may reproach the Greeks, I have brought these things in to refute them from their own fables.

(28) Meet the Jews with this question: "Is it more difficult for an old woman, barren and past the age of bearing, to bear, or for a virgin in the flower of youth to have a child?" Sara was barren, and menstruation had long ceased, but contrary to nature she bore a child. It is contrary to nature for a barren woman to bear, and for a virgin to bear. Either reject both or accept both. For it is the same God who wrought the one and effected the other. For you will not

---

103 Osee 9.12 (Sept.).
104 Cf. Mich. 5.2.
105 Cf. *ibid.*
106 Cf. Osee 2.22.
107 Luke 1.45.
108 I.e., Athena.
109 See, e.g., Euripides' *Bacchae*.

dare to say that that was possible for God, but not this. Again, it was surely unnatural for a man's hand to be changed in a single hour into a different appearance and to be again restored. How then was Moses' hand made white as snow and at once restored to its natural appearance? But you say that God, by so willing, changed it. Is it that in one case God has the power, but in this other He has not? That sign, indeed, was for the Egyptians only; but this sign was given to the whole world. Which is more difficult, O you Jews, for a virgin to give birth, or for a rod to be changed into a living thing? You confess that under Moses a perfectly straight rod, being changed into a serpent, struck with fear him who had cast it, so that he who held it fled from it as from a serpent; for it truly was a serpent; but he fled, not because he was afraid of what he held, but in dread of Him who had changed it. The rod had the fangs and eyes of a serpent; now if eyes that see are produced from a rod, cannot a child be born of a virgin's womb at God's will? I pass over the fact that the rod of Aaron brought forth in one night that which other trees do not produce in many years. For who does not know that a rod, when it has lost its bark, will never germinate, even if planted in the midst of rivers? But since God is not a servant of the nature of trees, but rather the creator of their nature, the fruitless, dry and barkless rod flowered and blossomed and brought forth almonds. For the sake of the typical high-priest God gave fruit, beyond nature, to the rod. Can it be that He would not allow a virgin to bear a child, for the sake of the true High-priest?

(29) These are goodly arguments to recall; but the Jews still object; they do not assent to the statements about the rod, unless they are persuaded by similar marvelous and praeternatural births. Therefore, question them thus: "Of whom was Eve begotten in the beginning? What mother conceived her who had no mother?" But Scripture says she was born from Adam's side. Now then, if Eve was born, without

a mother, from the side of a man, may not a child be born, without a man, from the womb of a virgin? A debt of gratitude was due from womankind; for Eve was begotten of Adam, not conceived of a mother, but, as it were, brought forth from man alone. Mary, then, paid the debt of gratitude when, not of man, but immaculately of her own self, she conceived of the Holy Spirit by the power of God.

(30) But let us take something more impressive. The production of bodies from bodies, though strange is, nevertheless, possible. For the dust of the earth to become man is still more wonderful. For a mass of clay to take on the vesture and splendor of eyes is surely more wonderful. For simple dust to issue forth at once into firm bones, soft lungs, and various other members, is a wonderful thing. For dust to become animated and traverse the earth by its own motion, and build houses, is a wonderful thing. For clay to teach and speak, and be a craftsman and a king, is wonderful. Whence, O most ignorant Jews, was Adam made? Did not God take the dust of the earth and fashion that marvelous frame? Is it possible for clay to be changed into an eye, but not for a virgin to bear a son? Can it be that what, as men think, is impossible, comes to pass rather than that which is of itself possible?

(31) Let us remember these things, brethren, and use them as weapons of defense. Let us not endure the heretics who teach that Christ's coming was in appearance only. Let us abhor too those who say that the birth of the Savior was from a man and a woman, daring to assert that He was begotten of Joseph and Mary, because it is written: "He took unto him his wife."[110] For let us recall Jacob who, before he received Rachel, said to Laban: "Give me my wife."[111] For just as she before the marriage state was called the wife of Jacob, so Mary also, because of her betrothal, was called the

---

110 Matt. 1.26.
111 Gen. 29.21.

wife of Joseph. Note the exactness of the Gospel, when it says: "Now in the sixth month the angel Gabriel was sent from God to a town of Galilee, called Nazareth, to a virgin betrothed to a man named Joseph,"[112] and what follows. Again, when the enrolling took place, and Joseph went up to be enrolled, what does the Scripture say? "And Joseph also went up from Galilee . . . to register together with Mary his espoused wife, who was with child."[113] For though she was with child, it does not say "with his wife," but "with his espoused wife." For: "God sent his Son," Paul says, not born of a man and a woman, but "born of a woman"[114] only, that is, of a virgin. We have already shown that a virgin is also called a woman. For He who makes virgin souls was born of a virgin.

(32) But you wonder at the event; she who bore Him also wondered, and said to Gabriel: "How shall this happen, since I do not know man?"[115] But he says: "The Holy Spirit shall come upon thee, and the power of the Most High shall overshadow thee; and therefore the Holy One to be born of thee shall be called the Son of God."[116] His generation was pure and undefiled; for where the Holy Spirit is, there all defilement has been taken away; unsullied was the birth in the flesh of the Only-begotten from the Virgin. If the heretics deny the truth, the Holy Spirit will convict them; the overshadowing power of the Most High will be wroth; in the day of judgment Gabriel will confront them face to face; the place of the manger which received the Lord will put them to shame. The shepherds will bear witness, who then received the good tidings; and the army of the angels praising and saying: "Glory to God in the highest, and peace on earth among men of good will";[117] and the temple, into which He

---

112 Luke 1.26, 27.
113 Luke 2.4, 5.
114 Gal. 4.4.
115 Luke 1.34.
116 *Ibid.* 35.
117 Luke 2.14.

was brought on the fortieth day; and the pair of turtle doves offered for Him; and Simeon, who then took Him into his arms; and the prophetess, Anna, who was present.

(33) Therefore, since God bears witness and the Holy Spirit adds His testimony, and Christ says: "Why do you seek to put me to death," a man "who has spoken the truth to you?"[118] let the heretics who deny His manhood be silent; for they speak against Him who said: "Feel me and see; for a spirit does not have flesh and bones, as you see I have."[119] Let the Lord born of the Virgin be worshiped, and let the virgins recognize the crown of their own state. Let the order of Solitaries also acknowledge the glory of chastity; for we men are not deprived of the dignity of chastity. The Savior passed the nine months period in the womb of the Virgin; but the Lord was a man for thirty-three years; so that if a virgin glories because of the nine months, so much the more may we glory because of the many years.

(34) But let us all, by the grace of God, run the race of chastity, "young men too, and maidens, old men and boys,"[120] not pursuing wantonness but praising the name of Christ. Let us be conscious of the glory of chastity, for its crown is angelic and its perfection above man. Let us respect our bodies, which are to shine as the sun; let us not for the sake of a little pleasure defile so great and noble a body; for the sin is fleeting and of the passing hour, but the shame lasts many years and forever. Those who live chastely are as angels walking upon the earth; the virgins have their portion with Mary the Virgin. Let all vain ornament be put aside, and every harmful glance, all wanton gait and flowing robe and perfume enticing to pleasure. Let the perfume for all be the prayer of sweet odor and good works, and the sanctification of our bodies, that the Lord born of the Virgin may say of us also, both the men who practice chastity and the women

118 John 7.20; 8.40.
119 Luke 24.39.
120 Ps. 148.12.

who wear its crown: "I will dwell and move among them, I will be their God and they shall be my people,"[121] to whom be glory forever and ever. Amen.

---

121 2 Cor. 6.16.

INDICES

GENERAL INDEX

(This index mainly covers the actual translations from St. Cyril and the notes that accompany them. The indexing of the Introduction has concentrated upon the proper names. In general, the authors and works named in the Select Bibliography are not indexed.)

INDEX OF HOLY SCRIPTURE

(BOOKS OF THE OLD TESTAMENT)

CPSIA information can be obtained
at www.ICGtesting.com
Printed in the USA
BVHW081340280120
570726BV00002B/172